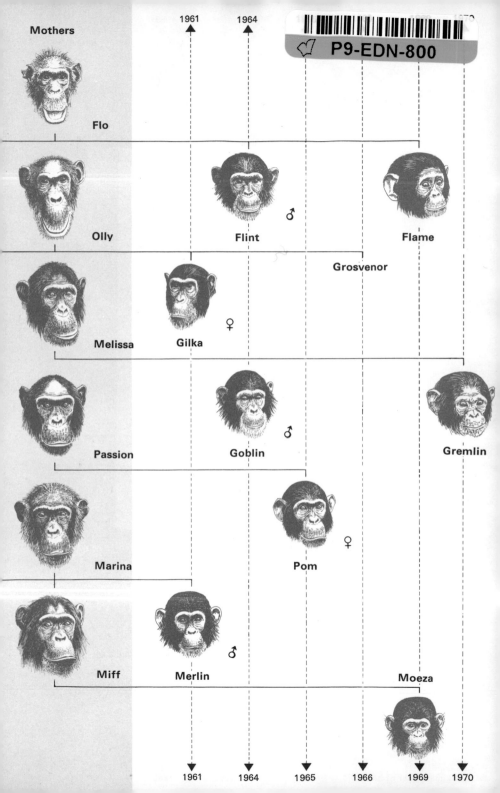

Mothers

Flo

Olly

Flint ♂

Flame

Grosvenor

Melissa

Gilka ♀

Passion

Goblin ♂

Gremlin

Marina

Pom ♀

Miff

Merlin ♂

Moeza

1961   1964   1965   1966   1969   1970

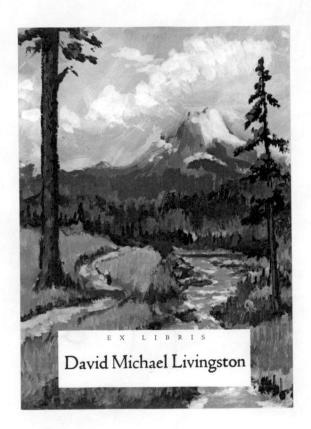

EX LIBRIS

David Michael Livingston

IN THE SHADOW
OF MAN

IN
THE SHADOW
OF MAN

by Jane van Lawick-Goodall
Photographs by Hugo van Lawick

HOUGHTON MIFFLIN COMPANY BOSTON

To Vanne, Louis, Hugo—
and in memory of David Graybeard

ACKNOWLEDGMENTS

I SHOULD HAVE BEEN UNABLE to study chimpanzees or write this book without the help and encouragement of a great many people, and I should like to express, however inadequately, my most profound thanks to all of them. First, of course, my gratitude lies with Dr. L. S. B. Leakey. It was he who originally suggested that I should study chimpanzees, he who found money to finance my early field work, and he who arranged for me to write up my results for a Ph.D. dissertation at Cambridge University. Last—but by no means least—it was through Louis's recommendation that Hugo came to photograph the chimpanzees.

I am tremendously grateful to the Tanzania government, its President, Mwalimu Julius Nyerere, and many of its officials for permitting us to conduct our research in the Gombe Stream area, and for giving us at all times help and assistance. I was initially helped by the Head and officials of the Tanzania Game Department, and I am particularly grateful to David Anstey, who assisted my mother and me when we first set up camp, and to the African Game Scouts Adolf, Saulo David, and Marcel, who were stationed in the Gombe Stream when the area was a game reserve. More recently, since the Gombe became a national park, we have received cooperation and assistance from Dr. John Owen, former Director of Tanzania National Parks, and his successor, Mr. S. ole Saibul. My thanks are due also to other members of the national parks staff, especially to Mr. J. Stevenson, Director of the Southern National Parks, and to the African Game Rangers stationed in the park.

My thanks are due also to government officials and many friends in Kigoma who throughout the years have done so much to help our research, as well as to give us personal assistance in countless ways.

I am very much indebted to Mr. Leighton Wilkie, who granted the funds that enabled me to venture forth on my field work in 1960 and who has, more recently, granted a further donation to our work. My gratitude to the National Geographic Society is sincere and of the greatest magnitude. The Society took over the financing of my research in 1961, supported the entire project at Gombe until 1968, and is continuing to make a major annual contribution today. In particular I should like to express my deepest thanks to Dr. Melville Bell Grosvenor, President and Editor from 1957 to 1967, to Dr. Melvin M. Payne, his successor as President, and to Dr. Leonard Carmichael, Chairman of the Research Committee, for their long-standing encouragement and support. I thank, too, the other members of the Board, and the staff and members of the Society, especially Mr. Robert Gilka, Miss Joanne Hess, Miss Mary Griswold, and Mr. Dave Boyer, who have gone out of their way to help us on many occasions.

In 1969 we received a substantial grant from the Science Research Council of Great Britain, and more recently we have received further financial support from the Wenner-Gren Foundation for Anthropological Research, the World Wildlife Fund, the East African Wildlife Society, and the L. S. B. Leakey Foundation. To these organizations, as well as to a number of private individuals who have made contributions to our research from time to time, I express our deep gratitude. Finally, I should like to convey my most sincere appreciation and thanks to the Grant Foundation of New York, which, as this book goes to press, has just given us a most generous sum of money; this, spread over the next three years, will enable us to make firm plans in advance for the continuity of the various facets of our research.

My profound thanks are due to Professor Robert Hinde of the Sub-Department of Animal Behaviour, Cambridge University, who not only supervised the analysis and writing up of results for my doctoral degree but who has been instrumental in obtaining some funds for the research and devoted much time and effort to helping us in other ways. I am also deeply grateful for the help given to us by Professor David Hamburg of the Stanford University School of Medicine. It is due to his efforts that our research center has now become affiliated with Stanford University, and I am planning many future projects in close collaboration with him. He has also been active in enabling us to acquire substantial grants for our research. Both Robert Hinde and Dave Hamburg kindly agreed to become scientific advisers to our research program. I am very appreciative, also, of the keen interest in our work and encouragement shown by Professor A. S. Msangi, Dean of the Faculty of Science of the University College of Dar es Salaam.

It is difficult to find adequate words to thank Hugo for all that he has done for me and for the research. He has built up a magnificent collection of photographs and a unique documentary film record of chimpanzee behavior, and it is to a large extent due to his constant help, administrative ability, and persistence that the Gombe Stream Research Centre was formed and is flourishing today. I am sure I could never have embarked on such a project on my own. Hugo's patience and understanding of both his chimpanzee subjects and his wife are remarkable. I must try also to thank my mother for all that she has done for me throughout the years, most particularly for her courage and cheerfulness during the early months when she shared with me the most primitive of living conditions. On many occasions, too, her advice and suggestions have proved invaluable. I am indebted to both my mother and to Hugo for the many valuable comments and criticisms they made when I was writing this book.

There are many people who have directly or indirectly made contributions to our research and helped us personally, and it is not possible to mention them all by name. I should, however, like to thank Dr. Bernard Verdcourt of Kew Botanical Gardens, who initially drove me to the Gombe Stream and later identified many food plants, and to Dr. Gillet of the East African Herbarium, who also identified plant specimens. My thanks are due also to the Pfizer Laboratories, which so generously supplied us with complimentary polio vaccine during the terrible epidemic at the Gombe Stream. I am also extremely grateful to Professor Douglas Roy, Drs. Anthony and Sue Harthoorn and Dr. Bradley Nelson, all of whom assisted in the tranquilization and operation on the chimpanzee Gilka. I am grateful to Mr. M. J. Richmond and Miss Dan, who have helped us with a great deal of general administration in Nairobi, and to George Dove, who has given us valuable assistance and advice on many occasions.

Next I should like to express my most sincere thanks to all the African staff and helpers who have done so much, throughout the years, to make our work easier and our life more pleasant. Particularly my thanks are due to Hassan and Dominic, Rashidi, Soko, Wilbert, and Short, who during the early years were at times my only companions in the bush. I thank also the many others: Sadiki, Ramadthani, Juma, Mpofu, Hilali, Jumanne, Kasim Ramadhani, Kasim Selemani, Yahaya, Aporual, Habibu, Alfonse, and Adreano. I should also like to express our gratitude to Iddi Matata and Mbrisho for the courtesy they have always shown us and the way in which they have made us feel welcome in their country. Perhaps this is the place also to thank Mucharia and Moro, who helped me so much by looking after my son while I was working on this book.

My thanks are due to Kris Pirozynski, who looked after our camp in the early days and to my sister Judy, who took some of the earliest photographs of chimpanzees in the wild. I am grateful, too, to Nicholas and Margaret Pickford, who worked at the center for a year as administrators, and to Baron and Baroness Godert and Bobbie van Lawick-de Marchant et d'Ansembourg, who also helped us in this capacity for three months.

I should like to acknowledge the work of Dr. Peter Marler and Dr. Michael Simpson. Both worked at the Gombe Stream on their own studies: Dr. Marler recorded chimpanzee calls over a two-month period and Dr. Simpson spent eighteen months working on social grooming. The results of these studies will be of value to our understanding of chimpanzee behavior. My thanks are due to Tim and Bonnie Ransom, Leanne Taylor, and Nicholas Owens, whose observations on the baboon troops at Gombe enabled us to learn more about the chimpanzees' predatory attempts on baboons and other chimpanzee-baboon interactions. Tim and Bonnie were extremely helpful when we changed the feeding system in 1968. I thank, too, John McKinnon, who worked at the Gombe on insect behavior, but devoted much time to helping us with our study of chimpanzees.

Finally I reach the point when I must attempt to express my thanks and gratitude to the students who as research assistants have so greatly increased our understanding of chimpanzee behavior. It is difficult in a short space to convey adequately my appreciation of the hard work, patience, and dedication that have in many instances gone into the careful accumulation of the long-term records on individual chimpanzees on which I have drawn so freely in the writing of this book. Without these students a longitudinal study of this sort could not be undertaken and this book could never have been written. At this point I should especially like to acknowledge the help of Edna Koning and Sonia Ivey, who worked so hard in the early pioneering days when our chores were seldom over before ten or eleven o'clock at night.

Some assistants have remained with us for a short time only, yet they too have made their contributions to the research: Sue Chaytor, Sally Avery, Pamela Carson, Patti Moehlman, Nicoletta Maraschin, June Cree, Janet Brooks, Sanno Keeler, Sally Puleston, Ben Gray, and Neville Washington. Others have stayed a full year as my research assistants, helping to accumulate data in the all-important long-term records: Caroline Coleman, Cathleen Clarke, Carole Gale, Dawn Starin, Ann Simpson.

Yet other students, after working for a year on the long-term records, have stayed on to start their own research projects in different aspects of behavior. Alice Sorem Ford worked on mother-infant interactions; I am particularly grateful to her hard work during the difficult time when each chimpanzee was given oral polio vaccine. Geza Teleki is now writing a report on meat-eating behavior in the Gombe Stream chimpanzees. Lori Baldwin is studying the relationship between adult female chimpanzees and David Bygott is studying those between adult males, with emphasis on dominance and aggression. Both Lori and David have been accepted by Cambridge University to work for their doctoral degrees. I am very grateful indeed to David for the superb line drawings of chimpanzees which he has made for the appendixes of this book. Seven other research assistants, at present working at Gombe, also plan to work there for a second year: Harold Bauer, Ellen

Drake, Margaretha Hankey, Ann Pusey, Gerald Rilling, Richard Wrangham, and Sean Sheehan, who with his wife will open up a second observation area, to the south of the park, for the promotion of tourism. I wish to thank all of them for their hard work, enthusiasm, and cooperation. I should also like to express appreciation to Dr. Helmut Albrecht, who has recently joined our research team as Senior Scientist; I am sure that his two-year sojourn at Gombe will be a happy one for all concerned. I have a special word of thanks to Patrick McGinnis, who is currently finishing the writing of his doctoral dissertation on reproductive behavior at Cambridge University. Pat has worked at the Gombe Stream for nearly four years, and on many occasions not only been in charge of the research but kept the place running almost single-handed when other students were away or sick. The Gombe Stream will seem quite strange when he finally leaves.

Now comes the most difficult part of these acknowledgments—that of trying to express my debt of gratitude to Ruth Davis, who lost her life while studying chimpanzees at the Gombe Stream. Ruth was not strong, yet she was one of the hardest workers we have had, and sometimes drove herself to near exhaustion. She chose to study the individualities of the adult male chimpanzees; she spent long arduous hours in the mountains observing and following her subjects, and sometimes typed out her notes until late in the evenings. It may have been due to physical exhaustion that one day, in 1968, Ruth fell from the edge of a precipice and was instantly killed. Her body was only found after a search of six days, during which many people took part, including the Kigoma police, national parks officials, and numerous volunteers from the surrounding villages. We were immensely grateful to all of these people.

It is impossible to find proper words to express my deep regret and sorrow at this terrible tragedy. Ruth's death was a great personal loss to all of us who knew her, and particularly to her fiancé, Geza Teleki. She was buried in the national park in the country that she loved so much during her life; her grave is surrounded by the forest and reverberates, from time to time, with the calling of the chimpanzees as they pass by.

My greatest admiration and deepest sympathy go to Ruth's

parents, who visited the Gombe Stream for the first time under the tragic circumstances of their daughter's burial. Despite their distress they were able to assure us that we should not feel ourselves at all responsible for the accident. Ruth, they told us, had known the happiest time of her life during her year with the chimpanzees, and in the work had found true fulfillment.

Ruth met her death while doing work that she really wanted to do, in the wilderness of the mountains that she loved; her careful study has given us added insight into the personalities of some of the chimpanzees. Ruth, I know, would wish me to end my acknowledgments with a tribute to the chimpanzees themselves, those amazing creatures who can teach us so much about ourselves even while we become increasingly fascinated by them in their own right. To David Graybeard and Flo in particular we owe much.

FOREWORD

ONCE IN A GENERATION, there occurs a piece of research that changes man's view of himself. The reader of this book has the privilege of sharing such an experience.

Of all the vast array of creatures on earth, none so closely resembles man as the chimpanzee. Indeed, recent biological research has shown that these resemblances are even more profound than we had anticipated. Whether one examines the nature of immune responses, the structure of blood proteins, or even the structure of the hereditary material itself (DNA), the chimp is closer to man than is any other species. Moreover, the circuitry of the brain is remarkably similar to man's. And the laboratory investigations of such pioneers as Yerkes and Köhler suggested that chimps have remarkable behavioral capacities. So students of human behavior have long been interested in learning what chimps could do in their natural habitat, unencumbered by constraints of a laboratory or a zoo. As one decade followed another without reliable information on this subject, it became increasingly doubtful whether the mystery of chimp behavior in nature could be solved before the chimps themselves became extinct under man's relentless pressure —a pressure that has eliminated so many species all over the earth.

The difficulties of solving the mystery were formidable—many experts thought insurmountable. Chimps live in dense forests, difficult of access and dangerous in many ways. There was no reason to believe they would permit close-range observation. There was much reason to doubt that a human observer could see enough behavior to make dependable observations; and some reason to doubt whether the observer could survive the effort over a long period of time. So, those of us who have had a persistent interest in this subject were inclined to despair that it could ever be clarified.

Then, in the early 1960s, reports began trickling back from Tanganyika that a young woman named Goodall was making a sustained and courageous effort; but the chimps were not cooperative. They stayed away from her, kept her at a great distance—often about five hundred yards—and threatened her if she took them by surprise. She suffered from malaria and a variety of hardships. Two years passed with only a scattering of close-range observations, and four years passed before truly abundant observations were possible. Yet she persisted—in itself one of the remarkable stories of our time. And at last the mystery of man's closest relative in nature began to yield to scientific scrutiny.

Today the study is in its eleventh year, with an excellent staff pursuing systematically many facets of chimp behavior. This study is unique in the history of research on animal behavior—partly because of the special place of the chimp in nature, but also because individual animals have been recognized and studied in all their individuality, because rich, close-range observations are accurately recorded, because there is a superb photographic record made by Hugo van Lawick, because changes in the life cycle have been carefully followed for a decade, because the individual animals have been studied in the context of their own community, because their habitat has not been disrupted, and because the study has in all respects been conducted with great care and integrity.

The picture of chimpanzee life that emerges is fascinating. Here is a highly intelligent, intensely social creature capable of close and enduring attachments, yet nothing that looks quite like human love, capable of rich communication through gestures, postures, facial expressions, and sounds, yet nothing quite like human language. This is a creature who not only uses tools effectively but also *makes* tools with considerable foresight; a creature who does a little sharing of food, though much less than man; a creature gifted in the arts of bluff and intimidation, highly excitable and aggressive, capable of using weapons, yet engaging in no activity comparable to human warfare; a creature who frequently hunts and kills small animals of other species in an organized, cooperative way, and seems to have some zest for the process of hunting, killing, and eating the prey; a creature whose repertoire of acts in aggression, deference, reassurance, and greeting bear uncanny similarities to human acts in similar situations.

Clearly, the chimpanzee bears extraordinary interest for man; and this study far exceeds any other in clarifying the chimpanzee's place in nature.

For me the reading of this beautifully written book helps to put man in a new perspective—significantly closer to other living organisms, sharing a common heritage of behavioral tendencies, yet also distinctive in crucial ways. More than any book of this generation, it helps one to see down the very long road we have traveled to our present predicaments, and to see—with modesty and yet with heightened appreciation—man's place in nature.

DAVID A. HAMBURG, M.D.
Stanford University School of Medicine

CONTENTS

IN THE SHADOW
OF MAN

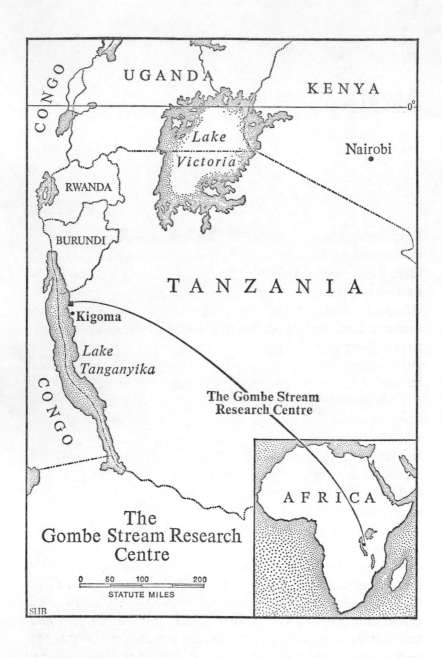

CONGO

UGANDA

KENYA

0°

Lake
Victoria

Nairobi

RWANDA

BURUNDI

TANZANIA

Kigoma

Lake
Tanganyika

The Gombe Stream
Research Centre

CONGO

AFRICA

The
Gombe Stream Research
Centre

0   50   100   200

STATUTE MILES

SHB

1

BEGINNINGS

SINCE DAWN I had climbed up and down the steep mountain slopes and pushed my way through the dense valley forests. Again and again I had stopped to listen, or to gaze through binoculars at the surrounding countryside. Yet I had neither heard nor seen a single chimpanzee, and now it was already five o'clock. In two hours darkness would fall over the rugged terrain of the Gombe Stream Chimpanzee Reserve. I settled down at my favorite vantage point, the Peak, hoping that at least I might see a chimpanzee make his nest for the night before I had to stop work for the day.

I was watching a troop of monkeys in the forested valley below when suddenly I heard the screaming of a young chimpanzee. Quickly I scanned the trees with my binoculars, but the sound had died away before I could locate the exact place, and it took several minutes of searching before I saw four chimpanzees. The slight squabble was over and they were all feeding peacefully on some yellow plumlike fruits.

The distance between us was too great for me to make detailed observations, so I decided to try to get closer. I surveyed the trees close to the group: if I could manage to get to that large fig without frightening the chimpanzees, I thought, I would get an excellent view. It took me about ten minutes to make the journey. As I moved cautiously around the thick gnarled trunk of the fig I realized that the chimpanzees had gone; the branches of the fruit tree were empty. The same old feeling of depression clawed at me.

Once again the chimpanzees had seen me and silently fled. Then all at once my heart missed several beats.

Less than twenty yards away from me two male chimpanzees were sitting on the ground staring at me intently. Scarcely breathing, I waited for the sudden panic-stricken flight that normally followed a surprise encounter between myself and the chimpanzees at close quarters. But nothing of the sort happened. The two large chimps simply continued to gaze at me. Very slowly I sat down, and after a few more moments, the two calmly began to groom one another.

As I watched, still scarcely believing it was true, I saw two more chimpanzee heads peering at me over the grass from the other side of a small forest glade: a female and a youngster. They bobbed down as I turned my head toward them, but soon reappeared, one after the other, in the lower branches of a tree about forty yards away. There they sat, almost motionless, watching me.

For over half a year I had been trying to overcome the chimpanzees' inherent fear of me, the fear that made them vanish into the undergrowth whenever I approached. At first they had fled even when I was as far away as five hundred yards and on the other side of a ravine. Now two males were sitting so close that I could almost hear them breathing.

Without any doubt whatsoever, this was the proudest moment I had known. I had been accepted by the two magnificent creatures grooming each other in front of me. I knew them both—David Graybeard, who had always been the least afraid of me, was one and the other was Goliath, not the giant his name implies but of superb physique and the highest-ranking of all the males. Their coats gleamed vivid black in the softening light of the evening.

For more than ten minutes David Graybeard and Goliath sat grooming each other, and then, just before the sun vanished over the horizon behind me, David got up and stood staring at me. And it so happened that my elongated evening shadow fell across him. The moment is etched deep into my memory: the excitement of the first close contact with a wild chimpanzee and the freakish chance that cast my shadow over David even as he seemed to gaze into my eyes. Later it acquired an almost allegorical significance, for of all living creatures today only man, with his superior brain, his superior intellect, overshadows the chimpanzee. Only man casts his shadow of doom over the freedom of the chimpanzee in the forests with his guns and his spreading settlements and cultivation. At that moment, however, I did not think of this. I only marveled in David and Goliath themselves.

The depression and despair that had so often visited me during the preceding months were as nothing compared to the exultation I felt when the group had finally moved away and I was hastening down the darkening mountainside to my tent on the shores of Lake Tanganyika.

It had all begun three years before when I had met Dr. L. S. B. Leakey, the well-known anthropologist and paleontologist, in Nairobi. Or perhaps it had begun in my earliest childhood. When I was just over one year old my mother gave me a toy chimpanzee, a large hairy model celebrating the birth of the first chimpanzee infant ever born in the London zoo. Most of my mother's friends were horrified and predicted that the ghastly creature would give a small child nightmares; but Jubilee (as the celebrated infant itself was named) was my most loved possession and accompanied me on all my childhood travels. I still have the worn old toy.

Quite apart from Jubilee, I had been fascinated by live animals from the time when I first learned to crawl. One of my earliest recollections is of the day that I hid in a small stuffy henhouse in order to see how a hen laid an egg. I emerged after about five hours. The whole household had apparently been searching for me for hours, and my mother had even rung the police to report me missing.

It was about four years later, when I was eight, that I first decided I would go to Africa and live with wild animals when I grew up. Although when I left school at eighteen I took a secretarial course and then two different jobs, the longing for Africa was still very much with me. So much so that when I received an invitation to go and stay with a school friend at her parents' farm in Kenya I handed in my resignation the same day and left a fascinating job at a documentary film studio in order to earn my fare to Africa by working as a waitress during the summer season in Bournemouth, my home town; it was impossible to save money in London.

"If you are interested in animals," someone said to me about a month after my arrival in Africa, "then you should meet Dr. Leakey." I had already started on a somewhat dreary office job, since I had not wanted to overstay my welcome at my friend's farm. I went to see Louis Leakey at what is now the National Museum of natural history in Nairobi, where at that same time he was Curator. Somehow he must have sensed that my interest in animals was not just a passing phase, but was rooted deep, for on the spot he gave me a job as an assistant secretary.

I learned much while working at the museum. The staff all were keen naturalists full of enthusiasm and were happy to share some of their boundless knowledge with me. Best of all, I was offered the chance, with one other girl, of accompanying Dr. Leakey and his wife Mary on one of their annual paleontological expeditions to Olduvai Gorge on the Serengeti plains. In those days, before the opening up of the Serengeti to tourists, before the discoveries of *Zinjanthropus* (Nutcracker man) and *Homo habilis* at Olduvai, the area was completely secluded: the roads and tourist buses and light aircraft that pass there today were then undreamed of.

The digging itself was fascinating. For hours, as I picked away at the ancient clay or rock of the Olduvai fault to extract the remains of creatures that had lived millions of years ago, the task would be purely routine, but from time to time, and without warning, I would be filled with awe by the sight or the feel of some bone I held in my hand. This—this very bone—had once been part of a living, breathing animal that had walked and slept and propagated its species. What had it really looked like? What color was its hair; what was the odor of its body?

It was the evenings, however, that gave those few months their special enchantment for me. When the hard work of the day was finished at about six o'clock, then Gillian, my fellow assistant, and I were free to return to camp across the sun-parched arid plains above the gorge where we had sweated all day. Olduvai in the dry season becomes almost a desert, but as we walked past the low thornbushes we often glimpsed dik-diks, those graceful miniature antelopes scarcely larger than a hare. Sometimes there would be a small herd of gazelles or giraffes, and on a few memorable occasions we saw a black rhinoceros plodding along the gorge below.

Once we came face to face with a young male lion: he was no more than forty feet away when we heard his soft growl and peered around to see him on the other side of a small bush. We were down in the bottom of the gorge where the vegetation is comparatively thick in parts; slowly we backed away while he watched, his tail twitching. Then, out of curiosity I suppose, he followed us as we walked deliberately across the gorge toward the open, treeless plains on the other side. As we began to climb upward he vanished into the vegetation and we did not see him again.

Toward the end of our time at Olduvai Louis Leakey began to talk to me about a group of chimpanzees living on the shores of Lake Tanganyika. The chimpanzee is found only in Africa, where it ranges across the equatorial forest belt from the west coast to a point just east of Lake Tanganyika. The group Louis was referring to comprised chimpanzees of the Eastern or Longhaired variety, *Pan troglodytes schweinfurthi,* as they are labeled by taxonomists. Louis described their habitat as mountainous, rugged, and completely cut off from civilization. He spoke for a while of the dedication and patience that would be required of any person who tried to study them.

Only one man, Louis told me, had attempted to make a serious study of chimpanzee behavior in the wild, and Professor Henry W. Nissen, who had done this pioneering work, had only been able to spend two and a half months in the field—in French Guinea. Louis said that no one could expect to accomplish much in such a short time; two years would scarcely be long enough. Much more Louis told me during that first talk. He was, he said, particularly interested in the behavior of a group of chimpanzees living on the shores of a lake—for the remains of prehistoric man were often found on a lakeshore and it was possible that an understanding of chimpanzee behavior today might shed light on the behavior of our stone age ancestors.

I could hardly believe that he spoke seriously when, after a pause, he asked me if I would be willing to tackle the job. Although it was the sort of thing I most wanted to do, I was not qualified to undertake a scientific study of animal behavior. Louis, however, knew exactly what he was doing. Not only did he feel that a university training was unnecessary, but even that in some ways it might have been disadvantageous. He wanted someone with a mind uncluttered and unbiased by theory who would make the study for no other reason than a real desire for knowledge; and, in addition, someone with a sympathetic understanding of animals.

Once I had agreed wholeheartedly and enthusiastically to undertake the work, Louis embarked on the difficult task of raising the necessary funds. He had to convince someone of the need for the study itself, and also that a young and unqualified girl was the right person to attempt it. Eventually the Wilkie Foundation in Des Plaines, Illinois, agreed to contribute a sum sufficient to cover the necessary capital expenses—a small boat, a tent, and air fares—and an initial six months in the field. I shall always be immensely grateful to Mr. Leighton Wilkie, who, trusting Louis's judgment, gave me the chance to prove myself.

By this time I was back in England, but as soon as I heard the news I made arrangements to return to Africa. The government officials in Kigoma, in whose area I would be working, had agreed to my proposed study, but they were adamant on one score: they would not hear of a young English girl living in the bush alone without a European companion. And so my mother, Vanne Goodall, who had already been out to Africa for a few months, volunteered to accompany me on my new venture.

When we reached Nairobi in 1960 everything at first went well. The Gombe Stream Chimpanzee Reserve (now the Gombe National Park), the home of my chimpanzee group, fell under the jurisdiction of the Tanganyika Game Department, and the Chief Game Warden was most helpful in sending the necessary permits for me to work in the reserve. He also sent much useful information about the conditions there—the altitude and temperature, type of terrain and vegetation, the animals I might expect to encounter. Word had come through that the small aluminum boat Louis had bought had arrived safely in Kigoma. And Dr. Bernard Verdcourt, Director of the East African Herbarium, volunteered to drive Vanne and me to Kigoma; he would be able to collect plant specimens on the way, and also in the botanically little-known Kigoma area.

Just as we were ready to leave came the first setback. The District Commissioner of the Kigoma region sent word that there was trouble among the African fishermen on the beaches of the chimpanzee reserve. The Game Ranger for the area had gone there to try to sort things out, but in the meantime it would not be possible for me to begin my work.

Fortunately Louis immediately put forward the suggestion that I should make a short trial study of the vervet monkeys on an island in Lake Victoria. Within a week Vanne and I were on his motor launch chugging lazily over the shallow muddy water of the lake to uninhabited Lolui Island. With us were Hassan, captain of the little launch, and his assistant, both Africans of the Kakamega tribe. Hassan, who later joined me at the chimpanzee reserve, is a wonderful person. Always calm and rather stately, he is wonderful in an emergency, and with his sense of humor and intelligence makes a fine companion. At that time he had worked for Louis for nearly thirty years.

It was three weeks before we received a radio message recalling us to Nairobi, and those three weeks were full of enchantment. At night we slept on the boat anchored just off the island and were lulled by the gentle rocking swell of the lake. Every morning just before sunrise Hassan rowed me ashore in the dinghy and I remained on the island watching the monkeys until dusk—or even later on those evenings when the moon was bright. Then I met Hassan on the lakeshore and he rowed me back to the boat. Over our meager supper, usually consisting of baked beans, eggs, or tinned sausages, Vanne and I exchanged our news of the day.

The short study of the troop of monkeys taught me a good deal about such things as note-taking in the field, the sort of clothes to wear, the movements a wild monkey will tolerate in a human observer and those it will not. Although the chimpanzees reacted quite differently in many ways, the things I learned at Lolui were very helpful when I started work at the Gombe Stream

I was sorry, in a way, when the expected message came one evening, for it meant leaving the vervets just as I was beginning to learn about their behavior, just as I had become familiar with the different individuals of the troop. It is never easy to leave a job unfinished. Once we reached Nairobi, however, I could think of nothing save the excitement of the eight-hundred-mile journey to Kigoma—and the chimpanzees. Nearly everything had been ready

before we left for Lolui, so it was only a few days before we were
able to set off with Bernard Verdcourt for Kigoma.

The journey itself was fairly uneventful, although we had three
minor breakdowns and the Land-Rover was so badly overloaded
with all our equipment that it swayed dangerously if we went too
fast. When we reached Kigoma, however, after a dusty three days
on the road, we found the whole town in a state of chaos. Since
we had left Nairobi violence and bloodshed had erupted in the
Congo, which lay only some twenty-five miles to the west of
Kigoma, on the other side of Lake Tanganyika. Kigoma was over-
run by boatloads of Belgian refugees. It was Sunday when we drove
for the first time down the avenue of mango trees that shade
Kigoma's one main street. Everything was closed, and we could
find no official to help us.

Eventually we ran the District Commissioner to earth, and he
explained, regretfully but firmly, that there was no chance at all
of my proceeding to the chimpanzee reserve. First it was necessary
to wait and find out how the local Kigoma district Africans would
react to the tales of rioting and disorder in the Congo. It was a blow,
but there was little time for moping.

We booked ourselves a room each at one of the two hotels. This
luxury did not last long, because another boatload of refugees
arrived that evening and every available inch of space was needed.
Vanne and I doubled up, squeezing ourselves into the small amount
of room left over after we had crammed in all our equipment from
the Land-Rover. Bernard shared his room with two homeless Bel-
gians, and we even got out our three camp beds and lent them to
the harassed hotel owner. Every room was crammed, but these
refugees were in paradise compared to those temporarily housed
in the huge warehouse, normally used for storing cargo on its way
across the lake to or from the Congo. There everyone slept in long
rows on mattresses or merely blankets on the cement floor, and
queued up in their hundreds for the scant meals that Kigoma was
able to provide for them.

Very soon Vanne, Bernard, and I had made the acquaintance
of a number of Kigoma's residents. We offered to help with the
catering and this offer was eagerly accepted. On our second evening in Kigoma we three and a few others made two thousand

Spam sandwiches. These were finally stacked neatly in wet cloths in large tin trunks that were carted off to the warehouse. Later we helped to hand them out to the refugees, together with soup, some fruit, chocolate, cigarettes, and drinks. I have never been able to face tinned Spam since.

Two evenings later most of the refugees had gone, carried off by a series of extra trains to Tanganyika's capital, Dar es Salaam. The hustle of activity was over, but still we were not allowed to leave for the chimpanzee reserve. We all became somewhat depressed. My funds did not permit Vanne and me to stay on at the hotel, so we decided to put up a temporary camp somewhere. When we inquired where we could do this, we were directed to the grounds of the Kigoma prison. This was not as bad as it sounds, since the grounds, which are beautifully kept, overlook the lake and at that time of year the citrus trees all around were groaning under the weight of sweet-smelling oranges and tangerines. The mosquitoes in the evening were terrible, though.

During our period of enforced inactivity we came to know the tiny town of Kigoma quite well—it is more like a village by European or American standards. The hub of activity was down by the lakeshore, where the natural harbor offers anchorage to the boats plying up and down the lake to Burundi, Zambia, Malawi, and across to the Congo in the west. Near the lake, too, are the government administrative offices, the police station, the railway station, and the post office.

One of the most fascinating aspects of any small town in Africa is the colorful fruit and vegetable market, where the merchandise is offered for sale in small piles, each of which has been accurately counted and priced. In Kigoma market we found that the more prosperous traders operated from under a lofty stone awning; the others sat on the red earth of the main market square, their wares neatly set out on sacking or on the ground itself. Bananas, green and yellow oranges, and dark purple, wrinkled passion fruits were displayed in profusion, and there were bottles and jars of glowing red cooking oil made from the fruit of oil nut palms.

Kigoma boasts one main street, which slopes upward from the administrative center and runs through the main part of Kigoma. On either side it is flanked by tall shady mango trees and countless tiny stores, or *dukas,* as they are called throughout East Africa. It amazed us, as we walked through Kigoma, that so many stores could survive when they all appeared to sell similar goods. Again and again we saw piles of kettles and crockery, sneakers and shirts, torches and alarm clocks. Most stores were brightened by great squares of brilliantly colored material sold in pairs to the African women and known as *kangas.* One square is wrapped around under the arms and hangs down just below the knees; the other becomes a headdress. Outside some of the dukas a tailor worked at his foot-operated sewing machine, and an old Indian sat in the dust outside the tiny shoe shop using his feet like extra hands to hold the leather as he sewed and tacked and glued shoes together. He was so skillful that it was a delight to watch him.

We became better acquainted with several Kigoma residents during these days; they were mostly government officials and their wives, and we found them very friendly and hospitable. One evening Vanne, not wanting to rebuff any of our new-found friends, accepted two offers of a hot bath. Bernard, who was convinced that we were both slightly mad anyway, drove her stoically from house to house to keep her appointments without giving her away.

When we had been in Kigoma just over a week David Anstey, the Game Ranger who had been sorting out the troubles between the fishermen at the Gombe Stream Reserve, returned to Kigoma. He and the District Commissioner had a long conference, the outcome of which was that I was given official permission to proceed to the Gombe Stream. By this time I had almost given up hope of ever seeing a chimpanzee; I had convinced myself that at any minute we would be ordered back to Nairobi. When I found myself on the government launch that had been lent to us for transporting all our equipment, including our twelve-foot dinghy, the expedition had taken on a dreamlike quality. As the engine sprang to life and the anchor was drawn, we waved goodbye to Bernard and were soon steaming out of Kigoma harbor and turning northward along the eastern shores of the lake. I can remember looking down into the incredibly clear water and thinking to myself, I expect the boat will sink, or I shall fall overboard and be eaten by a crocodile. But good luck was with us.

2

EARLY DAYS

I RETAINED THE STRANGE FEELING that I was living in a dream world throughout the twelve-mile journey from Kigoma to our camping place in the Gombe Stream Chimpanzee Reserve. It was the middle of the dry season, and the shoreline of the Congo, though it was only some twenty-five miles distant, was not even faintly discernible to the west of long, narrow Lake Tanganyika. The fresh breeze and the deep blue of the water, choppy with small waves and flecked with white foam, combined to make us feel that we were at sea.

I gazed at the eastern shoreline. Between Kigoma and the start of the chimpanzee sanctuary the steep slopes of the rift escarpment, which rise twenty-five hundred feet above the lake, are in many places bare and eroded from years of tree felling. In between, small pockets of forest cling to the narrow valleys where fast-flowing mountain streams rush down to the lake. The coastline is broken into a series of elongated bays often separated by rocky headlands that jut out into the lake. We steered a straight course, proceeding from headland to headland and noticing that the little canoes of the fishermen hugged the shoreline. David Anstey, who was traveling with us to introduce us to the local African inhabitants of the area, explained that sometimes the lake becomes suddenly rough, with fierce winds sweeping down the valleys and churning the water into a welter of spray and waves.

All along the shoreline fishing villages clung to the mountain slopes or nestled in the mouths of the valleys. The dwellings were mostly simple mud and grass huts, although even in those days there were a few larger buildings roofed with shiny corrugated iron—that curse, for those who love natural beauty, of the modern African landscape.

When we had traveled about seven miles, David pointed out the large rocky outcrop marking the southern limits of the chimpanzee reserve. Once past the boundary we noticed that the country changed suddenly and dramatically: here the mountains were thickly wooded and intersected by valleys supporting dense tropical forests. Even here we noticed a number of fishermen's huts dotted at intervals along the white beaches: David explained that these were temporary structures. The Africans had permits to fish during the dry season and to dry their catch on the beaches of the reserve itself. When the rains began, the fishermen returned to their home villages outside the chimpanzee reserve. It was among these men that the recent trouble had broken out—some argument between the fishermen of two different villages as to which of them had the right to a certain stretch of beach.

Since that day I have often wondered exactly what it was I felt as I stared at the wild country that so soon I should be roaming. Vanne admitted afterward to have been secretly horrified by the steepness of the slopes and the impenetrable appearance of the valley forests. And David Anstey told me several months later that he had guessed I would be packed up and gone within six weeks. I remember feeling neither excitement nor trepidation but only a curious sense of detachment. What had I, the girl standing on the government launch in her jeans, to do with the girl who in a few days would be searching those very mountains for wild chimpanzees? Yet by the time I went to sleep that night the transformation had taken place.

After a two-hour journey the launch dropped anchor at Kasekela, where the two government Game Scouts had their headquarters. David Anstey had suggested that, at least until we were familiar with the area, we should camp somewhere near their huts. As our dinghy approached the white sandy beach we saw that quite a crowd had gathered to watch our arrival: the two scouts, the few Africans who had permission to live permanently at the reserve so that the scouts should not be completely isolated, and some of the fishermen from nearby huts. We stepped ashore, splashing into the sparkling wavelets, and were greeted first by the scouts and then, with great ceremony, by the honorary headman of Kasekela village, old Iddi Matata. He was a colorful figure with his red turban, red European-style coat over flowing white robes, wooden shoes, and white beard. He made a long speech of welcome to us in Swahili, of which I understood only fragments, and we presented him with a small gift that David had advised us to buy for him.

The formalities over, Vanne and I followed David for about thirty yards along a narrow track leading from the beach through thick vegetation to a small natural clearing. With the help of David and the African scouts the large tent Vanne and I would share was soon up. Behind the tent flowed a small gurgling stream, and the clearing was shaded by tall oil nut palms. It was a perfect campsite. Fifty yards or so distant, under some trees on the beach, we set up another small tent for Dominic, the cook we had employed before leaving Kigoma.

When our camp was organized I slipped away to explore. The tall grass of the lower mountain slopes had been burned off by a recent bush fire, and the charcoal-encrusted ground was slippery. It was about four o'clock, but still the sun burned down fiercely and I was hot and sweating by the time I had climbed high enough to look down over the flat lake and the broad valley, lush and green in contrast to the blackened mountainside on which I stood.

I sat on a big flat rock, hot from the sun. Soon a troop of about sixty baboons passed by, searching the newly burned ground for the remains of baked insects. Some of them climbed trees when they saw me and shook the branches with jerky, threatening movements, and two of the big males started their loud alarm bark. But on the whole the troop was not very worried by my presence, and soon moved slowly on, busy with its own affairs. I also saw a bushbuck, a graceful chestnut animal slightly larger than a goat, with sturdy spiraling horns. He stared at me, motionless, and then suddenly turned and bounded away, barking like a dog and flashing the white underside of his tail.

I only stayed out on the mountain about three-quarters of an hour, but when I returned, almost as black as the slopes on which

I had been scrambling, I no longer felt an intruder. That night I pulled my camp bed into the open and slept with the stars above me twinkling down through the rustling fronds of a palm tree.

The next morning, though I was eager to go out looking for chimpanzees, I soon found that to start with, anyway, I was not to be my own master. David Anstey had arranged for a number of the local Africans to come and meet Vanne and me. He explained that they were all worried and resentful; they could not believe a young girl would come all the way from England just to look at apes, and so the rumor had spread that I was a government spy. Naturally I was very grateful to David for sorting things out for me right at the start, but my heart sank when I heard the plans he had made for me.

First it was agreed that the son of the chief of Mwamgongo, a large fishing village to the north of the chimpanzee reserve, should accompany me. He would make sure that when I saw one chimpanzee I did not write down in my book that I had seen ten or twenty. Later I realized that the Africans were still hoping to reclaim the thirty square miles of the reserve for themselves: if I stated that there were more chimpanzees than in fact there were, the Africans felt the government could then make a better case for keeping the area a protected reserve. Second, David felt that for the sake of my prestige I should employ an African to carry my haversack.

Since I was convinced the only way to establish contact with shy animals was to move about alone, I was upset to think I must be encumbered by two companions. Then came the final blow— I also had to have one of the Game Scouts with me. I felt depressed and miserable when I went to bed that night.

When I woke up the next morning, however, everything was new and exciting and my gloom soon vanished. I had arranged to meet the chief's son at a valley near the northern boundary, for my Game Scout, Adolf, had reported seeing chimpanzees while patrolling there the day before. David had some business in Mwamgongo village so he took me, together with Adolf and Rashidi, my "porter," in his boat and dropped us off at the appointed place.

The chief's son came toward us, followed by five or six other Africans, and I had a sudden horror that they would all insist on coming with me. My fears were quickly allayed. The young man asked where I planned to go and I pointed vaguely toward the steep thickly forested slopes of the valley. He looked rather taken aback and began to talk quietly and earnestly with his friends in Kiha, the language of the local Ha tribesmen. A few moments later he again approached and told me he felt rather unwell and would not go with me that day. Later I found out he had expected that I would merely ride up and down the lakeshore in a boat, counting any chimpanzees I saw. The idea of clambering about in the mountains did not appeal to him at all, and I never saw him again.

Just as we were leaving, two fishermen ran up and asked us to follow them for a moment. They led us to a tree behind one of the temporary huts: the bark was gashed in a hundred places. There, we learned, a lone bull buffalo had chased one of the fishermen the night before. The man had managed to climb to safety but the buffalo had charged at the slender tree time after time. Whether the men were merely making a report to the Game Scout or whether they were trying to impress upon me the hazards of their country I do not know, but the memory of that battered tree haunted me for weeks when I was crawling about in the thick undergrowth of the valley forests.

After this we set off up the Mitumba Valley, and I soon found myself walking through the sort of African forest of which I had always dreamed. There were giant buttressed trees festooned with lianas and here and there brilliant red or white flowers that gleamed through the dark foliage. We moved along beside a fast-flowing shallow stream, often wading across when the going was easier on the opposite side. Now and then a kingfisher or some other forest bird flashed past, and once a troop of redtail monkeys leaped across a gap overhead, their coppery tails glinting. The forest canopy, over a hundred feet above us, shut out most of the sunlight and there was little undergrowth along the valley bottom.

When we had been traveling for about twenty minutes Adolf left the stream and led us up the side of the valley. Almost at once the going became much more difficult. The trees were smaller and the undergrowth was thick and tangled with vines, so we had to crawl most of the time. Presently Adolf stopped under an enormous tree. I looked up and saw that it was laden with small orange and red fruits. Down below the ground was littered with broken-off twigs and partly eaten fruits. This was the *msulula* tree where the chimpanzees had been feeding the day before. I had not intended to go right up to the tree and, hoping that we had not disturbed any chimpanzees, I quickly told my guides that I wanted to watch from farther away—from the other side of the valley.

Ten minutes later we were settled in a small grassy clearing at about the same height as the msulula tree and directly opposite. I discovered afterward that it was, in fact, the only really good open space from which one could watch the tree. Rashidi's trained eye had spotted it instantly, whereas I, at that time, would never have noticed it. It seemed very quiet and peaceful, away from the rushing of the stream. Some cicadas were shrilling incessantly, and there were some bird songs and the occasional bark or scream of a baboon.

All at once in the valley below I heard the calling of a group of chimpanzees. I had heard chimpanzees in the zoo, of course, but out here in the African forest the sound was thrilling beyond words. First one chimp gave a series of low resonant "pant-hoots" —loud hooting calls connected by audible inhalations of breath. These grew louder and louder, until in the end the chimpanzee was almost screaming. Halfway through his calling another joined in, and then another. I had read of chimpanzees drumming on tree trunks when I went through Dr. Nissen's report. Now I heard the strange echoing sound for myself, reverberating throughout the valley, interspersed with the wild chorus of pant-hoots.

The group was very close to the msulula tree, and I waited with every sense alert, staring into the forest opposite. Even so, it was Rashidi who saw the first movement as a chimpanzee climbed up a palm trunk and into the branches of the giant tree. It was followed by another and another and another, each climbing in orderly procession. I counted sixteen in all, some large, some much smaller. One was a mother with a tiny infant clinging to her tummy.

Excited as I was, I could not help feeling disappointed. Although the chimpanzees remained for two hours in the tree, I saw little except an occasional glimpse of a black arm reaching out from the foliage and pulling bunches of fruit out of sight. And then, one after the other and in complete silence the whole group climbed down the palm tree ladder and vanished into the forest. That was what amazed me most—sixteen chimpanzees in one tree and yet the only sounds I had heard had been the calls announcing their arrival.

A few minutes after the last chimpanzee had gone, when I was still searching the valley with my binoculars in the hope of seeing the group climbing into another tree, I was horrified to hear Adolf and Rashidi announce that we must return because it was their time for eating. I remonstrated in vain. Until I felt myself on firmer ground I dared not order them to stay, nor did I dare risk David's displeasure by remaining without my escorts. As we filed back through the forest, however, I determined that things would be different in the future.

The msulula continued to bear fruit for another ten days, and Rashidi and Adolf took turns to accompany me, taking their midday meals with them. For three nights, in fact, we slept there, Rashidi and Adolf huddled close together in the glow of a small campfire, and myself, farther back, wrapped up in a blanket.

I saw many chimpanzees during those ten days. Sometimes large groups climbed up and fed on the msulula fruits, and sometimes there were only two or three individuals in a group. Twice I saw a completely solitary male who fed for over an hour by himself. I soon realized that the groups were not stable: once, for instance, fourteen chimps arrived together but left in two different groups, the second climbing down a full half hour after the first. And, judging from the subsequent sounds, they went off in different directions. On another occasion I saw two small groups meet high in the tree, with much screaming and rushing about through the branches. Then they quieted, fed peacefully together, and, so far as I could tell, moved off together. I found out too that some groups comprised only adult males, some only females and youngsters, and others consisted of males, females, and youngsters all together.

I was, however, far from satisfied. I saw very few interactions between individual chimpanzees—the foliage of the msulula was far too thick, and when I twice tried to watch from nearer I failed dismally: once the chimps saw me on their way to the tree and fled, and on the second occasion all I saw of the four who fed for an hour almost above me was a very brief glimpse as they climbed up, and subsequently down, the palm tree ladder.

Later I realized how lucky I had been during the fruiting of the msulula tree. I probably learned more during those ten days than I did during the eight depressing weeks that followed. Search as we would, we found no other large fruiting tree or group of fruiting trees. We went up most of the twelve valleys of the reserve, but the undergrowth was often very thick, and although the sound of the streams drowned any noise we made it also effectively camouflaged the sounds that might have warned us of the whereabouts of chimps. Those we did see were usually so close by the time we came upon them that they fled instantly. I now can well imagine how many times they must have seen us coming and silently vanished without our ever being aware of their presence.

We had slightly better luck when we climbed the ridges between the valleys, but again the chimps either hurried away at the sight of us, even when we were five hundred yards away and on the other side of a ravine, or else were so far off that it was impossible to see any details of their behavior. For a while I wondered whether it was because there were three of us that the chimpanzees seemed so frightened, but even when I left my two companions on some high peak, from which they could keep an eye on me, and tried to get closer to some distant group on my own, the reaction of the chimps was the same. They fled.

In between the disappointing days, when we only saw chimps too far off to observe properly or for a few minutes close by before they fled, were even worse days when we saw no chimps at all. The more I thought of the task I had set myself, the more despondent I became. Nevertheless, those weeks did serve to acquaint me with the rugged terrain. My skin became hardened to the rough grasses of the valleys and my blood immune to the poison of the tsetse fly, so that I no longer swelled hugely each time I was bitten. I became increasingly surefooted on the treacherous slopes, which were equally slippery whether they were bare and eroded, crusted with charcoal, or carpeted by dry, trampled grass. Gradually, too, I became familiar with many of the animal tracks in the five valleys that became my main work area.

I encountered many of the other denizens of the mountains during our daily wanderings: huge gray bushpigs with their silvery spinal crests; groups of banded mongooses rustling through the leaves in search of insects; the squirrels and the striped and spotted

elephant shrews of the thick forests. Gradually, too, I sorted out
the many different kinds of monkeys that can be found in the
Gombe Stream area. Most often we came across troops of baboons;
sometimes they accepted our presence quite calmly, like the group
I met that first afternoon, but some troops barked persistently and
noisily until we, or they, had moved out of sight. In each of the
valleys there were two or three small groups of redtail monkeys
and a few blue monkeys. There were much larger troops of red
colobus monkeys, numbering sixty or more, each of which ranged
over a couple of valleys. Occasionally we came across a solitary
silver monkey with its black face framed by a white band of hair.
There were even a few troops of vervet monkeys, down by the lakeshore, to remind me of my monkey-watching days on Lolui Island.

In particular I liked to watch the red colobus. They are large
monkeys, and occasionally I fleetingly mistook the adult males
for chimpanzees, because in some lights the dark brown hair of
their backs looks black, and they sit upright on the branches, holding an overhead bough with one hand more like apes than monkeys. But their long, thick hanging tails soon revealed their true
identity. When I got close to them and they peered down at me
from the branches, their faces reminded me of surprised maiden
aunts wearing ginger-red golliwog wigs.

Rashidi taught me a great deal about bush lore, and how to find
my way through seemingly impenetrable forest. Despite my initial
disappointment when I had heard that I was not allowed to be
alone, I was grateful for his help during those early days. Soon he
had to leave me, to return for a while to his village. Since I found
that Adolf the scout was not suited to long arduous hours in the
mountains without food, I had a succession of other African companions during the next few months. There was Soko, from
Nyanza, whose name caused much amusement among the local
Africans, for this is their word for chimpanzee. Next came the
enormously tall and willowy Wilbert, who always looked immacu-
late even after scrambling on his belly along a pig trail; and finally
Short, who, as his name implies, was very small. All three were
tough men who had spent their lives working in the bush with
animals, and I enjoyed their company and learned much during the
days they worked for me.

3

FIRST OBSERVATIONS

About three months after our arrival, Vanne and I fell ill at the same time. It was undoubtedly some sort of malaria, but since we had been told by no lesser person than the doctor in Kigoma that there was no malaria in the area we had no drugs with us. How he came to believe such a strange fallacy I cannot imagine. We were too naive to question him at that time. For nearly two weeks we lay side by side on our low camp beds in our hot, stuffy tent sweating out the fever. Occasionally we mustered the strength to take our temperatures; neither of us felt like reading so there was nothing else to do to pass the time. Vanne had a temperature of 105 degrees almost constantly for five days, and it dropped slightly only during the coolness of the nights. Afterward we were told that she had been lucky to pull through at all. To make everything worse, the whole camp was pervaded, throughout our illness, by the most terrible smell—rather like bad cabbage water. It was the flower of some tree—I forget its name now—I always think of as the "fever flower tree."

Dominic, our cook, was wonderful during those days. He begged us to go into Kigoma to see a doctor, and when we pleaded that we felt much too ill to face the three-hour journey in our little boat, he made up for our lack of medical attention by constantly fussing over us. One night Vanne wandered out of the tent in a delirium and fell, unconscious, by one of the palm trees. I never knew she had left the tent. It was Dominic who found her at about three in the morning and assisted her back to bed. Later he told us that he came along several times each night to make sure his "Memsahibs" were all right.

As soon as the fever left me I was impatient to start work again. Nearly three months had sped away, and I felt that I had learned nothing. I was frantic—in a couple of months my funds would run out. I could not bear the thought of any of my African companions seeing me in my weak state and so, risking official displeasure, I set off alone one morning for the mountain I had climbed on my first afternoon—the mountain that rose directly above our camp. I left at my usual time, when it was still cool, in the first glimmerings of dawn. After ten minutes or so my heart began to hammer wildly, I could feel the blood pounding in my head, and I had to stop to catch my breath. Eventually I reached an open peak about one thousand feet above the lake. It offered a superb view over the home valley, so I decided to sit there for a while and search for signs of chimpanzees through my binoculars.

I had been there some fifteen minutes when a slight movement on the bare burned slope just beyond a narrow ravine caught my eye. I looked around and saw three chimps standing there staring at me. I expected them to flee, for they were no farther than eighty yards away, but after a moment they moved on again, quite calmly, and were soon lost to sight in some thicker vegetation. Had I been correct, after all, in my assumption that they would be less afraid of one person completely alone? For even when I had left my African companions behind and approached a group on my own, the chimps had undoubtedly been fully aware of what was going on.

I remained on my peak, and later on in the morning a group of chimps, with much screaming and barking and pant-hooting, careered down the opposite mountain slope and began feeding in some fig trees that grew thickly along the streambanks in the valley below me. They had only been there about twenty minutes when another procession of chimps crossed the bare slope where earlier I had seen the three. This group also saw me since I was very conspicuous on the rocky peak. Although they all stopped and stared and then hastened their steps slightly as they moved on again, the chimpanzees did not run in panic. Presently, with violent swaying of branches and wild calling, this group joined the chimpanzees already feeding on figs. After a time they settled down to feed quietly together, and when they finally climbed down from the trees they moved off in one big group. For part of the way, as they walked up the valley, I could see them following each other in a long, orderly line. Two small infants were perched like jockeys on their mothers' backs. I even saw them pause to drink, each one for about a minute, before leaping across the stream.

It was by far the best day I had had since my arrival at Gombe, and when I got back to camp that evening I was exhilarated, if exhausted. Vanne, who had been far more ill than I and was still in bed, was much cheered by my excitement.

That day, in fact, marked the turning point in my study. The fig trees grow all along the lower reaches of the stream and that year the crop in our valley was plentiful, lasting for eight weeks. Every day I returned to my peak, and every day chimpanzees fed on the figs below. They came in large groups and small groups, singly and in pairs. Regularly they passed me, either moving along the original route across the open slope just above me or along one or other of the trails crossing the grassy ridge below me. And because I always looked the same, wearing similar dull-colored clothes, and never tried to follow them or harass them in any way, the shy chimpanzees began to realize, at long last, that after all I was not so horrific and terrifying. Also, I was usually alone on my peak; there was no need for my African companions to follow me up and down, since they knew where I was going to be. When Short had to leave I decided to employ no other African, and although Adolf and afterward Saulo David, the new scout, often came up in the evenings to make sure I was all right, mostly I was completely on my own.

My peak quickly became the Peak. It is, I think, the very best vantage point for watching chimpanzees in the whole of the Gombe Stream sanctuary. From higher up there is, indeed, a magnificent view in all directions, but the chimpanzees seldom move about near the top of the rift escarpment; most of their food is lower in the mountains. From the Peak I was able to look southward over our home valley and also, if I walked just a few yards to the north, I could look down into the basin of lower Kasekela Valley, a thick, almost circular pocket of forest. I quickly found that it was easy to cross the upper Kasekela Valley approximately on the level through a fairly open wood, where on several occasions I came across a small herd of about sixteen buffalo. To the north of Buffalo Wood another open ridge offered a good view over the upper reaches of the narrow, steepsided Mlinda Valley.

I carried a small tin trunk up to the Peak and there kept a kettle, some coffee, a few tins of baked beans, a sweater, and a blanket. A tiny stream trickled through Buffalo Wood. It was almost non-existent in the dry season, but I scooped out a shallow bowl in the gravelly streambed and so was able to collect enough of the sparkling clear water for my needs. When the chimpanzees slept near the Peak I often stayed up there too—then I didn't have to trudge up the mountain in the morning. I was able to send messages down to Vanne with whichever of the Game Scouts climbed to the Peak in the evening so that she always knew when I was planning to stay out for the night.

For about a month I spent most of each day either on the Peak or overlooking Mlinda Valley where the chimps, before or after stuffing themselves with figs, ate large quantities of small purple fruits that tasted, like so many of their foods, as bitter and astringent as sloes or crab apples. Piece by piece, I began to form my first somewhat crude picture of chimpanzee life.

The impression that I had gained when I watched the chimps at the msulula tree of temporary, constantly changing associations of individuals within the community was substantiated. Most often I saw small groups of four to eight moving about together. Sometimes I saw one or two chimpanzees leave such a group and wander off on their own or join up with a different association. On other occasions I watched two or three small groups joining to form a larger one.

Often, as one group crossed the grassy ridge separating the Kasekela Valley from the fig trees in the home valley, the male chimpanzee, or chimpanzees, of the party would break into a run, sometimes moving in an upright position, sometimes dragging a fallen branch, sometimes stamping or slapping the hard earth. These charging displays were always accompanied by loud pant-hoots and afterward the chimpanzee frequently would swing up into a tree overlooking the valley he was about to enter and sit quietly, peering down and obviously listening for a response from below. If there were chimps feeding in the fig trees they nearly always hooted back, as though in answer. Then the new arrivals would hurry down the steep slope and, with more calling and screaming, the two groups would meet in the fig trees. When groups of females and youngsters with no males present joined other feeding chimpanzees, usually there was none of this excitement; the newcomers merely climbed up into the trees, greeted some of those already there, and began to stuff themselves with figs.

While many details of their social behavior were hidden from me by the foliage, I did get occasional fascinating glimpses. I saw one female, newly arrived in a group, hurry up to a big male and hold her hand toward him. Almost regally he reached out, clasped her hand in his, drew it toward him, and kissed it with his lips. I saw two adult males embrace each other in greeting. I saw youngsters having wild games through the treetops, chasing around after each other or jumping again and again, one after the other, from a branch to a springy bough below. I watched small infants dangling happily by themselves for minutes on end, patting at their toes with one hand, rotating gently from side to side. Once two tiny infants pulled on opposite ends of a twig in a gentle tug-of-war. Often, during the heat of midday or after a long spell of feeding, I saw two or more adults grooming each other, carefully looking through the hair of their companions.

At that time of year the chimps usually went to bed late, making their nests when it was too dark to see properly through binoculars, but sometimes they nested earlier and I could watch them from the Peak. I found that every individual, except for infants who slept with their mothers, made his own nest each night. Generally this took about three minutes: the chimp chose a firm foundation such as an upright fork or crotch, or two horizontal branches. Then he reached out and bent over smaller branches onto this foundation, keeping each one in place with his feet. Finally he tucked in the small leafy twigs growing around the rim of his nest and lay down. Quite often a chimp sat up after a few minutes and picked a handful of leafy twigs, which he put under his head or some other part of his body before settling down again for the night. One young female I watched went on and on bending down branches until she had constructed a huge mound of greenery on which she finally curled up.

I climbed up into some of the nests after the chimpanzees had left them. Most of them were built in trees that for me were almost impossible to climb. I found that there was quite complicated interweaving of the branches in some of them. I found, too, that the nests were never fouled with dung; and later, when I was able to get closer to the chimps, I saw how they were always careful to defecate and urinate over the edge of their nests, even in the middle of the night.

During that month I really came to know the country well, for I often went on expeditions from the Peak, sometimes to examine nests, more frequently to collect specimens of the chimpanzees' food plants, which Bernard Verdcourt had kindly offered to identify for me. Soon I could find my way around the sheer ravines and up and down the steep slopes of three valleys—the home valley, the Pocket, and Mlinda Valley—as well as a taxi driver finds his way about in the main streets and byways of London. It is a period I remember vividly, not only because I was beginning to accomplish something at last, but also because of the delight I felt in being completely by myself. For those who love to be alone with nature I need add nothing further; for those who do not, no words of mine could ever convey, even in part, the almost mystical awareness of beauty and eternity that accompanies certain treasured moments. And, though the beauty was always there, those moments came upon me unaware: when I was watching the pale flush preceding dawn; or looking up through the rustling leaves of some giant forest tree into the greens and browns and black shadows that occasionally ensnared a bright fleck of the blue sky; or when I stood, as darkness fell, with one hand on the still-warm trunk of a tree and looked at the sparkling of an early moon on the never still, sighing water of the lake.

One day, when I was sitting by the trickle of water in Buffalo Wood, pausing for a moment in the coolness before returning from a scramble in Mlinda Valley, I saw a female bushbuck moving slowly along the nearly dry streambed. Occasionally she paused to pick off some plant and crunch it. I kept absolutely still, and she was not aware of my presence until she was little more than ten yards away. Suddenly she tensed and stood staring at me, one small forefoot raised. Because I did not move, she did not know what I was—only that my outline was somehow strange. I saw her velvet nostrils dilate as she sniffed the air, but I was downwind and her nose gave her no answer. Slowly she came closer, and closer—one step at a time, her neck craned forward—always poised for instant flight. I can still scarcely believe that her nose actually touched my knee; yet if I close my eyes I can feel again, in imagination, the warmth of her breath and the silken impact of her skin. Unexpectedly I blinked and she was gone in a flash, bounding away with loud barks of alarm until the vegetation hid her completely from my view.

It was rather different when, as I was sitting on the Peak, I saw a leopard coming toward me, his tail held up straight. He was at a slightly lower level than I, and obviously had no idea I was there. Ever since arrival in Africa I had had an ingrained, illogical fear of leopards. Already, while working at the Gombe, I had several times nearly turned back when, crawling through some thick undergrowth, I had suddenly smelled the rank smell of cat. I had forced myself on, telling myself that my fear was foolish, that only wounded leopards charged humans with savage ferocity.

On this occasion, though, the leopard went out of sight as it started to climb up the hill—the hill on the peak of which I sat. I quickly hastened to climb a tree, but halfway there I realized that leopards can climb trees. So I uttered a sort of halfhearted squawk. The leopard, my logical mind told me, would be just as frightened of me if he knew I was there. Sure enough, there was a thudding of startled feet and then silence. I returned to the Peak, but the feeling of unseen eyes watching me was too much. I decided to watch for the chimps in Mlinda Valley. And, when I returned to the Peak several hours later, there, on the very rock which had been my seat, was a neat pile of leopard dung. He must have watched me go and then, very carefully, examined the place where such a frightening creature had been and tried to exterminate my alien scent with his own.

As the weeks went by the chimpanzees became less and less afraid. Quite often when I was on one of my food-collecting expeditions I came across chimpanzees unexpectedly, and after a time I found that some of them would tolerate my presence provided they were in fairly thick forest and I sat still and did not try to move closer than sixty to eighty yards. And so, during my second month of watching from the Peak, when I saw a group settle down to feed I sometimes moved closer and was thus able to make more detailed observations.

It was at this time that I began to recognize a number of different individuals. As soon as I was sure of knowing a chimpanzee if I saw it again, I named it. Some scientists feel that animals should be labeled by numbers—that to name them is anthropomorphic—but I have always been interested in the *differences* between individuals, and a name is not only more individual than a number but also far easier to remember. Most names were simply those which, for some reason or other, seemed to suit the individuals to whom I attached them. A few chimps were named because some facial expression or mannerism reminded me of human acquaintances.

The easiest individual to recognize was old Mr. McGregor. The crown of his head, his neck, and his shoulders were almost entirely devoid of hair, but a slight frill remained around his head rather like a monk's tonsure. He was an old male—perhaps between thirty and forty years of age (the longevity record for a captive chimp is forty-seven years). During the early months of my acquaintance with him, Mr. McGregor was somewhat belligerent. If I accidentally came across him at close quarters he would threaten me with an upward and backward jerk of his head and a shaking of branches before climbing down and vanishing from my sight. He reminded me, for some reason, of Beatrix Potter's old gardener in *The Tale of Peter Rabbit*.

Ancient Flo with her deformed, bulbous nose and ragged ears was equally easy to recognize. Her youngest offspring at that time were two-year-old Fifi, who still rode everywhere on her mother's back, and her juvenile son, Figan, who was always to be seen wandering around with his mother and little sister. He was then about six years old; it was approximately a year before he would attain puberty. Flo often traveled with another old mother, Olly. Olly's long face was also distinctive; the fluff of hair on the back of her head—though no other feature—reminded me of my aunt, Olwen. Olly, like Flo, was accompanied by two children, a daughter younger than Fifi, and an adolescent son about a year older than Figan.

Then there was William, who, I am certain, must have been Olly's blood brother. I never saw any special signs of friendship between them, but their faces were amazingly alike. They both had long upper lips that wobbled when they suddenly turned their heads. William had the added distinction of several thin, deeply etched scar marks running down his upper lip from his nose.

Two of the other chimpanzees I knew well by sight at that time were David Graybeard and Goliath. Like David and Goliath in the Bible, these two individuals were closely associated in my mind because they were very often together. Goliath, even in those days of his prime, was not a giant, but he had a splendid physique and the springy movements of an athlete. He probably weighed about one hundred pounds. David Graybeard was less afraid of me from the start than were any of the other chimps. I was always pleased when I picked out his handsome face and well-marked silvery beard in a chimpanzee group, for with David to calm the others, I had a better chance of approaching to observe them more closely.

Before the end of my trial period in the field I made two really exciting discoveries—discoveries that made the previous months of frustration well worth while. And for both of them I had David Graybeard to thank.

One day I arrived on the Peak and found a small group of chimps just below me in the upper branches of a thick tree. As I watched I saw that one of them was holding a pink-looking object from which he was from time to time pulling pieces with his teeth. There was a female and a youngster and they were both reaching out toward the male, their hands actually touching his mouth. Presently the female picked up a piece of the pink thing and put it to her mouth: it was at this moment that I realized the chimps were eating meat.

After each bite of meat the male picked off some leaves with his lips and chewed them with the flesh. Often, when he had chewed for several minutes on this leafy wad, he spat out the remains into the waiting hands of the female. Suddenly he dropped a small piece of meat, and like a flash the youngster swung after it to the ground. Even as he reached to pick it up the undergrowth exploded and an adult bushpig charged toward him. Screaming, the juvenile leaped back into the tree. The pig remained in the open, snorting and moving backward and forward. Soon I made out the shapes of three small striped piglets. Obviously the chimps were eating a baby pig. The size was right and later, when I realized that the male was David Graybeard, I moved closer and saw that he was indeed eating piglet.

For three hours I watched the chimps feeding. David occasionally let the female bite pieces from the carcass and once he actually detached a small piece of flesh and placed it in her outstretched hand. When he finally climbed down there was still meat left on the carcass; he carried it away in one hand, followed by the others.

Of course I was not sure, then, that David Graybeard had caught the pig for himself, but even so, it was tremendously exciting to know that these chimpanzees actually ate meat. Previously scientists had believed that although these apes might occasionally supplement their diet with a few insects or small rodents and the like they were primarily vegetarians and fruit eaters. No one had suspected that they might hunt larger mammals.

It was within two weeks of this observation that I saw something that excited me even more. By then it was October and the short rains had begun. The blackened slopes were softened by feathery new grass shoots and in some places the ground was carpeted by a variety of flowers. The Chimpanzees' Spring, I called it. I had had a frustrating morning, tramping up and down three valleys with never a sign or sound of a chimpanzee. Hauling myself up the steep slope of Mlinda Valley I headed for the Peak, not only weary but soaking wet from crawling through dense undergrowth. Suddenly I stopped, for I saw a slight movement in the long grass about sixty yards away. Quickly focusing my binoculars I saw that it was a single chimpanzee, and just then he turned in my direction. I recognized David Graybeard.

Cautiously I moved around so that I could see what he was doing. He was squatting beside the red earth mound of a termite nest, and as I watched I saw him carefully push a long grass stem down into a hole in the mound. After a moment he withdrew it and picked something from the end with his mouth. I was too far away to make out what he was eating, but it was obvious that he was actually using a grass stem as a tool.

I knew that on two occasions casual observers in West Africa had seen chimpanzees using objects as tools: one had broken open palm-nut kernels by using a rock as a hammer, and a group of chimps had been observed pushing sticks into an underground bees' nest and licking off the honey. Somehow I had never dreamed of seeing anything so exciting myself.

For an hour David feasted at the termite mound and then he wandered slowly away. When I was sure he had gone I went over to examine the mound. I found a few crushed insects strewn about, and a swarm of worker termites sealing the entrances of the nest passages into which David had obviously been poking his stems. I picked up one of his discarded tools and carefully pushed it into a hole myself. Immediately I felt the pull of several termites as they seized the grass, and when I pulled it out there were a number of worker termites and a few soldiers, with big red heads, clinging on with their mandibles. There they remained, sticking out at right angles to the stem with their legs waving in the air.

Before I left I trampled down some of the tall dry grass and constructed a rough hide—just a few palm fronds leaned up against the low branch of a tree and tied together at the top. I planned to wait there the next day. But it was another week before I was able to watch a chimpanzee "fishing" for termites again. Twice chimps arrived, but each time they saw me and moved off immediately. Once a swarm of fertile winged termites—the princes and princesses, as they are called—flew off on their nuptial flight, their huge white wings fluttering frantically as they carried the insects higher and higher. Later I realized that it is at this time of year, during the short rains, when the worker termites extend the passages of the nest to the surface, preparing for these emigrations. Several such swarms emerge between October and January. It is principally during these months that the chimpanzees feed on termites.

On the eighth day of my watch David Graybeard arrived again, together with Goliath, and the pair worked there for two hours. I could see much better: I observed how they scratched open the sealed-over passage entrances with a thumb or forefinger. I watched how they bit the ends off their tools when they became bent, or used the other end, or discarded them in favor of new ones. Goliath once moved at least fifteen yards from the heap to select a firm-looking piece of vine, and both males often picked three or four stems while they were collecting tools, and put the spares beside them on the ground until they wanted them.

Most exciting of all, on several occasions they picked small leafy twigs and prepared them for use by stripping off the leaves. This was the first recorded example of a wild animal not merely *using* an object as a tool, but actually modifying an object and thus showing the crude beginnings of tool*making*.

Previously man had been regarded as the only tool-making animal. Indeed, one of the clauses commonly accepted in the definition of man was that he was a creature who "made tools to a regular and set pattern." The chimpanzees, obviously, had not made tools to any set pattern. Nevertheless, my early observations of their primitive tool-making abilities convinced a number of scientists that it was necessary to redefine man in a more complex manner than before. Or else, as Louis Leakey put it, we should by definition have to accept the chimpanzee as Man.

I sent telegrams to Louis about both of my new observations—the meat-eating and the toolmaking—and he was of course wildly enthusiastic. In fact, I believe that the news was helpful to him in his efforts to find further financial support for my work. It was not long afterward when he wrote to tell me that the National Geographic Society in the United States had agreed to grant funds for another year's research.

4

CAMP LIFE

"MEMSAHIB! MEMSAHIB!" The voice gradually penetrated the depths of my sleep. I sat up. "Please come. You are wanted," said the voice, disembodied, from behind the light of a small hurricane lamp. It was Adolf. When I asked him what was wrong he was vague, but I gathered it was something to do with a sick baby.

By this time Vanne was awake too, and so we both put on a few clothes and followed Adolf through the darkness. He led us to the small village on the other side of the stream, down on the beach. There the two Game Scouts lived, together with the honorary headman, old Iddi Matata, his large family, and about a dozen fishermen in their temporary dry-season huts. Presently we arrived at the large mud-brick and thatched hut of old Iddi. It was past midnight, but everyone was awake, talking and laughing in the smoke-filled main room. Two children scuttled into the shadows as we went in and Iddi's chief wife, who was nursing her twin sons, smiled a greeting to us. Adolf took us to a doorway leading into a smaller room, where it looked very dark, and stood aside for us to go in. And then we realized what it was we were called for. A young woman lay on the earth floor, and beside her a tiny baby still attached to its mother by the umbilical cord. Quite obviously the afterbirth was somehow stuck.

The father was there, looking rather worried, and one young girl; no one else seemed to be paying much attention to the situation. We were faced with a dilemma: we knew nothing about midwifery; we wanted to try to help but knew that if anything happened to the mother during our ministrations we should be held responsible. We soon discovered that the baby had been born five hours earlier and that it was a first child. The mother, it seemed, felt only a little pain but was very cold. We suggested that the cord should be cut and the baby wrapped up, but this was greeted with horrified protest. Such conduct would apparently violate time-honored traditions.

I went for a blanket and some brandy, and roused Dominic to make hot tea. These things seemed to bring back some life and energy to the poor mother. Vanne and I both felt convinced that some of the other African women there must know far more about childbirth than we did, so we went out to talk to Iddi's head wife with Adolf, who was still hanging around to translate. She agreed to come and see what she could do as soon as the twins had finished their feeding. It was not long before she came in with a brighter lamp and some warm palm nut oil, with which she massaged the girl on her belly and between her thighs, meanwhile gently pulling at the cord. Ten minutes later the afterbirth was delivered. Then, at last, old Iddi came in and, with a pair of ceremonial scissors, proudly cut the cord of his grandchild and himself tied the knot. We asked Dominic to make the mother some soup, congratulated the father, who was beaming with relief, and retired to our beds—having actually done very little but feeling that we had accomplished quite a lot.

This excursion into midwifery was but one of Vanne's medical tasks. As custom demanded in those days, we had arrived at the Gombe Stream well supplied with simple medicines—aspirins and ointments, Elastoplast and Epsom salts—and quite soon after our arrival Vanne found herself running a well-attended clinic every morning.

David Anstey, before he left, had told the neighboring Africans that Vanne and I would be pleased to try to treat small ailments, and quite a number had arrived during the first few days—mainly, I suspect, to have a good look at these two strange white women who had so surprisingly abandoned civilization. But then one day a very sick man with a hugely swollen leg was helped to our camp. He had two deep tropical ulcers on the lower part of his leg; after Vanne had done some preliminary cleaning she realized to her horror that the ulceration had already begun to eat away the bone. Although she begged the man to go to the Kigoma hospital, he absolutely refused—people only went there to die. And so Vanne treated him herself with an old-fashioned cure, a saline drip. Every morning and every afternoon the patient sat down with a large bowl of blood-warm salted water which he dripped very slowly over his sores. After three weeks the swelling had gone and the wounds were clean. Subsequently it was only a matter of time before he was completely healed.

Word spread fast. After that Vanne's clinics were enormous, and people trudged along the beaches or over the mountains for long distances. One of Rashidi's sons, eight-year-old Jumanne—Swahili for Tuesday—appointed himself as Vanne's orderly and helped her almost every morning, mixing the Epsom salts, pouring out water for aspirin, cutting the Elastoplast. He was particularly helpful in spotting those who sneaked around to join the queue again hoping for a second dose. The only payment Jumanne required was a small piece of Elastoplast on some microscopic—or sometimes imaginary—wound.

Vanne's clinics not only cured many maladies but, most importantly, helped us to establish good relations with our new neighbors. The suspicions that were rife on our arrival were soon dispelled. The Africans continued to think we were both slightly crazy, but they were prepared to be friendly when they realized we were genuine. Nor was it long before some of them became interested in the work I was doing. One day Dominic told me he had heard of an old man, Mbrisho, who had watched four chimpanzees chasing away a lion with sticks. This man lived in a village up in the hills, just outside the eastern boundary of the reserve. Would I like to go and talk to Mbrisho and see where the incident had taken place? It seemed an unlikely story, but I knew that lions had occasionally been observed in the area by previous Game Rangers. Also, I was curious to visit Bubango village and see the country on the other side of the rift. So early one morning I set off with a man from the village as my guide and tall willowy Wilbert to interpret—since his English was quite good and my Swahili was still very bad.

It was a long hot climb, and took four hours of pretty steady walking. We passed a procession of African women walking down to the temporary fishing huts on the beach, balancing great bundles on their heads with graceful ease and chattering and laughing like brightly colored birds. At one point, when I had stopped to watch a troop of red colobus monkeys, six men passed us on their climb to the village. One of them was old, with a slightly bent back and silver hair, but he seemed quite unconcerned by the steepness of the ascent and the heat of the sun. These men walked with the special springy stride of mountain folk, and each time they placed their stout staffs onto the ground they exhaled their breath with an eerie flutelike whistle.

As we climbed higher the countryside changed. Increasing numbers of trees were festooned with the feathery gray-green lichen of the upper slopes, and the open spaces were covered with short springy grass, so that I was reminded of the Sussex downs. From the top of the rift the view was superb. In those days, rolling forested country stretched away to the east as far as I could see. Today much of the forest has been cleared, and African huts and cultivation have marched from all sides toward the boundary of the chimpanzee sanctuary.

The village of Bubango sprawled below us, just on the other side of the mountaintop. It was larger than I had expected. There were groves of banana and palm trees clustered in the greenness of a valley, and on the slopes of the hillside many patches of cassava or *muhoge*, as it is known locally. Cassava root, ground into a fine white flour and subsequently cooked with water into a porridge, is a staple diet in the area. The huts were mostly rather small and simple, with mud walls and thatched roofs, and a crisscross of tracks, worn bare by the passage of countless human feet, led from the huts to the stream and to the patches of cultivation. Small children herded goats and sheep, and I even saw a few cows grazing here and there.

The little hut of old Mbrisho stood off to the side of the main dirt track that wound down through the village from the top of the escarpment. He welcomed us in, gave us tea and some delicious doughy African cakes, and beamed widely as he told me the lion story in his slow, deep voice. Every so often his conversation was punctuated by a long drawn-out *naaaahm*. Mbrisho always uses this word, and I have never been able to discover exactly what it means.

It soon became evident that it was not Mbrisho who had seen the chimps and the lion but some long dead relative, so I was none the wiser about that when I left. I had gained a firm and staunch friend in old Mbrisho, nevertheless; he never fails to bring a gift of eggs, carefully wrapped in a piece of cloth, when he comes down the mountain to visit our camp. And when a man lives off the land and is old, a few eggs are a valuable present, one we are proud to accept.

Mbrisho, like most of the able-bodied men of the surrounding villages, was a fisherman until he "retired." The principal catch is the small sardine-sized *dagaa*, which is caught at night in orange- or red-dyed nets shaped like gigantic butterfly nets. Each canoe, manned by two fishermen, is equipped with two or more bright kerosene pressure lamps: the fish, attracted by the light, rise to the surface and are scooped up in the net. Whenever a big shoal is sighted the fishermen start to sing, stamping with their feet, banging against the boat with paddle or net handle, and this apparently encourages the fish to rise. When fishing is good it sounds as though all the human inhabitants for miles around are having a fantastic party on the lake.

After the bottom of a canoe is filled with fish the catch is paddled back to the shore, where other men start spreading it out on special drying beds of fine gravel. If fishing is good each canoe may return two or three times a night, and the rising sun is reflected from millions and millions of tiny scales that seem to change the beaches to silver.

During the day the fishermen, or their wives or children, periodically work their way up and down the drying beds, prodding at the fish with long sticks, turning them so that the sun dries them evenly on both sides. In the evening the catch is gathered up into sacks while the men who will go out fishing sit around their grass huts talking, and their womenfolk prepare the evening meal of *ugali*, or cassava porridge, mixed with dried dagaa that have been fried in red palm nut oil.

When the moon is bright the dagaa are no longer attracted toward the lamps of the canoes and during this period the dried fish are taken to Kigoma for sale. Mostly they are loaded onto the small thirty-foot motorized boats that ply up and down the lakeshore. At the peak of the season these water taxis, as we call them, are loaded with sack upon sack of fish, for the dagaa industry is a profitable one. A great deal is sold locally but even more is railed away to other parts of East Africa and to the great copper mines of Nyanza in the south.

The fishermen who do not go to Kigoma return to their home villages to visit their families, and so for ten days or so each month the beaches of the Gombe Stream are deserted. It was at this time that I loved walking along the lakeshore when my work took me to some distant valley. In the early morning I occasionally met the lumbering shape of a hippo returning to the water after a night feeding on the lush grass along the lakeshore. Bushbucks and bush-pigs often moved along the beaches between the valleys, and once I saw a small herd of buffalo, looking huge and very black against the white sand. There was always a chance, too, of seeing some of the smaller animals—one of the mongooses, perhaps, or a slender dainty genet with its ringed tail, or a larger thickset civet cat.

One evening when I was wading in the shallows of the lake to pass a rocky outcrop, I suddenly stopped dead as I saw the sinuous black body of a snake in the water. It was all of six feet long, and from the slight hood and the dark stripes at the back of the neck I knew it to be a Storm's water cobra—a deadly reptile for the bite of which there was, at that time, no serum. As I stared at it an incoming wave gently deposited part of its body on one of my feet. I remained motionless, not even breathing, until the wave rolled back into the lake, drawing the snake with it. Then I leaped out of the water as fast as I could, my heart hammering.

A few weeks before, I had encountered another cobra—one of the white-lipped variety which, aiming for its victim's eyes, can spit venom from as far as six feet and cause temporary or even permanent blindness. At the time I had been standing looking over the valley and had glanced down to see the snake gliding between my legs. It had paused momentarily, testing the canvas of my shoe with its sensitive flickering tongue. But I felt no fear whatsoever, for there had been no chance of a sudden wave dashing it against me and making it frightened, no suction of water that might coil it around my ankle. There is something utterly unnerving about a snake in the water.

Lake Tanganyika is one of the few areas of fresh water in East Africa which is virtually free of the dread bilharzia snail, at least in the Kigoma and Gombe area, and the water is cool, sparkling clean, and excellent for swimming. In those early days I never had time for swimming—not that I felt any great desire to plunge into the water after my experience with the snake, and after hearing about Chiko's experience. Chiko was Dominic's wife, who with her little girl had joined us soon after our arrival at Gombe. One day when she was standing in the shallow water doing her washing there was a sudden swirling a few feet away, and with a shriek she leaped out onto the shore, staring in horror at the place where but a moment before she had seen a crocodile. It wasn't a very big crocodile—I had myself seen it a few times swimming in the lake— but I should not have liked to meet it in the water. Chiko's experience, however, became the joke of the moment—every African I met for the next few weeks was laughing about the crocodile that tried to grab my cook's wife. Dominic himself, when first he told me, laughed till the tears ran down his cheeks.

It is when the fishermen leave their huts during the full moon that the baboons come into their own on the beaches. All along the shoreline, where there are drying beds, the troops gather, searching through the pebbles for leftover scraps of dried fish. They sift through the sand around the huts too, probably looking for specks of cassava scattered where the women pounded the roots into flour for porridge. The Africans remove anything of value when they leave the beaches because the baboons are very destructive. I have watched them pulling apart a whole roof as they searched through the thatch for insects, and they move in and out of the huts as though they own them, eating anything edible, investigating or pulling apart anything that is not.

The baboons very soon made themselves at home around our camp, too, and Vanne quickly learned never to leave the tents unguarded. About two weeks after our arrival she went for a short walk; when she returned it was to find our belongings strewn in all directions, and one blasé male baboon sitting by the overturned table polishing off the loaf that Dominic had baked that morning.

Vanne was particularly incensed by the way the others barked at her from the surrounding trees, as though challenging her right to her own home. It was not long after this episode that Vanne, during a visit to the camp loo, or *choo,* as it is known in East Africa, looked up to see five large male baboons sitting around in a semicircle watching her. She told me that evening she had felt frightfully embarrassed for a moment.

It was far worse when one morning Vanne, who had been dozing after my early departure, suddenly heard a small sound in the tent. She opened her eyes and there, silhouetted in the entrance, she saw a huge male baboon. He and she remained motionless for a few moments and then he opened his mouth in a tremendous yawn of threat. In the gray light Vanne could just see the gleam of his teeth and she thought her last hour had come. With a sudden yell she sat bolt upright in bed, waving her arms—and her unwelcome visitor fled. He was a horrible baboon, that one, an old male who took to hanging around our camp at all hours of the day, lurking in the undergrowth and dashing out whenever opportunity presented to steal a loaf of bread or some other item of food. We called him Shaitani, which is Swahili for devil, and we were immensely relieved when he suddenly disappeared.

In those days food was precious; not only because of our limited budget but also because both Vanne and I hated "Kigoma days"—when we had to go into the town to renew our supplies and collect our mail. We went as infrequently as possible, but once every three or four weeks we had to make the expedition. We used to set off at about six in the morning when the lake was usually calm, and had breakfast at the hotel when we arrived. Then we trailed around doing the shopping, bargaining at the fruit and vegetable market, ordering tinned goods for the next month, and queuing in the post office. We always had a pleasant interlude at midday, since we were invariably invited to lunch by one or other of the friends we had made during our initial stay in Kigoma. They often tried to persuade us to stay the night, and most of them thought I was merely being antisocial when I explained it was bad enough to leave my work for one day and that I couldn't think of staying away for a second.

At first we used to take Dominic with us on these expeditions.

He was amazingly loyal and would bargain heatedly in the market so that we should not be overcharged by as much as a farthing. Nevertheless, after a while we realized that it was better to leave Dominic to look after camp. The locally made beer, brewed from fermented bananas, is strong, and drinking is Dominic's weakness. On several occasions we could not find him at all when it came to the appointed time to leave; once he did not turn up again for a week and we had to manage without him. And then there was the day when, though we did manage to find him in time to return with us, he was in a very merry state. Laughing at nothing, he accompanied us to the boat and half stepped, half fell in. He is an intelligent man, and often very amusing when a bit drunk. He soon had Vanne and me laughing with him. We were a gay party as we cast off and chugged out of Kigoma Bay.

By this time it was almost dark because the search for Dominic had delayed us. Normally I steered a course quite close to shore, but that evening the water was dotted with fishermen's canoes being paddled out from the shore and they were hard to see in the dusk. So I drove the boat along half a mile or more from the beach. Quite suddenly, when we were about a quarter of the way home, the engine stopped. Nothing we did produced even a spark, and none of us knew anything about engines. All we could do was row to shore.

Dominic announced proudly that he would row us in. Seating himself centrally he seized the two oars, settled himself, and gave a mighty pull. He caught a whopping "crab" and the next instant was lying flat out on top of one of the large baskets of fruit from the market. He could not get out for laughing. Eventually we hauled him back to the seat and I said I would row. This was too much for his sense of propriety—at least he must take one oar. For the next ten minutes we proceeded to turn small circles around his oar. Finally I persuaded him that I could manage, that I loved rowing more than anything, and off we set.

When we eventually reached the beach we found to our delight that one of the water taxis was anchored there. A crowd of fishermen soon gathered around us, and before long the driver of the taxi was found. After much arguing he agreed to transport us and our boat back to camp. But Dominic was incensed at the price we were to be charged. Telling us to wait, he vanished into the night before we could stop him.

We had a long wait, but we didn't want to leave without Dominic; also, we were grateful to him for thinking of our purse—it was indeed very slender. Thirty minutes later he returned with four stalwart Africans. These men, Dominic informed us, would *paddle* us home. They were friends of his, and they would only charge us a quarter of the price demanded by the motorized water taxi. This sounded marvelous until we discovered that even with eight men rowing hard it would take more than eight hours to get home. I think Dominic never quite forgave us for taking the faster vessel and allowing ourselves to be robbed.

It was not long after this that Vanne, who had gone to Kigoma without me, had a much worse experience. Dominic was not with her, but Wilbert had asked to go in because he wanted to do some shopping. He and Vanne parted in the morning, and arranged to meet back at the boat at five o'clock. When he finally appeared, half an hour late, Vanne's heart sank: here was another victim of Kigoma's banana beer! Wilbert, staggering slightly, swayed up to the boat and then, to Vanne's horror, pulled out a knife, which he waved around while with staring eyes he began to mutter incoherently about death and revenge.

Vanne later admitted that she had been frightened, for Wilbert, willowy though he appeared, was a very large man, and he looked terrifying with his eyes bloodshot and the blade of the knife glinting in the evening sun. However, she kept her head, spoke to him quietly, and asked him to let her look after the knife in case he cut himself getting into the boat. To her surprise he stared hard at her and then a bewildered expression came over his face. He lurched toward her, handed her the knife, and without another word climbed into the boat. He was very quiet during the trip home. We never did discover what it was all about, and Wilbert never asked for his knife back again.

How lucky I was to have a mother like Vanne—a mother in a million. I could not have done without her during those early days. She ran the clinic and ensured the goodwill of my neighbors, she kept the camp neat, she pressed and dried for me the specimens of the chimps' food plants that I collected, and, above all, she helped me to keep up my spirits during the depressing weeks when I could get nowhere near the chimps. How nice it was to come back in the evening and find a warm welcome. How pleasant to be able to discuss the events of the day, frustrating or exciting, over the fire during supper, and to hear the gossip of camp.

Vanne put up with the most primitive conditions without a murmur. We lived in those early days on baked beans, corned beef, and other tinned meat and vegetables, since we had no refrigerator. We bathed at night in a tiny canvas "tub" supported at each corner by a wooden frame and filled with a few inches of water—too hot when one got in and cold when one got out a few moments later. Sometimes giant hairy spiders took refuge in our tent, and twice Vanne woke in the morning to see the flattened, evil-looking body of a deadly giant centipede clinging to the roof of the tent above her bed. Also, there was an element in the water that disagreed with Vanne's never strong stomach, so she seldom if ever felt one hundred percent fit.

Five months after our arrival Vanne had to return to England. The authorities in Kigoma no longer worried about me being on my own. I was by then part of the Gombe Stream landscape and, thanks to Vanne's clinics, I enjoyed excellent relations with the local inhabitants. Just before Vanne left we were joined by Hassan, our old friend from Lake Victoria. We were overjoyed to see him, and Vanne was able to go knowing that I was in reliable hands. Hassan would drive the little boat and do the awful "Kigoma days" on his own, and if anything happened, Hassan somehow would cope. For Hassan had often proved himself in times of crisis during his thirty years with Louis.

My fire seemed lonely when Vanne had gone. Even Terry, the toad, who had become our nightly companion, served only to remind me of the times Vanne and I had laughed at him together as he gorged himself on the insects around the lamp. And on the evenings when Crescent, the genet, came softly toward the tent to take a banana, I found myself wishing Vanne were there to share in my appreciation of her slender grace.

As the weeks passed, however, I accepted aloneness as a way of life and I was no longer lonely. I was utterly absorbed in the work, fascinated by the chimps, too busy in the evenings to brood.

In fact, had I been alone for longer than a year I might have become a rather strange person, for inanimate objects began to develop their own identities: I found myself saying "Good morning" to my little hut on the Peak, "Hello" to the stream where I collected my water. And I became immensely aware of trees; just to feel the roughness of a gnarled trunk or the cold smoothness of young bark with my hand filled me with a strange knowledge of the roots under the ground and the pulsing sap within. I longed to be able to swing through the branches like the chimps, to sleep in the treetops lulled by the rustling of the leaves in the breeze. In particular, I loved to sit in a forest when it was raining, and to hear the pattering of the drops on the leaves and feel utterly enclosed in a dim twilight world of greens and browns and dampness.

5

THE RAINS

Soon after Vanne's departure the light rains of the Chimpanzees' Spring gave place to the long rains. Showers became deluges that sometimes lasted with unabated fury for two hours or more. One of those wild storms occurred a week or so after the change of seasons. For two hours I had been watching a group of chimpanzees feeding in a huge fig tree. It had been gray and overcast all morning, with thunder growling in the distance.

At about noon the first heavy drops of rain began to fall. The chimpanzees climbed out of the tree and one after the other plodded up the steep grassy slope toward the open ridge at the top. There were seven adult males in the group, including Goliath and David Graybeard, several females, and a few youngsters. As they reached the ridge the chimpanzees paused. At that moment the storm broke. The rain was torrential, and the sudden clap of thunder, right overhead, made me jump. As if this were a signal, one of the big males stood upright and as he swayed and swaggered rhythmically from foot to foot I could just hear the rising crescendo of his pant-hoots above the beating of the rain. Then he charged off, flat-out down the slope toward the trees he had just left. He ran some thirty yards, and then, swinging round the trunk of a small tree to break his headlong rush, leaped into the low branches and sat motionless.

Almost at once two other males charged after him. One broke off a low branch from a tree as he ran and brandished it in the air before hurling it ahead of him. The other, as he reached the end of his run, stood upright and rhythmically swayed the branches of a tree back and forth before seizing a huge branch and dragging it farther down the slope. A fourth male, as he too charged, leaped into a tree and, almost without breaking his speed, tore off a large branch, leaped with it to the ground, and continued down the slope. As the last two males called and charged down, so the one who had started the whole performance climbed from his tree and began plodding up the slope again. The others, who had also climbed into trees near the bottom of the slope, followed suit. When they reached the ridge, they started charging down all over again, one after the other, with equal vigor.

The females and youngsters had climbed into trees near the top of the rise as soon as the displays had begun, and there they remained watching throughout the whole performance. As the males charged down and plodded back up, so the rain fell harder, jagged forks or brilliant flares of lightning lit the leaden sky, and the crashing of the thunder seemed to shake the very mountains.

My enthusiasm was not merely scientific as I watched, enthralled, from my grandstand seat on the opposite side of the narrow ravine, sheltering under a plastic sheet. In fact it was raining and blowing far too hard for me to get at my notebook or use my binoculars. I could only watch, and marvel at the magnificence of those splendid creatures. With a display of strength and vigor such as this, primitive man himself might have challenged the elements.

Twenty minutes from the start of the performance the last of the males plodded back up the slope for the last time. The females and youngsters climbed down from their trees and the whole group moved over the crest of the ridge. One male paused, and with his hand on a tree trunk, looked back—the actor taking his final curtain. Then he too vanished over the ridge.

I continued to sit there, staring almost in disbelief at the white scars on the tree trunks and the discarded branches on the grass— all that remained, in that rain-lashed landscape, to prove that the wild "rain dance" had taken place at all. I should have been even more amazed had I known then that I would only see such a display twice more in the next ten years. Often, it is true, male chimpanzees react to the start of heavy rain by performing a rain dance, but this is usually an individual affair.

As the rainy season progressed the grass shot up until it was over twelve feet in some places, and even on the exposed ridges it often reached heights of at least six feet. When I left the tracks that I knew—if indeed I could find them at all—I could not tell where I was going and had to stop every so often and climb a tree to get my bearings. Also, I was no longer able to sit down wherever I happened to be or wherever was convenient when I came across a group of chimpanzees, for usually my view would then be totally obscured by grasses. I have never been able to work with binoculars for long periods of time when standing, so I had either to bend down hundreds of grass stems or else climb a tree. As the rainy season progressed I became increasingly arboreal in my habits, but despite my love for trees it was not very satisfactory, because I lost time both in looking for a suitable tree and in breaking away branches that obstructed my view of the chimps. And when there was a wind, which was often, I couldn't keep the binoculars steady anyway.

I found it difficult, also, to shield my binoculars from the rain. I made a sort of tube from a sheet of plastic which kept out much of the wet, and I pulled a large piece of plastic material forward over my head, like a peaked cap, when I was watching chimps. Even so, there were many days when I couldn't use my binoculars because the lenses were clouded over inside with droplets of condensed moisture.

Also, when it was not actually raining the long grass remained drenched nearly all day either with rain or the heavy nightly dew, and there were periods when I seemed to be wet through for days on end. I think I spent some of the coldest hours of my life in those mountains, sitting in clammy clothes in an icy wind watching chimpanzees. There was even a time when I dreaded the early morning climb to the Peak: I left my warm bed in the darkness, had my slice of bread and cup of coffee by the cozy glow of a hurricane lamp, and then had to steel myself for the plunge into that icy, water-drenched grass. After a while, though, I took to bundling my clothes into a plastic bag and carrying them. There was no one to see my ascent, and it was dark anyway. Then, when I knew there were dry clothes to put on at my destination, the shock of the cold grass against my naked skin was a sensual pleasure. For the first few days my body was crisscrossed by scratches from the tooth-edged grass, but after that my skin hardened.

One morning, in the first light of dawn, I plodded up the last steep slope to the Peak. As I reached the top my foot seemed to freeze in midair, for no less than four yards from me, a lone buffalo lay, half hidden in the long grass. He must have been asleep, or surely he would have heard me; and luckily the breeze was blowing his rich cowlike scent my way. Had it been the other way around . . . As it was, I was able to creep quietly away, and he was not disturbed.

It was at this time, too, that a leopard actually passed within a few yards of me as I sat in some long grass. I never knew he was there until I saw the white tip of his tail just ahead of me, and there was no time to retreat. So I just held my breath. I doubt if he ever knew how close to a human being he had been.

On the whole I loved that rainy season at the Gombe. It was cool most of the time and there was no heat to distort long-distance observations. The crunching of my feet on the crackling leaf carpet of the forest floor in the dry season had always bothered me, but when the leaves became soft and damp during the rains I could move through the trees silently, and catch more than fleeting glimpses of some of the shyer creatures. Best of all, of course, I was continuously learning more and more about chimpanzees and their behavior.

In the dry season the chimpanzees, I knew, usually rested on the ground at midday; I had often glimpsed them lying stretched out in the shade. In the rainy season, though, the ground is frequently sodden and I found that the chimpanzees made quite elaborate day nests on which to rest. To my surprise they often made these while it was still actually raining and then sat hunched up, with their arms around their knees and their heads bowed, until the rain stopped. In the mornings they got up later and at times, after feeding or just sitting about, made new nests and lay down again only two or three hours later. I suppose this was because they sometimes had such miserably wet and cold nights that they couldn't sleep, and so were tired in the morning. They usually went to bed earlier, too. Often when I left the chimps in their nests, soaking wet from a late afternoon storm, I felt not only sorry for them but guilty because I was returning to a warm meal, dry clothes, and a tent. And I felt even worse when I woke in the middle of the night to hear the rain lashing down on the canvas and thought of all the poor huddled chimps shivering on their leafy platforms while I snuggled cozily into my warm bed.

Sometimes at the beginning of a storm a chimpanzee would shelter under an overhanging trunk or tangle of vegetation, but then, when the rain began to drip through, he usually emerged and just sat in the open, hunched and looking miserable. Small infants appeared to fare the best in a heavy storm. Quite often I saw old Flo, who of all the females was least afraid of me at that time, sitting hunched over two-year-old Fifi. At the end of a deluge Fifi would crawl from her mother's embrace looking completely dry. Flo's son Figan, about four years older than Fifi, often swung wildly through the tree on such occasions, dangling from one hand and kicking his legs, leaping from branch to branch, jumping up and down above Flo, until she was showered with debris and she hunched even lower to avoid the twigs that lashed her face. It was a good way of keeping his blood warm—rather like the wild rain display with which older males frequently greeted the start of heavy rain.

As the weeks went by I found that I could usually get closer to a group of chimpanzees when it was cold and wet than when the weather was dry. It was as though they were too fed up with the conditions to bother about me. One day I was moving silently through the dripping forest. Overhead the rain pattered onto the leaves and all around it dripped from leaf to leaf to the ground. The smell of rotten wood and wet vegetation was pungent; under my hands the tree trunks were cold and slippery and alive. I could feel the water trickling through my hair and running warmly into my neck. I was looking for a group of chimps I had heard before the rain began.

Unexpectedly, only a few yards ahead of me, I saw a black shape hunched up on the ground with its back to me. I hunched down onto the ground myself: the chimp hadn't seen me. For a few minutes there was silence save for the pattering of the rain, and then

I heard a slight rustle and a soft *hoo* to my right. Slowly I turned my head, but saw nothing in the thick undergrowth. When I looked back, the black shape that had been in front of me had vanished. Then came a sound from above. I looked up and there saw a large male directly overhead: it was Goliath. He stared down at me with his lips tensed and very slightly shook a branch. I looked away, for a prolonged stare can be interpreted as a threat. I heard another rustle to my left, and when I looked I could just make out the black shape of a chimp behind a tangle of vines. Ahead I saw two eyes staring toward me and a large black hand gripping a hanging liana. Another soft *hoo,* this time from behind. I was surrounded.

All at once Goliath uttered a long drawn-out *wraaaa,* and I was showered with rain and twigs as he threatened me, shaking the branches. The call was taken up by the other dimly seen chimps. It is one of the most savage sounds of the African forests, second only to the trumpeting scream of an enraged elephant. All my instincts bade me flee, but I forced myself to stay, trying to appear uninterested and busy eating some roots from the ground. The end of the branch above me hit my head. With a stamping and slapping of the ground a black shape charged through the undergrowth ahead, veering away from me at the last minute and running at a tangent into the forest. I think I expected to be torn to pieces. I do not know how long I crouched there before I realized that everything was still and silent again, save for the *drip-drip* of the raindrops. Cautiously I looked around. The black hand and the glaring eyes were no longer there; the branch where Goliath had been was deserted; all the chimpanzees had gone. Admittedly, my knees shook when I got up, but there was the sense of exhilaration that comes when danger has threatened and left one unharmed—and the chimpanzees were surely less afraid of me.

It lasted for about five months, this period of aggression and hostility toward me following the initial fear and hasty retreat that had taken place whenever the chimps saw me. There is one other incident that stands out in my memory: it took place about three weeks after the one I have just described. I was waiting on one side of a narrow ravine, hoping that chimpanzees would arrive in a fruit-laden tree on the opposite slope. When I heard the deliberate footsteps of approaching chimpanzees behind me I lay down flat and kept still—for often, if the apes saw me on their way to feed, they changed their minds and fed elsewhere. Once they had started to feed, however, once they were surrounded by the delicious taste and sight and smell of the fruit, their hunger usually proved stronger than their distrust of me. On this occasion the footsteps came on and abruptly stopped, quite close. There was a soft *hoo,* the call of a worried, slightly fearful individual. I had been seen. I kept still, and presently the footsteps came even closer. Then I heard one chimpanzee run for a few yards; this was followed by a loud scream.

Suddenly I saw a large male chimpanzee climbing a tree only a couple of yards away. He moved over into the branches above my head and began screaming at me, short, loud, high-pitched sounds, with his mouth open. I stared up into his dark face and brown eyes. He began climbing down toward me until he was no more than ten feet above me and I could see his yellow teeth and, right inside his mouth, the pinkness of his tongue. He shook a branch, showering me with twigs. Then he hit the trunk and shook more branches, and continued to scream and scream and work himself into a frenzy of rage. All at once he climbed down and went out of sight behind me.

It was then that I saw a female with a tiny baby and an older child sitting in another tree and staring at me with wide eyes. They were quite silent and quite still. I could hear the old male moving about behind me and then his footsteps stopped. He was so close I could hear his breathing.

Without warning there was a loud bark, a stamping in the leaves, and my head was hit, hard. At this I had to move, had to sit up. The male was standing looking at me, and for a moment I believed he would charge; but he turned and moved off, stopping often to turn and stare at me. The female with her baby and the youngster climbed down silently and moved after him. A few moments later I was alone again. There was a sense of triumph: I had made real contact with a wild chimpanzee—or perhaps it should be the other way round.

When I looked back some years later at my description of that male, I was certain it was the bad-tempered, irascible, paunchy

J.B. The behavior fits in perfectly with the irritable, fearless character that I later came to know so well. I suppose he was puzzled by my immobility and the plastic sheet that was protecting me from the light rain. He simply had to find out exactly what I was and make me move—he must have known, from my eyes, that I was alive.

It was after incidents of this sort that I longed to return to camp and find Vanne there so that I could share with her the horror or the delight of the occasion. I told Dominic and Hassan about my encounter with the old male, and they in turn told old Iddi Matata. He came to see me the following evening and recounted the story of an African who had climbed halfway up a palm tree to collect the ripe fruit without noticing that a male chimp was feeding at the top. The ape suddenly saw him and rushed down, hitting out at the African's face as he passed. The man lost one eye. And so the rumor went around that I had some magic about me, that I went unharmed where others were hurt. This all helped my friendly relations with my African neighbors.

The long rains should end during April, I had been told. That year it was still raining in June, although less frequently. In between the cold gray days the whole area was like a gigantic tropical greenhouse. The moisture sucked by the sun from the lush vegetation of the mountains was trapped in the valleys, trapped between the long grass stems. Climbing the steep slopes was often a nightmare. Sometimes I felt I simply had to climb into a tree in order to breathe, and once I was up there I wondered why on earth our ancestors had ever left the branches. That May and June were the worst of all my early months—worse even than the time when the chimpanzees fled at my approach. I had several returns of fever and often it was an effort to lift a hand, so bad was the humidity, let alone struggle up mountains. And the chimpanzees, who had been feeding in large noisy groups, were splitting up more and more often into small units of two to six. Frequently such groups made no sounds all day as they wandered through the forests feeding on the fruit of the ubiquitous *mbula* tree, known as wild custard apples.

Gradually, however, the terrible humidity lessened, strong winds blew daily down through the valleys, and my spirits and health were restored. The wild fig season came around again, and this time, instead of watching from the Peak, I was able to move down into the valley and sit quite close to the trees where the chimpanzees fed each day.

Once, as I was watching a group in a tree about thirty yards away, I heard a slight rustle in the leaves behind me. I looked around. There about fifteen feet away sat a chimpanzee with his back to me. I was motionless, thinking he had not seen me, but after a few moments he glanced casually at me over his shoulder, then went on chewing. He stayed there for another ten minutes, sometimes giving me a quick look, before finally walking away. That was Mike, an adult male with a face almost as handsome as David Graybeard's. The incident took place a few weeks after that never to be forgotten day described at the beginning of the book, when David Graybeard and Goliath also sat calmly only a few feet away from me. Their original fear of me had gradually given place to aggression and hostility and now many of the chimps had begun to accept me as part of their normal, everyday landscape. A strange white ape, unusual to be sure, but not, after all, terribly alarming.

Toward the end of August my sister Judy arrived from England. The National Geographic Society, which was by then financing my research, had been interested in obtaining photographs for its magazine. The Society wanted to send a professional photographer, but I was terrified at the thought of a stranger arriving on the scene and ruining my hard-won relationship with the chimps. I suggested to Louis that Judy should come out—not because she had had any photographic experience, but because she looked like me and would be willing to sacrifice chances of getting pictures for the good of my work. The National Geographic Society did not finance her trip, but a British weekend newspaper, *Reveille*, took a gamble and paid all her expenses in return for a series of interviews with me when I returned to England.

Poor Judy. When she arrived it was virtually the end of the dry season—a dry season that had lasted no more than six weeks. I had built small hides near trees that I expected to fruit during September and October, but the crops were poor that year, and it rained nearly every day. Judy spent hours and hours waiting in hides in the pouring rain, trying to shelter herself and her photographic paraphernalia under a plastic sheet. The chimps hardly ever came, and when they did, it was raining too hard for Judy to take a single picture. However, during November things cheered up a bit, and she was able to take some of the first-ever pictures of chimpanzees using tools as they fished for termites. Also, she got some shots of me, and camp life and the fishermen, which made her trip worthwhile so far as her sponsors were concerned.

When Judy first arrived at the Gombe Stream she was surprised at my "emaciated" appearance. For eighteen months, apart from the occasional Kigoma day, or short periods when fever had laid me low, I had worked full time in the mountains. My alarm clock was always set for five-thirty in the morning, and after a slice of bread and a cup of coffee I would hurry off after my chimps. I never felt the need for food, and seldom for water, when I was roaming the forests. The cups of coffee made on the Peak were luxuries. And then, after returning to camp as darkness fell, always there were notes to transcribe; often I was working until far into the night. This routine was an effective way to lose weight.

Judy felt it her duty to "fatten me up." Accordingly, she ordered such things as porridge and custard, Bovril and Horlicks. But somehow I never felt like eating them, and, since Judy couldn't bear to see them wasted, she ate them instead.

In December we had to pack up camp—in a downpour, of course —and store all the equipment in Kigoma. Louis had managed to get me admitted to Cambridge University to work for a Ph.D. in ethology, the study of animal behavior. Louis met Judy and me in Nairobi and sent a cable to Vanne. It read: GIRLS ARRIVED SAFELY STOP ONE THIN ONE FAT.

6

THE CHIMPS COME
TO CAMP

NINETEEN SIXTY-ONE was a cold winter in England, and in Cambridge, with the winds whistling over the flat country straight from the icy wastes of Norway, the snow and the frost and the frozen water pipes seemed interminable. I felt utterly remote from Africa and the chimpanzees and all that I longed for most at that time. Of course I was immensely grateful for the privilege of going to Cambridge, and for the chance of working under the supervision of Professor Robert Hinde—but what was David Graybeard doing in the meantime? How were Goliath and Flo? What was I missing?

At last the spring thawed the hard ground; in two months I would be back in Africa. First I had two ordeals to face, and the thought of them terrified me far more than any encounter with enraged chimpanzees. I had to speak at two scientific conferences in London and in New York, since other scientists were avid for firsthand information about the ways of my chimpanzees. These milestones finally came and went, unbelievably the six-month exile was over, and I was heading for Africa again, crossing the vastness of the Sahara Desert in the lurid red dawn light that is so much an integral part of modern air travel.

Would the chimpanzees have forgotten me? Would I have to get them used to me all over again? I need not have worried. When I got back to the Gombe Stream Chimpanzee Reserve it seemed that the chimps were, if anything, *more* tolerant of my presence than before.

One evening I returned to camp and found Dominic and Hassan

very excited. A large male chimpanzee, they told me, had walked right into camp and spent an hour feeding from the palm tree that shaded my tent. The following evening I learned that the same chimp had paid another visit. I determined to stay down the next day to see if he came again.

It seemed strange to lie in my bed and watch the dawn break, to have breakfast in camp, to sit in my tent in the *daylight* to type out my previous day's notes on the typewriter I had brought back from England. And it seemed quite unbelievable when at about ten o'clock David Graybeard strolled calmly past the front of my tent and climbed the palm tree. I peeped out and heard him giving low-pitched grunts of pleasure as he poked the first red fruit from its horny case. An hour later he climbed down, paused to look, quite deliberately, into the tent, and wandered away. After all those months of despair, when the chimpanzees had fled at the mere sight of me five hundred yards away, here was one making himself at home in our very camp.

David Graybeard paid regular visits until the palm tree's fruit was finished, then he stopped coming. These oil nut palms do not all fruit at the same time, however, and so a few weeks later the hard nutlike fruits on another of the camp palms became red and ripe. David Graybeard resumed his daily visits.

I did not often stay to watch him, since there was a limit to the amount of information one could gain from watching a lone male guzzling palm nuts. Sometimes, though, I waited for him to come just for the intense pleasure of seeing him so close and so unafraid. One day as I sat on the veranda of the tent, David climbed down from his tree and then, in his deliberate way, walked straight toward me. When he was about five feet from me he stopped, and slowly his hair began to stand on end, until he looked enormous and very fierce. A chimpanzee may erect his hair when he is angry, frustrated, or nervous. Why had David now put his hair out? All at once he ran straight at me, snatched up a banana from my table, and hurried off to eat it farther away. Gradually his hair returned to its normal sleeked position.

After that incident I asked Dominic to leave bananas out whenever he saw David, and so, even when there were no ripe palm nuts, the chimp still wandered into camp sometimes, looking for bananas. His visits were irregular and unpredictable, and I no longer waited in my tent for him to come.

About eight weeks after my return to Gombe I had a slight attack of malaria. I stayed in bed and, hoping that David Graybeard might pass by, asked Dominic to set out some bananas. Late that morning David walked up to my tent and helped himself to the fruit. As he walked back toward the bushes I suddenly saw that a second chimpanzee was standing there, half hidden in the vegetation. It was Goliath. As David sat down to eat, Goliath went close to him, peering into his face. Then, as David rolled a banana skin wad around in his lower lip, squeezing out the last juices, occasionally pushing it forward and looking down at it over his nose, Goliath reached out one hand to his friend's mouth, begging for the wad. Presently David responded by spitting out the well-chewed mass into Goliath's hand, and then Goliath sucked on it in turn.

The next day Goliath followed David to camp again. I kept hidden right inside the tent, with the flap down, and peeped out through a small hole. This time Goliath, with much hesitation and with all his hair on end, followed David to the tent and seized some bananas for himself.

The following few weeks were momentous. I sent Hassan off to the village of Mwamgongo, to the north of the reserve, to buy a supply of bananas, and each day I put out a pile near my tent. Since the figs in the home valley were ripe again, large groups of chimps were constantly passing near camp. I spent part of my time up near the fig trees and the remainder waiting for David in camp. He came nearly every day, and not only did Goliath sometimes accompany him but William also, and occasionally a youngster.

One day, when David came by himself, I held a banana out to him in my hand. He approached, put his hair out, and gave a sudden soft exhalation rather like a cough, while at the same time he jerked his chin up. He was mildly threatening me. Suddenly he stood upright, swaggered slightly from foot to foot, slapped the trunk of a palm tree beside him with one hand, and then, very gently, took the banana from me.

The first time I offered Goliath a banana from my hand was very different. He too put his hair out, then seized a chair and charged past me, almost knocking me over. Next he sat and glow-ered from the bushes. It was a long time before he behaved as calmly in my presence as David; if I made a sudden movement and startled him he often threatened me vigorously, uttering a soft barking sound while rapidly raising one arm or swaying branches with quick, rather jerky movements.

It was exciting to be able to make fairly regular observations on the same individuals; previously I had found this almost impossible. Chimpanzees follow no set route on their daily wanderings, and so, except when a good fruit tree had been ripe, it had only been by chance that I had observed the same chimpanzee more than a few times in any one month. In camp, however, I was able to make detailed observations on social interactions of David, Goliath, and William to each other several times a week. Additionally, I often saw incidents involving one of the three when I was watching the chimpanzee groups feeding on figs in the home valley.

It was at this point when I began to suspect that Goliath might be the highest-ranking male chimpanzee in the area—and later I found that this in reality was the case. If William and Goliath started to move toward the same banana at the same time, it was William who gave way and Goliath who took the fruit. If Goliath met another adult male along a narrow forest track, he continued —the other stepped aside. Goliath was nearly always the first to be greeted when a newcomer climbed into a fig tree to join a feeding group of chimpanzees. One day I actually saw him driving another chimp from her nest in order to take it over for himself. It was nearly dark when I observed this from the Peak. The young female had constructed a large leafy nest and was peacefully lying there, curled up for the night. Suddenly Goliath swung up onto the branch beside her, and after a moment stood upright, seized an overhead branch, and began to sway it violently back and forth over her head. With a loud scream she leaped out of bed and vanished into the darkening undergrowth below; Goliath calmed instantly, climbed onto her vacated nest, bent over a new branch, and lay down. Five minutes later the ousted female was still constructing a new bed in the last glimmers of dusk.

William, with his long scarred upper lip and his drooping lower lip, was one of the more subordinate males in his relationships with other chimpanzees. If another adult male showed signs of

aggression toward him, William was quick to approach with gestures of appeasement and submission, reaching out to lay his hand
on the other, crouching with soft panting grunts in front of the
higher-ranking individuals. During such an encounter he would
often pull back the corners of his lips and expose his teeth in a
nervous grin. Initially William was timid in camp, also. When I
offered him a banana in my hand for the first time, he stared at it
for several moments, gently shook a branch in his frustration, and
then sat uttering soft whimpering sounds until I relented and put
the fruit on the ground.

It took much longer to determine David Graybeard's position
in the dominance hierarchy. In those early days I only knew that
he had a very calm and gentle disposition: if William or some
youngster approached him with submissive gestures, David was
quick to respond with a reassuring gesture, laying his hand on the
other's body or head, or briefly grooming him. Often, too, if Goliath
showed signs of excitement in camp—if I approached too closely,
for instance—David would reach out and lay his hand gently in
his companion's groin or make a few brief grooming strokes on
Goliath's arm. Such gestures nearly always seemed to calm the
more dominant male.

It was during these weeks that Hugo arrived at the Gombe
Stream. I had at last agreed that a professional photographer be
allowed to come and photograph the chimpanzees, and Louis had
recommended Hugo. The National Geographic Society had accepted the advice and given Hugo funds for filming the chimpanzees—partly to obtain a documentary film record of as much
behavior as possible, and partly in the hope of being able to prepare
a lecture film for their members.

Hugo was born in Indonesia, educated in England and Holland,
and, like myself, had always loved animals. He chose photography
as a career on the assumption that he would somehow and sometime get to Africa and film wild animals. After two years of working
in a film studio in Amsterdam he was accepted by Armand and
Michaela Denis to help with the filming of their well-known TV
program "On Safari." He arrived in Africa, in fact, one year after
I did.

While he was working for the Denises, Hugo came to know the

Leakeys, who were practically neighbors, and after two years he agreed to make a lecture film for the National Geographic Society on Louis's work at the Olduvai Gorge. During this period Louis decided that Hugo would be just the person to go to the Gombe Stream; he realized that Hugo was not only an excellent photographer but also that he had a real love and understanding of animals. Louis wrote to tell me about Hugo and his abilities. At the same time he wrote to Vanne telling her that he had found someone just right as a husband for Jane.

I still felt some apprehension as to how the chimpanzees would tolerate a man with a load of photographic equipment, but I realized the importance of getting a documentary film record of the chimpanzees' behavior. Also, there was David Graybeard—I did not anticipate that David would be too upset by the arrival of a stranger.

On Hugo's first morning at the Gombe Stream, David Graybeard arrived very early in camp, for he had nested nearby. I had decided that it might be best if David first got used to the new tent, and then to its occupant; so while David ate his bananas Hugo remained inside, peering out through the flaps. David scarcely glanced at the tent until his meal was finished. Then he walked deliberately over, pulled back one of the flaps, stared at Hugo, grunted, and plodded away in his usual leisurely manner.

To my surprise Goliath and even timid William, who arrived together a short while afterward, also accepted Hugo with very little fuss. It was as though they regarded him as merely part of the "furniture" of the camp. And so on his first day Hugo was able to get some excellent film of interactions—greeting, grooming, and begging for food—between the three males. And on his second day, Hugo was able to get some even more remarkable film—shots of chimpanzees eating a monkey.

Since that memorable day when I first had watched David Graybeard feeding on the carcass of a young bushpig, I had only once seen meat-eating again. On that occasion the prey had been a young bushbuck, but again I could not be sure that the chimps had caught it themselves. On this third occasion Hugo and I actually witnessed the hunt and kill.

It happened most unexpectedly. I had taken Hugo up to show

him the Peak and we were watching four red colobus monkeys that were evidently separated from their troop. Suddenly an adolescent male chimpanzee climbed cautiously up the tree next to the monkeys and moved slowly along a branch. Then he sat down. After a moment, three of the monkeys jumped away—quite calmly, it appeared. The fourth remained, his head turned toward the chimp. A second later another adolescent male chimp climbed out of the thick vegetation surrounding the tree, rushed along the branch on which the last monkey was sitting, and grabbed it. Instantly several other chimps climbed up into the tree and, screaming and barking in excitement, tore their victim into several pieces. It was all over within a minute from the time of capture.

We were too far away for Hugo to film the hunt, and anyway it happened so suddenly that he could hardly have expected to do so even had we been close enough. He did get some film of the chimpanzees eating their share of the kill, though from very far away.

After such a startlingly auspicious beginning, however, Hugo's luck changed. True, he was able to get a great deal of excellent movie film and still photographs of David, William, and Goliath. But he needed more than that for his documentary record. He needed film of as many aspects of the chimpanzees' life as possible —their life in the mountains and forests. And most of them fled from Hugo just as two years earlier they had fled from me; even Goliath and William distrusted him when they met him in the forest.

As I had done previous to Judy's visit, I had constructed a few ramshackle hides for Hugo, close to trees I expected to bear fruit. I had even stuck empty bottles through the walls to try to get the chimps accustomed to the sight of camera lenses. Somehow, though, they instantly detected the difference when they spied real lenses and, if they did arrive in the tree, they usually stared toward the hide and vanished silently. Poor Hugo—he lugged most of his camera equipment up and down the steep slopes himself so as not to create the added disturbance of taking an African porter with him. He spent long hours perched on steep rocky hillsides or down on the softer earth of the valley floors, which always seemed to harbor biting ants. Frequently no chimps came at all; when they did they often left before he could get even a foot of film.

However, it seemed that the chimps, having very slowly got used to one white-skinned ape in the area, and having then had the chance to study a second, very similar-looking ape in the person of my sister, took a relatively short time to accept a third. And David Graybeard hastened the process. Occasionally, when he saw Hugo or me, he would leave his group and come to see whether by any chance we had a banana. The other chimps watched intently.

When David, William, and Goliath had started visiting camp I had soon discovered that they loved chewing on cloth and cardboard; sweaty garments, presumably because of their salty flavor, were the most sought after. One day, when Hugo was crouched in a small hide by a large fruiting tree, a group of chimps climbed up and began to feed. They did not, it appeared, notice him at all. Just as he was beginning to film he felt his camera being pulled away from him. For a moment he couldn't imagine what was going on. Then he saw a black hairy hand pulling at the old shirt he had wrapped around his camera to camouflage the shiny surfaces of the lenses. Of course it was David Graybeard; he had walked along the valley path behind Hugo and then, when he got level with the hide, spied the tempting material. Hugo grabbed hold of one end and engaged in a frenzied tug-of-war until the shirt finally split and David plodded off to join the group in the tree with his spoils in one hand. The other chimps had watched these proceedings with apparent interest, and after that they tolerated Hugo's filming even though during the struggle with David most of the hide had collapsed.

In fact it was only a month after he arrived before most of the chimpanzees accepted not only Hugo but also his clicking, whirring cameras—provided he kept still and did not move around. The rains once again started early, and just as the weather had consistently ruined Judy's few photographic opportunities the year before, so it was with Hugo. Day after day he had sat in his hides, the sun shining, the lighting perfect—but with no chimpanzees to film. Then a group arrived, everything was just right, and, almost as though prearranged, it began to rain.

Nevertheless, over the weeks Hugo did get some first-rate material on chimpanzee behavior in the mountains. Also, he continued to film interactions between David, Goliath, and William in camp.

One of my problems, from the time when I first tried to tempt David and the others to the camp with bananas, had been that of the baboons. There was never a day when the troop did not pass through camp, and some of the males often remained on their own, as old Shaitani had done, in the hope that bananas would appear. One day, when David, William, and Goliath were sitting around a large pile of bananas, a particularly aggressive male baboon suddenly ran at them. William retired from the fray almost at once, his lips wobbling in his agitation, and, with the few bananas he had managed to seize, watched the ensuing battle from a safe distance. David also ran from the baboon when it first threatened him, but he then approached Goliath (who was calmly ignoring the commotion and finishing his bananas) and flung his arms around his friend. Next, as though made brave by the contact, he turned to scream and wave his arms at the baboon. Again the baboon threatened him, lunging forward, and again David rushed to embrace Goliath. This time Goliath responded; he got up, ran a few steps toward the baboon, and then leaped repeatedly into the air in an upright posture, waving his arms and uttering his fierce *waa* or threat bark. Although David Graybeard joined in, it was noticeable that he kept a few feet behind Goliath from the start. The baboon retreated, but a moment later, avoiding Goliath, it rushed to lunge and slap at David.

This happened over and over. Goliath leaped at the baboon and the baboon, avoiding him with ease, managed each time to hit out at David, no matter how the latter tried to hide behind his friend. Eventually it was David and Goliath who retreated, leaving the baboon to grab the spoils of victory and rush off to a safer distance. Hugo managed to film the entire incident, and it remains one of the best records of an aggressive encounter between chimpanzees and baboons.

The National Geographic Society had agreed to finance Hugo's work at the Gombe Stream until the end of November so that he would be able to film the chimpanzees using tools during the termite season. I expected this to start, as in previous years, during October. Although Hugo and I daily examined different termite mounds, we saw no signs of any activity until early November. Then, when Hugo had only just over two weeks longer at the Gombe, the termites began to cooperate. One day when Hugo made his pilgrimage to his favorite nest near camp, he saw a few moist spots. He scratched away the newly sealed-over passages, poked a grass down, and to his delight felt the insects grip on. The chimpanzees perversely showed no desire to eat termites. During the following week David, William, and Goliath passed the heap frequently but never paused to examine it. Hugo grew desperate. He even led David Graybeard to the termite nest one day, walking along ahead of him with a banana in one hand, and while the chimp sat eating the fruit, offered him a strawful of clinging termites. David glanced at them and then hit the straw from Hugo's hand with a soft threat cough.

However, during Hugo's last ten days, the chimpanzees finally demonstrated their skill in tool-using and toolmaking. Hugo was able to film and take still photographs of David, William, and Goliath working at the camp termite heap. It was exciting material, and Hugo hoped that it would help him to persuade the Geographic Society to let him return the following year and continue filming the chimpanzees.

When Hugo left at the end of November I was alone again. I still was not lonely, yet I was not as completely happy in my aloneness as I had been before he came. For I had found in Hugo a companion with whom I could share not only the joys and frustrations of my work but also my love of the chimpanzees, of the forests and mountains, of life in the wilderness. He had been with me into some of the wild, secret places where, I had thought, no other white person would ever tread. Together we had roasted in the sun and shivered under plastic covering in the rain. In Hugo I knew I had found a kindred spirit—one who had a deep appreciation and understanding of animals. Small wonder that I missed him when he was gone.

Christmas that year at the Gombe Stream was a day to remember. I bought an extra large supply of bananas and put them around a small tree I had decorated with silver paper and absorbent cotton.

Goliath and William arrived together on Christmas morning and gave loud screams of excitement when they saw the huge pile of fruit. They flung their arms around one another and Goliath kept patting William on his wide-open screaming mouth while William laid one arm over Goliath's back. Finally they calmed down and began their feast, still uttering small squeaks and grunts of pleasure, somewhat muffled and sticky through their mouthfuls of banana.

David arrived much later, on his own. I sat close beside him as he ate his bananas. He seemed extra calm, and after some time I very slowly moved my hand toward his shoulder and made a grooming movement. He brushed me away—but so casually that after a moment I ventured to try again. And this time he actually allowed me to groom him for at least a minute. Then he gently pushed my hand away once more. But he had let me touch him, tolerated physical contact with a human being—and he was a fully adult male chimpanzee who had lived all of his life in the wild. It was a Christmas gift to treasure.

I had invited some of the Africans and their children for tea. At first the children were very nervous and ill-at-ease, but when I produced paper hats and balloons and a few little toys they were so excited that their reserve was soon gone and they were laughing and chasing around and thoroughly enjoying themselves. Iddi Matata, in his stately way, also was entranced by the balloons.

When the party was over I felt a need to go up to the Peak for an hour or so by myself before darkness fell. Then I hurried down to enjoy the Christmas dinner Dominic had been talking about for days. He and Hugo had planned it in minute detail, from the stuffing of the chicken to the custard sauce for the plum pudding, before Hugo left. It was dark when I returned, my mouth watering in anticipation—only to find that Dominic meanwhile had been celebrating Christmas in his own way. Laid out on my table was one unopened tin of bully beef, an empty plate, a knife, and a fork. And that was my Christmas dinner. When I asked Dominic about the chicken and all the rest of it, he only laughed uproariously and repeated many times, "Tomorrow." Then he went off, giggling weakly, to the four-gallon can of local beer which, I later heard, had been brought down by a well-wisher from Bubango, the village on the mountaintop. Dominic made up for it when he cooked the meal next day, despite his king-size hangover.

Shortly after Christmas I had to leave the Gombe Stream myself for another term at Cambridge. My last two weeks were sad, for William fell ill. His nose ran, his eyes watered, and he constantly coughed—a dry hacking cough that shook his entire body. The first day of William's illness I followed him when he left camp, because by that time I was able to move about the forests with both William and David, although Goliath still threatened me if I tried to follow him. William went a few hundred yards along the valley, climbed into a tree, and made himself a large and leafy nest. There he lay until about three in the afternoon, wheezing and coughing, and sometimes apparently dozing. Several times he actually urinated while lying in his bed—behavior so unusual that I knew he surely must be feeling very poorly. When he finally got up he fed on a few bits and pieces of leaf and vine, wandered slowly back to camp, ate a couple of bananas, and then climbed into a tree beside my tent and made another nest.

That night I stayed out since there was a moon. At about one in the morning the clouds built up and covered the moon; soon it began to rain. I was crouched some distance up the steep slope of the mountain at a slightly higher level than William's nest, and when I shone my powerful torch in his direction I could just make out his huddled figure, sitting up in his wet bed with his knees up to his chin and his arms around his legs. For the rest of the night it rained on and off, and the silences between the pattering of the raindrops were punctuated by William's hacking cough. Once at the start of a really heavy deluge William gave a few rather tremulous pant-hoots and then was silent.

When he climbed down in the morning I saw that every few moments his body shook with violent spasms of shivering. When he shivered his long slack lips wobbled, but it was no longer funny. I longed to be able to wrap a warm blanket around him and give him a steaming-hot toddy. All I could offer were a few chilly bananas.

I was with William almost constantly for a week. He spent his days in the vicinity of camp, much of the time lying in different nests. Several times he joined David or Goliath briefly, but when they moved off up the mountainside he turned back as though he couldn't face a long journey.

One morning I was sitting near William a short way up the mountain above camp when a boat arrived with some visitors from Kigoma. By now, David Graybeard's fame had spread and people sometimes came for a Sunday afternoon in the hope of seeing him. I should of course have gone down to say hello, but I had become so attuned to William that I almost felt myself the chimps' instinctive distrust of strangers. When William moved down toward the tents, I followed him; when he sat in the bushes opposite my camp, I sat beside him. Together we watched the visitors. They had coffee and chatted for some time and then, since there was no sign of David, they left. I wondered what they would have thought if they had known I was sitting there with William, peering at them as though they had been alien creatures from an unknown world.

One morning, two days before I had to leave, William stole a blanket from Dominic's tent. He had been sitting chewing on it for a while when David Graybeard arrived and, after eating some bananas, joined William at the blanket. For half an hour or so the two sat peacefully side by side, each sucking noisily and contentedly on different corners. Then William, like the clown he so often appeared to be, put part of the blanket right over his head and made groping movements with his hands as he tried to touch David from within the strange darkness he had created. David stared for a moment, and then patted William's hand. Presently the two wandered off into the forest together, leaving me with the echo of a dry hacking cough and the blanket lying on the ground. I never saw William again.

7

FLO'S SEX LIFE

SEX APPEAL, that strange mystery, is a phenomenon as inexplicable and as obvious among chimpanzees as human beings. Old Flo, bulbous-nosed and ragged-eared, incredibly ugly by human standards, undoubtedly has more than her fair share of it. At one time I thought it was simply because she was an old and therefore experienced female that the males got so excited when she became sexually attractive. Now I know better, for there are some old females who are almost ignored at such times, and some young ones who are courted as frenziedly as Flo.

When a female chimpanzee comes into heat—or into estrus, as a scientist would say—the sex skin of her genital area becomes swollen. Such swellings vary somewhat in size; some females develop a pale pink protuberance that is fully as large as a three-pint bowl, whereas others have smaller protuberances. A swelling usually persists for about ten days before becoming flabby and wrinkled and then shrinking away to nothing again. Normally it occurs at a point midway between menstrual periods, which in the female chimp occur about every thirty five days. It is during her period of swelling that a female—whom I refer to frivolously as a "pink lady" —is courted and mated by the males.

By the time I returned to the Gombe Stream after my second sojourn at Cambridge—together with Hugo, who had, after all, persuaded the National Geographic Society that we needed more film on chimpanzee behavior—Flo and two of her three offspring had become fairly regular visitors to camp. Flo's daughter Fifi was about three and a half years old then. She still suckled from her mother for a few minutes every two or three hours, and jumped occasionally onto Flo's back, particularly if she was nervous or startled. I knew, too, that she still shared her mother's nest at night. Figan, Fifi's senior by some four years, had just attained puberty. Some young males of this age are fairly independent of their mothers, but Figan spent most of his days traveling about with Flo and Fifi. Faben, Flo's eldest known son, was seldom seen with his family that year; he was an adolescent of about ten years at the time.

When Hugo and I first returned to the Gombe Stream, Flo, Fifi, and Figan were still rather apprehensive when they came to camp. They spent most of the time lurking in the thick bushes around the clearing, only emerging to seize the bananas we put out for them. Gradually, however, they relaxed, particularly when David or Goliath was with them, and then they spent longer and longer out in the open. I still spent most of my time climbing the mountains, but when most of the chimpanzees moved far to the north or to the south, then I often stayed in camp, hoping that Flo would come.

Even in those days Flo looked very old. She appeared frail, with but little flesh on her bones, and thinning hair that was brown rather than black. When she yawned we saw that her teeth were worn right down to the gums. We soon found out that her character by no means matched her appearance: she was aggressive, tough as nails, and easily the most dominant of all the females at that time.

Flo's personality will become more vivid if I contrast it with that of another old female, Olly, who also began to visit camp at that time. Olly, with her long face and loose wobbling lips so sadly reminiscent of William, was remarkably different. Flo for the most part was relaxed in her relations with the adult males; often I saw her grooming in a close group with two or three males out in the forests, and in camp she showed no hesitation in joining David or Goliath to beg for a share of cardboard or bananas. Olly, on the other hand, was tense and nervous in her relations with others of her kind. She was particularly apprehensive when in close proximity to adult males, and her hoarse, frenzied pant-grunts rose to near hysteria if high-ranking Goliath approached her. She had a large pendulous swelling in the front of her neck which looked exactly like a goiter. It may have been one, since they are not uncommon among African women in the area; and if so it might account for much of her nervous behavior.

Olly tended to avoid large groups of chimps and often wandered about with only her two-year-old daughter Gilka for company. Sometimes she was accompanied by her eight-year-old son Evered; in fact it was he who first led his mother to our camp after coming several times himself with David and Goliath. Often, too, Olly and Flo traveled about together in the forests, and all four children were playmates of long standing. For the most part the relationship between Flo and Olly was peaceful enough, but if there was a single banana lying on the ground between them the relative social status of each was made very clear: Flo had only to put a few of her moth-eaten hairs on end for Olly to retreat, pant-grunting and grinning in submission.

Once a game between Flo's son Figan and Olly's son Evered turned into a serious squabble—as happens only too often when young males play together—and Flo rushed over at once, her hair on end, in response to Figan's loud screams. She flew at Evered and rolled him over and over until he managed to escape and run off screaming loudly. Olly hurried up too, uttering threatening barks and looking extremely agitated, but she did not dare join in, and so contented herself when all was over with approaching and, as though to appease the dominant female, laying a hand gently on Flo's back.

Flo was a far more easygoing and tolerant mother than Olly. When Fifi begged for food, whimpering and holding out her hand, Flo nearly always let the child take a banana. Sometimes she actually held one out to her. True, there were a few occasions when Fifi tried to take her mother's last banana and Flo objected; then mother and daughter rolled over on the ground as they fought for the fruit, screaming and pulling at each other's hair. Such incidents were rare, though. Gilka would never have dared to try such a thing. We rarely saw her even begging for Olly's bananas, and when she did she was usually ignored. She seldom got more than a taste of the skins until she got tame enough to come right up to us so that we could smuggle her a whole banana. And even then Olly often rushed up and wrenched the fruit away from her daughter.

Despite Flo's normally relaxed relation with the adult males, she did not usually compete for bananas with David or Goliath; rather, she waited until they had taken an armful before she ventured to attempt to get some for herself. And so, one morning in July 1963, Hugo and I were surprised to see Flo rushing up to join in as Goliath and David approached a pile of bananas. Then we saw that she was flaunting a large sexual swelling.

After seizing a heap of bananas but before taking a single bite, Goliath stood upright with all his hair on end, stared at Flo, and swaggered from foot to foot. As Flo approached, clutching some bananas herself, Goliath raised one arm in the air and made a sweeping gesture through the air with his banana-filled hand. Flo crouched to the ground, presenting Goliath with her pink posterior, and he mated her in the typical nonchalant manner of the chimpanzee, squatting in an upright position, one fruit-laden hand laid lightly on Flo's back and the other resting on the ground beside him.

Chimpanzees have the briefest possible intercourse—normally the male remains mounted for only ten to fifteen seconds. Nevertheless, before Goliath had done with Flo, Fifi was there. Racing up she hurled herself against Goliath, shoving at his head with both her hands, trying to push him off her mother. I expected Goliath to threaten the child, to hit at her, or at least to brush her aside. Instead he merely turned his head away and appeared to try to ignore Fifi altogether. As Flo moved away, Fifi followed, one hand laid over her mother's swelling, looking back over her shoulder at Goliath, who sat eating his bananas. For a moment Fifi stayed close to Flo, and then she went off to scrounge a banana.

A few minutes later David Graybeard approached Flo with his hair bristling. Sitting on the ground, he shook a little twig, staring at her as he did so. Flo instantly ran toward him, turned, and crouched to the ground; again Fifi raced up and pushed and shoved at David as hard as she could. And David also tolerated her interference.

After this the group settled down. David groomed Flo and then, since it was a hot morning, lay down to snooze. Goliath followed suit, and everything was peaceful. Not long afterward we saw Evered move slightly away from the group, looking over his shoulder at Flo, who was watching him. Then he squatted down with his shoulders hunched and his arms held slightly out from his body. This was the typical adolescent male courtship posture, and Flo responded at once, approaching and presenting as she had for the adult males. Goliath and David both looked up but otherwise ignored the incident. Fifi, as before, ran up and pushed at Evered, and he too ignored her.

The next day Flo arrived very early in the morning. Her suitors of the previous day were with her; once again they courted and mated with her before eating their bananas; once again Fifi rushed up each time and pushed at them. And then, from the corner of his eye, Hugo saw another black shape in the bushes. As we peered we saw another, and another, and another. Quickly we withdrew into the tent and looked through binoculars into the vegetation. Almost immediately I recognized old Mr. McGregor. Then Mike and J.B. Also there were Huxley, Leakey, Hugh, Rodolf, Humphrey—just about all the adult males I knew. And there were some adolescents, females, and youngsters in the group as well.

We remained inside the tent. Soon Flo moved up into the bushes and there was mated by every male in turn. Each time, Fifi got there and tried to push the suitor away. Once she succeeded: she jumped right onto Flo's back while Mr. McGregor was mating her mother, and pushed so hard that he lost his balance and tumbled back down the slope.

For the next week Flo was followed everywhere by her large male retinue. It was impossible for her to sit up or lie down without several pairs of eyes instantly swiveling in her direction, and if she got up to move on, the males were on their feet in no time. Every time there was any sort of excitement in the group—when they arrived at a food source, when they left their nests in the morning, when other chimps joined them—then, one after the other, all the adult males mated Flo. We saw no fighting over this very popular female; each male simply took his turn. Only once, when David Graybeard was mating Flo, did one of the other males show signs of impatience: irascible J.B. started to leap up and down as he swayed a large low branch so that the end beat down on David's head. But David merely pressed himself close to Flo and closed his eyes—and J.B. did not attack him.

The few adolescent males of the group, however, did not stand a chance. Normally these youngsters are able to take their turn, provided they wait until a flurry of sexual excitement has died down and the adult males are calm and satiated. Then, if an adolescent hunches his shoulders or shakes a branch at the female from a discreet distance she will usually move toward him in response. The older males, although they may glance at the mating pair, seldom object to these expressions of youthful passion. Flo, however, was an exceptionally popular female. We did sometimes see an adolescent hunching at Flo from behind some tree, but, though Flo herself usually got up and wandered toward him, several of the adult males instantly followed. It was as though they feared that Flo might try to escape. The proximity of his elders effectively nipped the amorous intentions of the adolescent at the start and he would retreat hastily to gaze at Flo from a safer distance.

Once we saw Evered sitting some distance from Flo and every so often glancing from her toward one or other of the adult males. It looked as if he was torn between desire and caution. He took a few tentative steps toward Flo and suddenly went off at a tangent, flicking at pieces of rock, throwing little handfuls of grass in the air, kicking at stones with his feet. Then he sat down and for the next ten minutes occasionally shook a branch as though to relieve his feelings.

On the eighth day of her swelling Flo arrived in camp with a torn and bleeding bottom. The injury must have just occurred. Within another couple of hours her swelling had gone. She looked somewhat tattered and exhausted by then and we were relieved for her sake that everything was over. At least we thought it was over, for normally a swelling only lasts about ten days. But five days later, to our utter astonishment Flo was fully pink again. She arrived, as before, with a large following of attendant males. This time her swelling lasted for three consecutive weeks, during which time the ardor of her suitors did not appear to abate in any way.

During this second period of pinkness we noticed that a strange sort of relationship had grown up between Flo and one of her suitors—a relationship of a type we have never seen since. The male was Rodolf (his real name is Hugo, but two named Hugo in one book are too confusing, and so I have given him Hugo's second name). Rodolf, in those days, was a high-ranking and enormously big and powerful chimpanzee, and he became Flo's faithful escort. He walked everywhere just beside or behind her, he stopped when she stopped, he slept in the nest closest to hers. And it was to Rodolf that Flo often hurried when she was hurt or frightened during those weeks, and he would lay his hand reassuringly on her or sometimes put one arm around her. Yet he did not protest in any way when other males mated with Flo.

During the final weeks Fifi became increasingly wary of the males; perhaps finally she had been threatened, or even attacked, by one of Flo's suitors. Whatever the reason, her gay assurance in life was gone for the time being. She stayed farther and farther away from the center of a group during any sort of excitement and she completely stopped interfering with her mother's sex life. She didn't even dare join a group that was loading up with bananas in camp—she who a couple of weeks earlier had actually taken fruits from the hands of the males that she tried to push from Flo.

The fact that Flo's milk had, quite obviously, dried up with the appearance of her sexual swelling may have affected Fifi's behavior too. A quick suck of milk, more than anything else, seems to calm an infant chimpanzee. If one of the males threatened Fifi, she could still run to Flo, still be embraced by her mother—but where was the comfort of a sudden flow of warm milk? Whenever the group was resting and peaceful during those hectic three weeks, Fifi went close to Flo and either groomed her or simply sat beside her with one hand on her mother's body. And when the group was on the move, Fifi, instead of running jauntily along ahead of Flo or bouncing along behind, took to riding again as though she were an overgrown baby. Not only did she frequently perch ridiculously on her mother's back, but she sometimes actually clung on in the ventral position under Flo's tummy with her back bumping along the ground.

One day Flo, with Fifi on her back, came into camp alone. Her fabulous swelling had gone, shriveled into a limp flap of wrinkled skin. She looked worn out, faded, incredibly tattered after her strenuous five weeks. There were two extra pieces torn from her ears and a variety of cuts and scrapes all over her body. That day she just lay around camp for several hours, looking utterly exhausted. She and Fifi left as they had arrived, on their own.

The following day a group of males was in camp when Flo appeared plodding along the path. The moment they spotted her they leaped up, their hair on end, and charged off to meet her. Flo, with a hoarse scream, rushed up the nearest palm tree. The males ran on, with David Graybeard for once in the lead. They stopped under her tree and gazed up for a moment before David, slowly and deliberately, began to climb the trunk. What took place we shall never know, for leaves hid the two from sight. A few moments later David reappeared and climbed slowly down the trunk again. He walked past the other five males and plodded back to camp. A moment later Flo reappeared and moved down toward the waiting group. She hesitated for a second before finally stepping to the ground. Then, crouching slightly, she turned and presented her shriveled posterior to her former suitors. Goliath carefully inspected the flabby skin, poking around for a moment and intently sniffing the end of his finger. Then he followed David back to camp, and it was Leakey's turn to inspect Flo. After Leakey came Mike and Rodolf, and finally old Mr. McGregor. Then they all trailed back to their interrupted meal, leaving Flo standing on the path staring after them. Who can tell what she was thinking?

After that Rodolf again attached himself to the old female, and for the next fortnight continued to travel around with her and her family; Figan, who had stayed away from his mother during most of her pinkness, was back with her also. One day, about a week after the last vestiges of Flo's swelling had subsided, Rodolf, who had been grooming her, suddenly pushed Flo roughly to her feet and feverishly inspected her bottom, repeatedly sniffing his finger, an eager glint in his eyes. Obviously her hormonal secretions gave no indication of imminent pinkness, and after a few moments he permitted Flo to sit down again and continued to groom her. We saw him behave thus on three different occasions. But Rodolf would have to wait close to five years before Flo again went pink.

I would follow the chimpanzees through the forest

Inquisitive African children visit our camp. *Copyright National Geographic Society*

With her clinic Vanne established friendly relations with the fishermen

Chimpanzees make nests to sleep in

My lookout place on the Peak
gave a commanding view

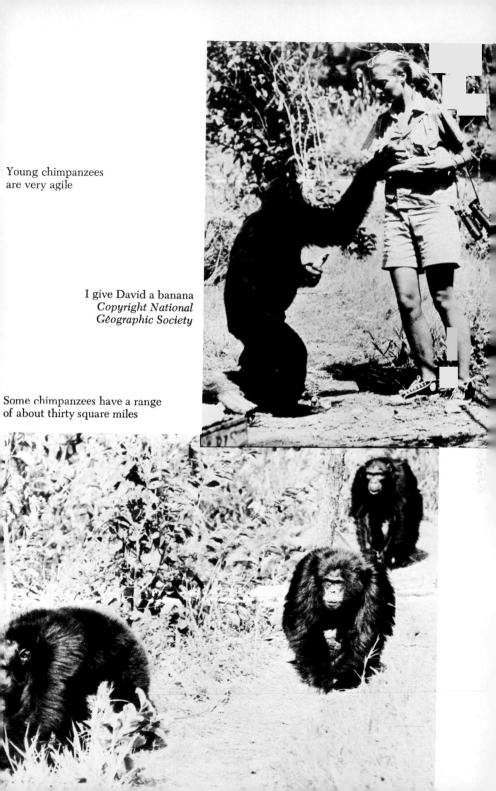

Young chimpanzees
are very agile

I give David a banana
*Copyright National
Geographic Society*

Some chimpanzees have a range
of about thirty square miles

Figan does a rain-dance

Hugo is an all-weather photographer

When David was attacked by this baboon he ran to
Goliath for reassurance. During the ensuing battle
Goliath repeatedly lunged at the baboon while David
sheltered behind him

When Flo became sexually attractive
and weaned her daughter, Fifi reverted
to infantile behavior

David, Goliath, and William raided my tent for cardboard to chew on

Rodolf escorted Flo but
did not stop other males
from mating with her

Leakey

Worzle

Mike

Goliath

McGregor

Melissa with Goblin

8

THE FEEDING STATION

THERE WERE TWO MAJOR RESULTS of Flo's memorable pinkness. First, she conceived. Second, the large number of chimpanzees who had accompanied her during those five weeks had all become accustomed to camp and bananas. They continued to visit us even when Flo was no longer the lure. And so it became worthwhile to think of setting up a feeding station on more permanent lines: a feeding station that would tempt the nomadic chimpanzees to camp whenever they happened to be in the vicinity, so that we should be able to make reasonably regular observations on a number of different, known individuals.

First of all we had to think of better ways of offering bananas than merely spraying them about on the ground. For one thing, an adult male, if he has the chance, will eat fifty or more bananas at a sitting; for another, we were having more and more trouble with the baboon troop. These were problems which took us another six years to solve, but at least when Hugo and I had to leave at the end of that year we had made a beginning. With Hassan's help we made a number of concrete boxes with steel lids opening outward. These boxes were sunk into the ground, the lids held shut by wires attached to handles some distance away. When pins holding the handles were released the wires became slack and the lids fell open.

Some of these boxes were installed by the time Kris Pirozynski, a young Polish mycologist, arrived in early December to study the microfungi of the Gombe Stream area. Kris had agreed to look after

camp and keep an eye on the chimps during the four months that
Hugo and I would be away. Hassan and Dominic would both stay
on to help him, and Dominic was excited at the prospect of making notes on the chimps each day.

By this time Hugo and I were very much in love. But was this,
we asked ourselves, simply the outcome of being thrown together
in the wilds, far from other European society? Would our feelings
change, perhaps, when we found ourselves back in civilization
again? We didn't think so; however, since both of us considered
marriage a very final step, we resolved to test our love. I was going
for a third term to Cambridge. Later Hugo would be joining me,
and together we would show the chimpanzee film to National
Geographic Society members in Washington, D.C. We would meet
again in the world of men rather than the world of apes; and then
we would know. As it turned out, we knew the very moment we
were separated.

I left Hugo about a week before Christmas. The day after Christmas (Boxing Day, as it is known in England) a cable arrived at
my family home in Bournemouth: WILL YOU MARRY ME STOP LOVE
STOP HUGO. In fact, I should have received the message on Christmas Eve, and although I replied immediately Hugo had had to
leave on safari and didn't receive my answer for five whole days—
not until he got to a place from where he could telephone through
to Nairobi.

We decided to be married in London after my Cambridge term
and our American lecture were over. Despite the difficulties of
planning a wedding when the parties concerned were scattered
between Cambridge, Nairobi, Amersfort in Holland, and Bournemouth, Hugo and I agreed afterward that we had never been to a
wedding we enjoyed more. A clay model of David Graybeard
crowned the wedding cake and huge colored portraits of David and
Goliath, Flo and Fifi, and other chimps looked down on the recep-
tion. Everything, from my dress to those of the two little bridesmaids and the arum lilies and daffodils, was white and yellow like
the spring sunshine that peeped in and out of the fluffy white
clouds. It was sad that Louis, after all his machinations and predictions, was unable to be with us, but he sent a speech on tape,
and he was represented by his daughter and by his granddaughter,
who was one of the bridesmaids.

Three weeks before our wedding we had received letters telling us that Flo had borne a son. Although we had not changed our wedding plans, we did cut our honeymoon to only three days in order to get back to the Gombe Stream as quickly as possible.

When we finally made it back to the chimps, after battling our way through flooded rivers, making detours around others, and finally putting the Land-Rover onto a train, Flo's new infant, whom we subsequently called Flint, was already seven weeks old. He was still incredibly tiny, still quite hairless on the pink underside of his tummy and chest. I can even recapture six years later the thrill of that first moment when Flo came close to us with Flint clinging beneath her. As his mother sat, Flint looked around toward us. His small, pale, wrinkled face was perfect, with brilliant dark eyes, round shell-pink ears, and slightly lopsided mouth—all framed by a cap of sleek black hair. He stretched out one arm and flexed the minute pink fingers, then gripped Flo's hair again and turned to nuzzle and rootle with his mouth until he located a nipple. Flo helped him, hitching him a few inches higher and into a better position for suckling. He fed for about three minutes and then appeared to sleep. When Flo moved away she carefully supported him, holding one hand under his back and walking on three limbs.

It was Dominic who had first seen Flo with her new baby. On the 28th of February she had been in camp, still very pregnant. The following day she had appeared with the tiny infant. She had been accompanied as usual by Fifi and Figan. Both had sat and stared at the baby, and Fifi had spent a lot of time grooming her mother. After that, Figan had seemed less and less interested in his new sibling, and Fifi had become increasingly fascinated.

Dominic and Kris had some other interesting news for us as well. A number of new chimpanzees, including several females, had become regular visitors to camp. Goliath was losing his top-ranking position to Mike. Melissa, one of the young females, seemed to be pregnant. And the chimpanzees were becoming more impossible in camp. J.B. had learned to dig boxes and wires out of the ground, so that Hassan had had to sink the boxes in concrete and lay expensive piping between box and handle for the wire. Then J.B. had dug up the pipes, so they had been put into concrete too. And Figan and Evered had started trying to pry open the steel lids with strong sticks; occasionally, if the wire was too slack, they succeeded. Even worse, from Kris's point of view, increasing numbers of the chimps had followed David's lead and begun wandering into his tent, taking his clothing and bedding. Finally he had organized things, stowing any material into tin trunks or stout wooden boxes. Then Goliath had started a craze for chewing canvas. Little groups of chimps had sat around tearing up and chewing chair seats, flaps of tents—even Kris's camp bed had been destroyed. And now, he told us, during the last few weeks it had become fashionable to chew wood; the back of one of Hassan's homemade cupboards had gone, and the leg of a wooden chair.

There was also rather alarming news: some of the bolder chimps had begun to raid the huts of the African fishermen and taken *their* clothing. We were worried lest someone, trying to defend his property, might anger or scare one of the big males and get badly hurt in consequence, because the fishermen would not realize the extent to which the chimps had lost their fear of men. We discussed the problem far into one night and eventually decided that as soon as possible we would move the feeding area farther up the valley.

The move was surprisingly easy. At the outset, with Hassan's help we installed more of the concrete banana boxes at the new site, and when these were ready we transported our tents and equipment there. This was all done after nightfall in order to disturb the chimps as little as possible with the comings and goings of the African porters.

There remained only the task of acquainting the chimps themselves with the new arrangements. One morning I waited at the new camp in the hope that some chimpanzees might pass by—in which case I would offer them bananas. Hugo was down at the beach camp, and we were in communication with one another by means of walkie-talkies. At about eleven o'clock Hugo's voice came through announcing that he had a big group down there, and was going to try to lead them the half mile or so to the new area. For a while there was silence, and then I heard him again, sounding frightfully out of breath; indeed, it was difficult to make out what he was saying. Eventually I gathered that he wanted me to throw out lots of bananas as far along the path toward beach camp as I could, and as quickly as I could.

I rushed about with armfuls of fruit and had just finished my task when Hugo appeared, running along with a box under one arm and a single banana in his other hand. He hurled the one fruit back along the path and collapsed beside me, gasping for breath, as the group of chimps which had been following him suddenly saw the bananas all over the path. With piercing shrieks of excitement they hugged and kissed and patted one another as they fell on the unexpected feast. Gradually their calls became muffled by sticky mouthfuls of banana.

Hugo then told me that he had shown a banana to David Graybeard, who had been among the six mature males of the group, picked up an empty box of the type we used for storing bananas, and started to run up the steep skiddy path leading to the new camp. He had not really expected the plan to work, but the trusting David, uttering loud barks of delight, had started after him, and the others had immediately followed. Hugo admitted that he had been terrified lest the excited chimps should catch up with him, snatch the box from his arms—and discover that the box was empty.

Within a very short time the chimpanzees all had discovered the new feeding area. In fact these nomads are accustomed to changes in feeding places—first the figs are ripe in one valley and then in another. So far as they were concerned the bananas, after an exceptionally long fruiting in one area, had become ripe in their strange underground boxes somewhere else.

At the new camp, far from the noise and bustle of the fishermen on the beaches, many of the chimps who had seemed tense and apprehensive before the move soon relaxed. In addition, a number of newcomers began to come for bananas. This was good because at that time some age groups were very badly represented in our group; we only had two juveniles, for instance, and only a few young adult females. As soon as we noticed a strange face peering from a tree we quickly hid in one of the tents and watched through the mosquito-netting windows. Then the stranger would only have to face the novelty of the tents and boxes without the added offense of human beings walking around. We used to tip big piles of bananas just outside the tent from storage boxes inside, and hope that the stranger would be able to beg a few from one or other of our chimps, or at least gather up and wad a few skins.

Often these strangers came many times as far as the trees around our camp, watching the strange goings-on of their fellows, before they actually ventured out into the open. Sometimes we were imprisoned within the hot stuffy tent for hours on end. But it was worth it.

One day Goliath appeared some distance up the slope with an unknown pink female close behind him. Hugo and I quickly put out a pile of bananas where both chimps could see the fruit and hid in the tent to watch. When the female saw our camp she shot up a tree and stared down. Goliath instantly stopped also, and looked up at her. Then he glanced at the bananas. He moved a short way down the slope, stopped, and looked back at his female. She had not moved. Slowly Goliath continued down, and this time the female climbed silently from the tree and we lost sight of her in the undergrowth. When Goliath looked around and saw that she had gone, he simply raced back. A moment later the female again climbed into a tree, followed by Goliath, who had every hair on end. He groomed her awhile but every so often glanced toward camp. Although he could no longer see the bananas he knew that they were there, and since he had been away for about ten days his mouth was probably watering.

In time he climbed down and once more walked toward us, stopping every few steps to stare back at the female. She sat motionless, but Hugo and I both had the distinct impression that she wanted to escape from Goliath's company. When Goliath had come a bit farther down the slope the vegetation obviously hid the female from his view because he looked back and then quickly climbed a tree. She was still sitting there. He climbed down, walked another few yards, and then shot up another tree. Still there. This went on for a further five minutes as Goliath proceeded toward the bananas.

When he reached the camp clearing Goliath faced an added problem—there were no trees to climb and he couldn't see the female from the ground. Three times he stepped into the open, then turned and rushed back up the last tree. The female did not move. Suddenly Goliath seemed to make up his mind and, at a fast canter, raced over to the bananas. Seizing only one he turned back and raced to climb his tree again. Still the female sat on the same branch. Goliath finished his banana and, as though slightly reassured, hastened back to the pile of fruit, gathered up a whole armful, and rushed back to the tree. This time the female had gone; while Goliath gathered the bananas she had climbed down from her branch, repeatedly glancing toward him over her shoulder, and vanished silently.

Goliath's consternation was amusing to watch. Dropping his bananas he raced up to the tree where he had left her, peered all around, and then he too vanished into the undergrowth. For the next twenty minutes he searched for that female. Every few minutes we saw him climbing up yet another tree, staring in every direction; but he never found her and finally gave up, returned to camp, and, looking quite exhausted, sat slowly eating bananas. Even so, he kept turning his head to gaze back up the slope.

I remember too when an old mother whom I knew well in the forests appeared for the first time at the outskirts of our clearing. She remained in the trees, watching, but her four-year-old son moved on into camp with the rest of the group. To our astonishment he actually came onto the veranda of the tent, and, as we crouched inside hardly daring to breathe lest we scare him, the corner of the flap was lifted and his small face stared in at us. Then, quite calmly, he lowered the flap and resumed his search for banana peels. He was the boldest youngster we ever encountered.

It was during these months that we first realized what an exceptionally gifted chimp was young Figan. As more and more chimps discovered the feeding area we soon found that we did not have sufficient concrete boxes. It took a long time to get the lids made in Kigoma and it became ever more difficult to make sure that the females and the youngsters had their share. So we took to hiding some fruits up in the trees, one here, one there. Youngsters such as Figan quickly learned to search for these while the adult males were busy loading up at the boxes. One day, sometime after the group had been fed, Figan spotted a banana that had been overlooked—but Goliath was resting directly underneath it. After no more than a quick glance from the fruit to Goliath, Figan moved away and sat on the other side of the tent so that he could no longer see the fruit. Fifteen minutes later, when Goliath got up and left, Figan without a moment's hesitation went over and collected the banana. Quite obviously he had sized up the whole situation: if he had climbed for the fruit earlier, Goliath almost certainly would have snatched it away. If he had remained close to the banana, he would probably have looked at it from time to time. Chimps are very quick to notice and interpret the eye movements of their fellows, and Goliath would possibly, therefore, have seen the fruit himself. And so Figan had not only refrained from instantly gratifying his desire but had also gone away so that he could not "give the game away" by looking at the banana. Hugo and I were properly impressed. But there was more to come.

Commonly when a chimpanzee gets up from a resting group and walks away without hesitation, the others will get up and follow. It does not need to be a high-ranking individual—often a fe male or a youngster may start such a move. One day when Figan was part of a large group and, in consequence, had not managed to get more than a couple of bananas for himself, he suddenly got up and walked away. The others trailed after him. Ten minutes later he returned by himself, and naturally got his share of bananas. We thought this was coincidence—indeed, it may have been on that first occasion—but after this the same thing happened over and over again: Figan led a group away and returned later for his bananas. Unquestionably he was doing it deliberately. One morning, after such a maneuver, he returned with his characteristic jaunty walk only to find that a high-ranking male had in the meantime arrived in camp and was sitting eating bananas. Figan stared at him for a few moments and then flew into a tantrum of screaming and hitting at the ground. Eventually he rushed off after the group he had led away earlier, his screams gradually receding in the distance.

That camp was a perfect spot for a newly married couple. Our tents were pitched in the dense shade of a small palm grove and we looked out over a natural grassy clearing that was brilliant for over four months with the scarlet blossoms of ten or more candelabra trees. Gleaming metallic sunbirds of many species flitted about during the day feeding on the nectar, and often in the evening a bushbuck picked his way daintily across the grass. At the far end of the clearing ran the stream, and there in the cold mountain water we washed in the evening. We cooked our own breakfasts and ate a couple of slices of bread for lunch; Hugo was determined I should not become a skeleton now that I was his wife. As darkness fell, Dominic and Sadiki, the local African we had employed to help with the work of the camp, came up with our supper and tidied camp.

Over and above the growing love that enriched our lives, and the beauty of the mountains and the forests around us, we were sharing work and experience we both enjoyed more than anything else—watching and learning about animals.

That year, among other things we discovered a new chimpanzee tool when we were out in the forest watching the old mother Olly with her two offspring, Gilka and Evered. Evered, as he climbed through a tree, suddenly stopped and, with his face close to the bark, peered into what looked like a small hollow. He picked a handful of leaves, chewed them for a moment, took them out of his mouth, and pushed them down into the hollow. As he withdrew them we saw the gleam of water. Quickly Evered sucked the liquid from his homemade sponge and poked it down into the hollow once more. At that moment Gilka came up and watched him closely. When he moved away she made a tiny sponge and pushed it into the hollow, but it seemed that all the water had gone. She dropped her sponge and wandered off. Later we saw the same behavior many times, for we had made an artificial water bowl in a fallen tree trunk in camp. Always the chimpanzees first crumpled and chewed the leaves, and that of course made their sponge much more absorbent. It is, in fact, another example of tool*making*.

Without doubt the most exciting thing that year was being able to record on paper and on film the week-by-week development of a wild chimpanzee infant—Flint. Flo and her family had been well known to us before; now they became an integral part of our lives. We learned a great deal about their behavior by means of objective recording of fact, but we also became increasingly aware of them as individual beings. Intuitively we "knew" things about them which as yet we could not begin to define in scientific terms. We began, though indeed "through a glass darkly," to understand what a chimpanzee really is.

Our only disappointment of the year was the fact that we had missed the first few weeks of Flint's life, but the birth of a baby to Melissa almost made up for that. The heat of the day was over and the sun low in the sky when we first saw the tiny infant. As Melissa came down the slope toward our camp she moved on three limbs, supporting the newborn with one hand. Every so often she stopped and seemed to disentangle something from the undergrowth; when she got closer we saw that this was the placenta, still attached to the baby by the umbilical cord.

Melissa came right up to us, quite unafraid for her infant. She seemed dazed, her eyes not quite focused, her movements slow and uncertain. When one of the mature males arrived, Melissa, usually so quick to greet another chimp, so anxious to ingratiate herself with her superiors, ignored him completely. Nor did she follow when shortly he left. She continued to sit, the baby cuddled between her thighs, her feet crossed under his tiny rump, her arm behind his head. For some time we could not see the infant at all, and then, as she finished her few bananas, she removed her encircling arm.

The baby's head fell back on her knees, and Melissa, looking down, stared long at the tiny face. Never had we imagined such a funny twisted-up little face. It was comical in its ugliness, with large ears, small, rather pursed lips, and skin incredibly wrinkled and bluish black rather than pink. His eyes were screwed tight shut against the fading light of the sun and he looked like some wizened gnome or hobgoblin. We christened him Goblin on the spot. Melissa gazed down at her son for fully two minutes before she placed one hand behind his back and set off to make her nest for the night.

Hugo and I followed, keeping well behind. Every fifteen steps or so Melissa stopped and sat for a few moments before moving on, still supporting the infant with one hand, the placenta still trailing. It was dusk when she reached a tall leafy tree and climbed up, and we could hardly see by the time she had finished making her bed. She made a very large one, using her feet and one hand, and it took her eight minutes instead of the usual three to five. Finally she lay down and all was quiet.

We left her and climbed back down the mountain to our forest home, rather silent as we thought of the young female, bewildered by the miracle of birth as so many other mothers have been throughout the centuries, animal and human alike. For the first time since leaving her own mother, Melissa was sharing her nest with another chimpanzee.

9

FLO AND HER FAMILY

OLD FLO LAY ON HER BACK in the early morning sunshine, her belly full of palm nuts, and suspended Flint above her, grasping one of his minute wrists with her large horny foot. As he dangled, gently waving his free arm and kicking with his legs, she reached up and tickled him in his groin and his neck until he opened his mouth in the play-face, or chimpanzee smile. Nearby Fifi sat staring at Flint, occasionally reaching out to touch her ten-week-old brother gently with one hand.

Faben and Figan, Flo's two elder sons, played with each other not far away. Since Flint's birth two and a half months earlier Faben had begun to move around with his family more frequently. Every so often, as their game became extra vigorous, I could hear the panting chuckles of chimpanzee laughter. All at once Faben, three or four years Figan's senior, began to play rather roughly, sitting down and kicking with the soles of his feet on Figan's bent head. After a few moments Figan had had enough. He left Faben, and, with his jaunty walk, approached Fifi and tried to play with her. At that moment Flo, gathering Flint to her breast, got up to move into the shade, and Fifi pulled away from Figan to follow her mother. Ever since Hugo and I had returned to the Gombe Stream when Flint was seven weeks old, Fifi had become increasingly fascinated by her new brother.

Flo sat down and began to tickle Flint's neck with small nibbling movements of her worn teeth, and Fifi once again sat close and reached out to make a few grooming movements on Flint's back.

Flo ignored this. Earlier, though, when Flint was not yet two months old, Flo had usually pushed Fifi's hand away each time she tried to touch Flint, and often the only way in which the child had been able to momentarily touch the infant had been by solicitously grooming Flo, working ever closer and closer to those places where Flint's hands gripped his mother's hair. Intently Fifi had groomed around the hands, occasionally briefly fondling the minute fingers and then, with a glance at Flo, hastily returning to her grooming.

Now, however, Flint was older and for the most part Fifi was permitted to touch him. As I watched, Fifi began to play with Flint, taking one hand and nibbling the fingers. Flint gave a soft whimper—possibly Fifi had hurt him—and instantly Flo pushed her daughter's hand away and cuddled her infant close. Frustrated, Fifi rocked slightly to and fro, twisting her arms behind her head and staring at Flint, her lips slightly pouted. It was not long before she reached out, gently this time, to touch him again.

I have always thought that human children become increasingly fascinating as they grow out of the helpless baby stage and begin to respond to people and things. Certainly a chimpanzee baby becomes more attractive as it grows older, not only to its mother and siblings but also to the other members of the community—and to mere human observers. For Hugo and me the privilege of being able to watch Flint's progress that year remains one of the most delightful of our experiences—comparable only to the joy we were to know much later as we watched our own son growing up.

When Flint was three months old he was able to pull himself about on Flo's body, taking handfuls of her hair, pulling with his arms and pushing with his feet. And at this time he began to respond when Fifi approached by reaching out toward her. Fifi became more and more preoccupied with him. She began to make repeated attempts to pull him away from his mother. At first Flo firmly prevented this, but even when Fifi persisted, continually pulling at her brother, Flo never punished her. Sometimes she pushed the child's hand away, sometimes she simply walked away, leaving Fifi rocking slightly, her limbs contorted. And sometimes, when Fifi was extra troublesome, Flo instead of repulsing her advances either groomed her or played with her quite vigorously.

These activities usually served to distract Fifi's attention, at least temporarily, from her infant brother.

As the year wore on it seemed that Flo, perhaps as a result of playing so often with her two younger children, became even more playful. Often, as the weeks passed, we saw her playing with both Figan and twelve-year-old Faben, tickling them or chasing with them round and round a tree trunk with Flint hanging on for dear life. On one occasion, in the middle of a romp with Faben, this old female lowered her balding head to the ground, raised her bony rump in the air, and actually turned a somersault. And then, almost as though she felt slightly ridiculous, she moved away, sat down, and began to groom Flint very carefully.

When Flint was thirteen weeks old we saw Fifi succeed in pulling him away from his mother. Flo was grooming Figan when Fifi, with infinite caution and many quick glances toward her mother's face, began to pull at Flint's foot. Inch by inch she drew the infant toward her—and all at once he was in her arms. Fifi lay on her back and cuddled Flint to her tummy with her arms and legs. She lay very still.

To our surpirse Flo for the first few moments appeared to take no notice at all. But when Flint, who had possibly never lost contact with his mother's body, reached around and held his arms toward her, pouting his lips and uttering a soft *hoo* of distress, Flo instantly gathered him to her breast and bent to kiss his head with her lips. Flint eagerly sought the reassurance of his mother's breast, suckling for a few moments before turning to look at Fifi again. And Fifi, her hands clasped behind her head, her elbows in the air, stared at Flint. Ten minutes later Fifi was again permitted to hold Flint for a short while but, once more, the moment Flint gave his tiny distressed whimper Flo rescued him; and Flint, as before, suckled briefly when he regained the security of his mother's arms.

After this not a day passed without Fifi pulling her infant brother away from Flo. As time went on Flint became accustomed to the arms of his sibling, and so she was able to hold him for longer periods before he uttered the tiny sound that for the next nine months would bring Flo hastening to his rescue. Flo even permitted Fifi to carry Flint when the family wandered through the forests. On those occasions when Flo and her family were part of a large group, however, Flo was more possessive of her infant. Then if Fifi moved away with Flint, Flo followed, uttering soft whimpers herself, until she caught up with the kidnaper and retrieved her infant. Even now Fifi was not punished; Flo simply reached forward, grabbed hold of her daughter's ankle, and then gathered Flint into her arms. Sometimes Fifi led her old mother a merry dance, around trees, under low vegetation, where Flo had to creep almost on her belly—even up into the trees. And sometimes, as if to prevent Flo from catching hold of her, she walked backward in front of her mother, grunting softly and bobbing up and down as though in submission, but not—until she was forced to—relinquishing Flint.

When Flint was very small his two elder brothers, although they sometimes stared at him, paid him little attention. Occasionally while he was grooming with his mother, Faben very gently patted the infant; Figan, though he was such an integral part of the family, seemed afraid to touch Flint in the early days. If, when Figan and Flo were grooming, the infant accidentally touched Figan, as in baby fashion he waved his arms about, Figan, after a quick glance at Flo's face, seemed to avoid looking at Flint. For Figan, though he was a vigorous adolescent male, still showed great respect for his old mother.

One occasion is vivid in my memory. Fifi had taken Flint and was sitting grooming the infant some ten yards from Flo. When Figan approached and sat beside his sister, Flint turned toward him and, with his wide-eyed gaze fixed on Figan's face, reached out to grasp his brother's chest hair. Figan started, and after a quick glance in Flo's direction raised his hands up and away from the infant. Then he stayed motionless, staring down at Flint, his lips tense. The infant pulled closer and nuzzled at Figan's breast, then all at once seemed afraid of the unfamiliar. Usually his only contacts were Flo and Fifi, and if he reached toward either of them they always responded by holding him close. With a slight pout Flint turned back to Fifi, but then, as though confused, he again reached to Figan with a soft whimper. At this Flo came hurrying to his rescue, and as she approached Figan too gave low worried cries, and raised his hands even higher as in the age-old gesture of surrender. Flo gathered up her infant and Figan lowered his hands slowly, as though dazed.

One day, when Flint was just less than five months old, Flo got up to go and, instead of pressing Flint to her belly, took his arm in one hand and hoisted him over her shoulder onto her back. There he remained for a few yards before he slipped down and clung to her arm. For a short distance Flo continued, with Flint gripping around her elbow; then she pushed him back under her tummy. The next day when Flo arrived in camp, Flint was clinging precariously to her back, hanging on to her sparse hair with his hands and feet. When Flo left she again pushed her son up onto her back, and again he clung there awhile before sliding down and dangling from one hand by her side. This time, after walking thirty yards or so, Flo pushed him once more onto her back. After this Flint nearly always rode on Flo's back or else dangled beside her while she walked the mountains. This was not surprising, since all infants after a certain age start riding their mothers rather than clinging on beneath; but we were astonished to see that Fifi, when next we saw her take Flint, also tried to push him onto her back. This was surely an example of learning by direct observation of her mother's behavior.

By the time Flint was five months old he had become an accomplished rider, and only occasionally slipped down to dangle beside Flo as she walked. If there was any sign of excitement among the group, of if Flo was about to move into thick undergrowth, then she always reached back and pushed Flint around so that he clung underneath as before. Soon he learned to wriggle under Flo of his own accord in response to the slightest touch.

About the same time Flint began to ride on Flo's back we first saw him take a step by himself. For some weeks previously he had been able to stand on the ground balanced on three limbs and clinging to Flo's hair with one hand; and occasionally he had taken a couple of steps in this manner. On this particular morning he suddenly let go of Flo and stood by himself, all four limbs on the ground. Then, very deliberately, he lifted one hand off the ground, moved it forward safely, and paused. He lifted a foot off the ground, lurched sideways, staggered, and fell on his nose with a whimper. Instantly Flo reached out and scooped him into her arms.

But that was the beginning. Each day after this Flint walked one or two steps farther, although for months he was incredibly wobbly. Constantly he got his hands and feet muddled up and fell—and always Flo was quick to gather him up. Often she kept one hand under his tummy as he tottered along.

Just after he began to walk Flint attempted to climb. One day we saw him standing upright, holding on to a tiny sapling with both hands and gripping it first with one foot and then the other. But he never managed to get both feet off the ground at once and after a few moments he fell backward onto the ground. Subsequently he repeated this performance several times and Flo, as she groomed Fifi, idly held one hand behind his back, preventing further tumbles. A week after his first attempt Flint was able to climb a short way quite easily. Like a human child, he found it much harder to get down by himself. Flo of course was very watchful—as indeed was Fifi—and one or other of his guardians reached to rescue him the moment he gave his soft whimper. Flo, in fact, often retrieved him when she noticed that the end of the branch on which he was swinging was beginning to bend and Flint was totally unaware of it. She was equally quick to seize him if she saw any sign of social excitement or aggression among other members of the group.

Gradually Flint learned to control his limbs slightly better when walking, although he still often relied on speed, rather than coordination, to get him from one place to another. He began to venture several yards away from Flo—and since any movement away from his mother was wildly exciting, and excitement set his hair on end, he tottered around like a fluffy black ball, his wide-eyed gaze fixed with concentration on some object or individual in front of him.

It was at this time that fascination for her small brother became almost an obsession of Fifi's. She spent nearly all her day playing with him, grooming him as he slept, or carrying him about with her. Flo, it seemed, was often far from displeased to shed from time to time part of her load of maternal responsibility. Provided that Fifi did not carry Flint out of sight, and provided there were no potentially aggressive males nearby, she no longer objected when Fifi kidnaped Flint. Nor did Flo seem to mind if other youngsters

approached Flint to play gently with him. But Fifi did. If she suddenly noticed Gilka, or another of her erstwhile playmates, close
to Flint, Fifi instantly abandoned whatever she was doing, rushed
over, and chased the youngster away, hair bristling, arms flailing,
and feet stamping the ground. Even chimps much older than
herself, provided they were subordinate to Flo, were threatened or
even attacked by aggressive Fifi. Presumably she acted on the assumption that if anything went wrong old Flo would hurry to her
assistance—and it was evident that the victims of her fury were
fully aware of this fact also.

Fifi, however, could not chase Faben or Figan away from Flint,
and as the infant grew up both of his elder brothers showed increasing interest in him. Often they would approach and play with
him, tickling him or pushing him gently to and fro as he dangled,
legs kicking, from a low branch. Sometimes when Figan was
playing with Flint, we saw Fifi hurry to the scene and try to initiate a game with Figan; many times she was successful. Then,
when the game was over, Fifi would hurry back to play with Flint
herself. Was she, perhaps, practicing the same technique of distraction that Flo had used so often on her?

When Flint tottered up to one of the adult males, Fifi could
scarcely interfere; she merely sat and stared as David, or Goliath,
or Mike reached out and time and again patted Flint or gently
embraced him. And as the weeks went by Flint, like a spoiled human child, wanted more and more attention. One day as he tottered
up to Mr. McGregor the old male got up and moved away. It was
not, I think, deliberate—it just happened that he was about to
leave. Flint stopped dead, staring with widening eyes at the male's
retreating rear, and then, stumbling along with frantic haste, repeatedly falling on his face, Flint followed. Continuously he uttered his soft whimper. Within moments Flo was rushing to
retrieve him. That was only the start of it, and for the next few
weeks Flint was always whimpering along after one or other of the
adult males who had not deigned to stop and greet him, or who had
walked away from the infant for any reason whatever. Often the
male concerned, uneasy perhaps at the little calls following in his
wake, would stop or turn back to pat Flint.

When Flint was eight months old he sometimes spent fifteen

minutes or so out of contact with Flo as he played or explored, but he was never far from her. He was somewhat steadier on his feet and he was able to join Fifi in some of her slightly rougher games, chasing around a grass tuft, or pulling himself on top of her as she lay on the ground and tickling her with his hands and mouth. It was at this time that the termiting season began.

One day when Flo was fishing for termites it became obvious that Figan and Fifi, who had been eating termites at the same heap, were becoming restless and wanted to leave. Old Flo, who had already fished for two hours and was herself only getting about two termites every five minutes, showed no signs of stopping. Being an old female, it was possible that she might continue for another hour at least. Several times Figan had set off resolutely along the track leading to the stream, but on each occasion, after repeatedly looking back at Flo, he had given up and returned to wait for his mother.

Flint, too young to mind where he was, pottered about on the heap, occasionally dabbing at a termite. Suddenly Figan got up again and this time approached Flint. Adopting the posture of a mother who signals her infant to climb onto her back, Figan bent one leg and reached back his hand to Flint, uttering a soft, pleading whimper. Flint tottered up to him at once, and Figan, still whimpering, put his hand under Flint and gently pushed him onto his back. Once Flint was safely aboard, Figan, with another quick glance at Flo, set off rapidly along the track. A moment later Flo discarded her tool and followed.

Hugo and I were amazed at this further example of Figan's ingenuity in getting his own way. Had his behavior really been deliberate? We couldn't be sure. A few days later Fifi did exactly the same thing. A week later we watched Faben take Flint to his breast after he too had tried several times to persuade his mother to follow him away from a termite heap. We had never seen Faben carrying Flint before.

As the termite season wore on there could be no doubt that Flo's older offspring were kidnaping Flint with the deliberate intent of getting their mother to stop, at least for the time being, her endless termiting. We saw all three of them taking Flint in this way on any number of occasions. They were not always successful. Often

Flint dropped off and ran back to his mother of his own accord. And sometimes, if Flo's hole was still yielding a good supply of termites, she hurried to retrieve Flint and then returned to the heap followed by the unsuccessful kidnaper—who usually tried again later.

Flint, of course, was too young to show any interest in eating termites; he occasionally sampled a mouthful of fig or banana but still received virtually all his nourishment from his mother's milk, and would continue to do so for another year. Once in a while he did poke at a crawling termite with his finger, and he played with discarded grass tools when he was wandering about on a termite heap. Also, he began to "mop" everything. When termites are spilled onto the surface of the heap, older chimps mop them up with the backs of their wrists: the termites become entangled in the hairs and are picked off with the lips. It was soon after the termite season began that Flint started to mop things—the ground, his own legs, his mother's back as he rode along, anything but termites. Actually, though he sometimes gazed intently for a few moments as his mother or one of his siblings worked, he was not really interested in this activity which so absorbed his elders.

Fifi, on the other hand, was a keen termite fisher, and when Flint, wanting to play with his sister, jumped onto her and scattered the insects from her grass stem, she was obviously irritated. Over and over she pushed him away roughly. Fifi still played with Flint frequently herself when she was not termiting, but, almost as though some spell had been broken, she never again showed quite the same fanatical preoccupation with him; she no longer protected him as consistently from social contact with other young chimps.

Flint then began to enlarge his circle of friends, since Fifi, particularly when she was working at a termite heap, often permitted Gilka or one of the other juveniles to approach and play with Flint. She no longer rushed up aggressively every time one or other of the adolescent females carried Flint around or groomed him or played with him. Flint, in fact, was growing up. Even when Fifi did devote all her attention to her little brother she could no longer treat him as her doll, for he had developed a mind of his own. If Fifi wanted to carry him in one direction and he wanted to go somewhere else, then he struggled away from her and went his way. Also, he was getting heavier. One day when Flint was sleeping in her lap and gripping tightly to her hair, it was obvious that he was hurting his sister. Fifi carefully detached first one hand and then the other, but as soon as they were loosened Flint, disturbed, gripped on again tightly. Finally, for the first time on record Fifi carried the infant back to Flo and pushed him in her mother's direction.

When Flint was one year old he was still wobbly on his legs but he was quick to bounce toward any game in progress, and eager to hurry over to greet any newcomer that joined his group. He was, in fact, beginning to take part in the social life of his community: a community which at that time was still unsettled as a result of the dramatic rise to overall dominance of Mike. Flint could scarcely have been aware of the battle of wills that had finally led to Goliath's defeat because it had started at the time of his birth. Flint grew up in a world where Mike undisputedly was supreme.

10

THE HIERARCHY

Mike's rise to the number one or top-ranking position in the chimpanzee community was both interesting and spectacular. In 1963 Mike had ranked almost bottom in the adult male dominance hierarchy. He had been the last to gain access to bananas, and had been threatened and actually attacked by almost every other adult male. At one time he even had appeared almost bald from losing so many handfuls of hair during aggressive incidents with his fellow apes.

When Hugo and I had left the Gombe Stream at the end of that year preparatory to getting married, Mike's position had not changed; yet when we returned four months later we found a very different Mike. Kris and Dominic told us the beginning of his story—how he had started to use empty four-gallon kerosene cans more and more often during his charging displays. We did not have to wait many days before we witnessed Mike's techniques for ourselves.

There was one incident I remember particularly vividly. A group of five adult males, including top-ranking Goliath, David Graybeard, and the huge Rodolf, were grooming each other. The session had been going on for some twenty minutes. Mike was sitting about thirty yards apart from them, frequently staring toward the group, occasionally idly grooming himself.

All at once Mike calmly walked over to our tent and took hold of an empty kerosene can by the handle. Then he picked up a second can and, walking upright, returned to the place where he had been sitting. Armed with his two cans Mike continued to stare toward the other males. After a few minutes he began to rock from side to side. At first the movement was almost imperceptible, but Hugo and I were watching him closely. Gradually he rocked more vigorously, his hair slowly began to stand erect, and then, softly at first, he started a series of pant-hoots. As he called, Mike got to his feet and suddenly he was off, charging toward the group of males, hitting the two cans ahead of him. The cans, together with Mike's crescendo of hooting, made the most appalling racket: no wonder the erstwhile peaceful males rushed out of the way. Mike and his cans vanished down a track, and after a few moments there was silence. Some of the males reassembled and resumed their interrupted grooming session, but the others stood around somewhat apprehensively.

After a short interval that low-pitched hooting began again, followed almost immediately by the appearance of the two rackety cans with Mike close behind them. Straight for the other males he charged, and once more they fled. This time, even before the group could reassemble, Mike set off again; but he made straight for Goliath—and even he hastened out of his way like all the others. Then Mike stopped and sat, all his hair on end, breathing hard. His eyes glared ahead and his lower lip was hanging slightly down so that the pink inside showed brightly and gave him a wild appearance.

Rodolf was the first of the males to approach Mike, uttering soft pant-grunts of submission, crouching low and pressing his lips to Mike's thigh. Next he began to groom Mike, and two other males approached, pant-grunting, and also began to groom him. Finally David Graybeard went over to Mike, laid one hand on his groin, and joined in the grooming. Only Goliath kept away, sitting alone and staring toward Mike. It was obvious that Mike constituted a serious threat to Goliath's hitherto unchallenged supremacy.

Mike's deliberate use of man-made objects was probably an indication of superior intelligence. Many of the adult males had at some time or another dragged a kerosene can to enhance their charging displays in place of the more normal branches or rocks; but only Mike apparently had been able to profit from the chance experience and learn to seek out the cans deliberately to his own advantage. The cans, of course, made several times more noise than a branch when dragged along the ground at speed, and eventually Mike was able to keep three cans ahead of him at once for about sixty yards as he ran flat-out across the camp clearing. No wonder that males previously his superiors rushed out of Mike's way.

Charging displays usually occur at a time of emotional excitement—when a chimpanzee arrives at a food source, joins up with another group, or when he is frustrated. But it seemed that Mike actually *planned* his charging displays; almost, one might say, in cold blood. Often when he got up to fetch his cans he showed no visible signs of frustration or excitement; that came afterward when, armed with his display props, he began to rock from side to side, raise his hair, and hoot.

Eventually Mike's use of kerosene cans became dangerous—he learned to hurl them ahead of him at the close of a charge. Once he got me on the back of my head, and once he hit Hugo's precious movie camera. We decided to remove all the cans, and went through a nightmare period while Mike tried to drag about all manner of other objects. Once he got hold of Hugo's tripod—luckily when the camera was not mounted—and once he managed to grab and pull down the large cupboard in which we kept a good deal of food and all our crockery and cutlery. The noise and the trail of destruction were unbelievable. Finally, however, we managed to dig things into the ground or hide them away, and like his companions Mike had to resort to branches and rocks.

By that time, however, his top-ranking status was assured, although it was fully another year before Mike himself seemed to feel quite secure in his position. He continued to display very frequently and vigorously, and the lower-ranking chimps had increasing reason to fear him, since often he would attack a female or youngster viciously at the slightest provocation. In particular, as might be expected, a tense relation prevailed between Mike and the formerly dominant male, Goliath.

Goliath did not relinquish his position without a struggle. His displays also increased in frequency and vigor and he too became more aggressive. There was a time, toward the start of this battle for dominance, when Hugo and I feared for Goliath's sanity. After attacking a couple of youngsters and charging back and forth dragging huge branches, he would sit, with hair on end, his sides heaving from exertion, a froth of saliva glistening at his half-open mouth, and a glint in his eyes that to us looked not far from madness. We actually had a soldered-mesh iron cage built in Kigoma and, when this had been set up in camp, we retreated inside when Goliath's temper was at its worst.

One day when Mike was sitting in camp, a series of distinctive, rather melodious pant-hoots with characteristic quavers at the close announced the return of Goliath, who for two weeks had been somewhere down in the southern part of the reserve. Mike responded immediately, hooting in turn and charging across the clearing. Then he climbed a tree and sat staring over the valley, every hair on end.

A few minutes later Goliath appeared, and as he reached the outskirts of the camp clearing he commenced one of his spectacular displays. He must have seen Mike, because he headed straight for him, dragging a huge branch. He leaped into a tree near Mike's and was motionless. For a moment Mike stared toward him and then he too began to display, swaying the branches of his tree, swinging to the ground, hurling a few rocks, and, finally, leaping up into Goliath's tree and swaying the branches there. When he stopped, Goliath immediately reciprocated, swinging about in the tree and rocking the branches. Presently, as one of his wild leaps took him quite close to Mike, Mike also displayed, and for a few unbelievable moments both of the splendid male chimpanzees were swaying branches within a few feet of each other until I thought the whole tree must crash to the ground. An instant later both chimps were on the ground displaying in the undergrowth. Eventually they both stopped and sat staring at each other. It was Goliath who moved next, standing upright as he rocked a sapling; when he paused Mike charged past him, hurling a rock and drumming with his feet on the trunk of a tree.

This went on for nearly half an hour: first one male and then the other displayed, and each performance seemed to be more vigorous, more spectacular than the one preceding it. Yet during all that time, apart from occasionally hitting one another with the ends of the branches they swayed, neither chimpanzee actually attacked the other. Unexpectedly, after an extra long pause, it looked as if Goliath's nerve had broken. He rushed up to Mike, crouched beside him with loud, nervous pant-grunts, and began to groom him with feverish intensity. For a few moments Mike ignored Goliath completely. Suddenly he turned and, with a vigor almost matching Goliath's, began to groom his vanquished rival. There they sat, grooming each other without pause for over an hour.

That was the last real duel between the two males. From then on it seemed that Goliath accepted Mike's superiority, and a strangely intense relationship grew up between the two. They often greeted one another with much display of emotion, embracing or patting one another, kissing each other in the neck; afterward they usually started grooming each other. During these grooming sessions it appeared that the tension between them was eased, soothed by the close, friendly physical contact. Afterward they sometimes fed or rested quite close to each other, looking peaceful and relaxed as though the bitter rivalry of the past had never been.

It is one of the most striking aspects of chimpanzee society that creatures who can so quickly become roused to frenzies of excitement and aggression can for the most part maintain such relaxed and friendly relations with each other. One day I followed Mike from camp, over the stream and for some way into the thick forest of the opposite mountain slope. With Mike were the old male J.B. and Flo with Flint, Fifi, and Figan. Eventually they stopped under some trees in one of those places where chimps love to rest stretched out in the shade. I sat down nearby. Fifi climbed high up into the tree and made herself a little nest; Figan and J.B. snoozed on the ground; Flo, with Flint sleeping on her lap, sat grooming Mike. At last they too lay down to rest.

Presently Mike reached out toward Flo's hand and began almost imperceptibly to play with her fingers. Soon she responded, gently grasping his hand, twisting and pulling away—only to reach out and grasp it again. After a few minutes Mike sat up and leaned over Flo, tickling her neck and her ticklish groin until, protecting Flint with one hand and parrying Mike with the other, Flo started to shake with panting gasps of chimpanzee laughter. After a while she could stand it no longer and rolled away from him. But she was roused, this ancient female with her stumps of teeth, and soon she was tickling Mike in the ribs with her bony fingers. Then it was Mike's turn to laugh and reach to grab her hands and tickle her again himself.

After ten minutes Flo evidently could endure the tickling no longer and she moved away, leaving Mike stretched out with a benign expression on his face. And yet just two hours earlier this same male had attacked Flo savagely, dropping a huge pile of his own bananas and pounding the old female unmercifully—just because she had presumed to take a few fruits for herself from a nearby box. How was it possible for her to enjoy such a relaxed interaction with Mike so soon? The secret perhaps lies in the fact that, although a male chimpanzee is quick to threaten or attack a subordinate, he is usually equally quick to calm his victim with a touch, a pat on the back, an embrace of reassurance. And Flo, after Mike's vicious attack, and even while her hand dripped blood where she had scraped it against a rock, had hurried after Mike, screaming in her hoarse voice until he had turned. As she approached him and crouched low in apprehension, he had patted her several times on her head and then, as she calmed, had given her a final reassurance by leaning forward to press his lips to her brow.

Would Mike have become the top-ranking male if my kerosene cans and I had not invaded the Gombe Stream? We shall never know, but I suspect he would have in the end. Mike has a strong "desire" for dominance, a characteristic very marked in some individuals and almost entirely lacking in others. Over and above this trait Mike has unquestionable intelligence—and amazing courage too. Soon after he had become the uneasy top-ranking male, when some of the high-ranking males turned on him, Mike had charged into camp, hurled a few rocks, and, in passing, briefly pounded on David Graybeard. David Graybeard in some ways was a coward, since he nearly always tried to avoid trouble, and, when he couldn't, he usually tried to hide behind a higher-ranking companion, such as Goliath. But when he became really roused to fury, he was a very dangerous chimpanzee.

On this occasion David, after running away from Mike screaming, turned and began to utter loud, fierce-sounding *waa* barks. He hurried over to Goliath and embraced him, then turned and again shouted toward Mike. By this time Hugo and I knew David well, and it was obvious that he was furious. Abruptly David ran forward a short way toward Mike and immediately Goliath joined him, adding his own fierce call to his friend's. Mike began to display, charging across the clearing toward another group of males. They fled, screaming, but then, since David and Goliath were still calling, they joined in too. Now it was five strong adult males, including the once top-ranking Goliath, against one. Again Mike charged across the clearing, and all at once, with David in the lead, the others were after him. Mike, screaming now, rushed up a tree and the others followed. Hugo and I felt sure that this was the showdown: now Goliath would regain his lost position.

To our amazement, Mike turned—instead of leaping away into the next tree and running away, he turned. He was still screaming but he began to sway branches violently, and the next moment he took a leap toward the five. In a flurry of fright they rushed down the tree, almost falling over one another in their haste, and fled with Mike after them. When Mike sat, hair on end, eyes glaring, the others stayed away from him, cowed. Mike had won a spectacular victory by bluff.

When I refer to Mike as the dominant male, what I really mean is that he became top-ranking among those individuals that we know, individuals whose normal range includes our home valley. Once I had become really familiar with all the chimpanzees of our community, I quickly realized from visits to the north and south of the reserve that there are in fact two other communities. Many of the individuals making up these groups seldom or never travel as far as our centrally located valley, but without doubt there is some intermixing between chimpanzees of the three communities.

One fully mature male, whose normal range, so far as we know, lay to the south, did start to visit our feeding station; he would come for a week or so at a time when he was in the vicinity and then disappear back to his normal haunts. Just before he died he became quite a regular visitor to camp, but his relationships with the males of our group were always rather tense. Quite often females from the northern or southern communities arrive at camp during their periods of sexual swelling, brought along by our males. Once they have discovered bananas some of them become fairly regular visitors, though others come only once or twice in a year.

On several occasions I have seen individuals from two of these main communities meet and mingle without aggression, feeding together side by side. But it seems that Mike himself is reluctant to mix with the chimps to the north and south of his domain. A few times when "strangers" called from a neighboring valley, Mike, after much displaying and calling, turned back, taking some of his group with him while others moved on to mix with the strangers.

A chimpanzee community is an extremely complex social organization. Only when a large number of individuals began to visit the feeding area and I could make regular observations on their interactions one with another did I begin to appreciate just how complex it is. The members who compose the community move about in constantly changing associations, and yet, though the society seems to be organized in such a casual manner, each individual knows his place in the social structure—knows his status in relation to any other chimpanzee he may chance upon during the day. Small wonder there is such a wide range of greeting gestures, and that most chimpanzees do greet each other when they meet after a separation. Figan, going up to an older male with a submissive pant-grunt, is probably affirming that he remembers quite well the little aggressive incident of two days before when he was thumped soundly on the back. "I know you are dominant. I admit it; I remember" is probably the sort of communication inherent in his submissive gesturing. "I acknowledge your respect; I shall not attack you just now" is implicit in the gentle patting movement of Mike's hand as he greets a submissive female.

As Hugo and I became increasingly familiar with Mike's community we began to learn more and more about the variety of relationships which existed between different adult chimpanzees. Some individuals only interacted when chance—such as a fruiting tree or a sexually attractive female—threw them together. Others moved about together frequently and showed an affectionate tolerance and regard for each other which we felt could best be described as friendship. As our study continued, we found that some friendships persisted over the years and others were of relatively short duration. We learned also to appreciate the different characteristics of male and female chimpanzees. And the more we learned, the more we were impressed by the obvious parallels between some chimpanzee and some human relationships.

Firm friendships, like that between Goliath and David Graybeard, seem to be particularly prevalent among male chimpanzees. Mike and the irascible, testy old J.B. traveled about in the same group very frequently. When I first knew them, J.B. was the higher-ranking of the two, but Mike's strategies with the kerosene cans served to subordinate J.B. along with all the other males. However, once things had settled down, with Mike secure in the top-ranking position, it became apparent that J.B. had also risen in the social ladder. When he was in a group with Mike, J.B. was able to dominate Goliath as well as other males who had held a higher rank than he before Mike's rise. These other males quickly accepted J.B. as second only to Mike, but Goliath asserted his old superiority over J.B. on many occasions when Mike was not part of the group. I well remember one day when Goliath threatened J.B., who had approached his box of bananas. J.B. at once moved away but began to scream loudly, looking across the valley in the direction that Mike had taken earlier. Mike must have been quite close, because within a few minutes he appeared, his hair on end, looking around to see what had upset his friend. Then J.B. ran toward the box where Goliath sat, and Goliath, with submissive pant-grunts, hastened to vacate his place—even though Mike took no further active part in the dispute.

There was another occasion when after eating about twenty bananas J.B. tried hard to break open another box. As he was a past master at breaking boxes, and they were hard to mend, Hugo and I tried to dissuade him from the idea by walking slowly to the box and sitting on it. J.B. did move away, but then he climbed a nearby tree and screamed, again staring in the direction taken by Mike when he had left earlier. That time, however (perhaps luckily for us), Mike must have been out of earshot, for he did not come back.

Leakey and Mr. Worzle were two other males who frequently traveled together. In temperament they were very different.

Leakey, like his namesake, was robust, high-ranking, and usually good-natured. Mr. Worzle, on the other hand, was always nervous, both in his dealings with other chimps and with human beings. He was very low-ranking and, even before he became really decrepit previous to his death, was subordinate to all the other adult males—and some of the adolescent males also. Nevertheless, the two spent hours in each other's company, grooming one another, feeding, and moving from place to place together, building their nests in the same or neighboring trees. When Leakey was with him, Mr. Worzle always seemed far more relaxed and confident.

Friendships of this sort are beneficial not only to the lower-ranking of the pair. One day, during the period when Goliath was losing his top-ranking position, he arrived in camp alone. He was tense and obviously anxious about something; every so often he stood upright to stare back along the way from which he had come, and he jumped at every sudden sound.

All at once Hugo and I noticed three males, one of whom was the high-ranking Hugh, standing at the top of a slight rise looking toward Goliath. They all had their hair slightly on end, and as they began running down the slope they reminded us of a gang of thugs. Goliath did not wait to see what they would do. With great speed and silence he ran in the opposite direction and vanished into the thick vegetation surrounding camp. The three rushed after him, and for the next five minutes they bustled about noisily in the undergrowth, obviously searching for Goliath. They were unsuccessful and ultimately emerged and began to eat bananas. Suddenly Hugo pointed. There, a short distance up the slope, I saw a head peeping cautiously from behind a tree trunk—Goliath's. Every time one of the three looked up Goliath bobbed back behind his tree, only to peer out after a few moments. Eventually we saw him moving off quietly up the slope.

The chimps slept near camp that night and very early, almost before dawn, we heard a sudden burst of pant-hooting from the direction of Goliath's nest. Hugh and the other two males were the first to arrive in camp, dark shapes in the gray light. While they were eating bananas we heard a burst of calling from the slope. A moment later Goliath charged down, dragging a huge branch and hurling it forward as he crossed the clearing. Without pausing he rushed at Hugh and began to attack him. It was a fierce battle, and Hugh came off very much the worst. Usually a male pounds his victim for a few seconds only, but this time the two combatants rolled over and over, grappling and hitting. Goliath then managed to leap onto Hugh, hanging on to his shoulder hair and stamping on his back with both feet.

It was just after the start of the fight that Hugo and I realized why Goliath was suddenly brave: we heard the deep, characteristic pant-hoots of David Graybeard and glimpsed him charging in his slow and magnificent fashion across the clearing and past the battling males. David must have joined his friend early that morning, and by his presence alone given Goliath the courage to face Hugh and his gang.

With the exception of David and Goliath, who bore no resemblance at all to each other, we have been able to detect similarities in either physical make-up or behavioral characteristics—or both—in all of the pairs of male friends that we have known. This was particularly striking in the case of Leakey and Mr. Worzle. Mr. Worzle had extraordinary eyes, for the part around the iris was white instead of being heavily pigmented with brown as in other chimpanzees. His eyes therefore exactly resembled those of a man. Leakey also showed the same unusual lack of pigmentation, though to a much lesser extent than Mr. Worzle. We suspect, therefore, that pairs of male friends may often be siblings.

The only two adult females we know who enjoyed this sort of friendship were almost certainly sisters; not only did they look alike facially, but they had the same massive build, and both were prone to perform charging displays, stamping on the ground and swaggering in a manner more typical of males. They were the only two adult females I ever saw playing with each other—rolling about on the ground, tickling one another and panting with laughter, each with her infant cradled in one arm.

The adult females of the chimpanzee community are almost always submissive to adult males, and to many of the older adolescent males. But they have their own dominance hierarchy, of which Flo for many years was supreme, respected and even feared by old and young females alike. Flo was exceptionally aggressive toward her own sex, and she would tolerate no insubordination from young adolescent males. Much of her confidence no doubt resulted from the fact that she was so often accompanied by her two eldest sons, and with the aggressive Fifi as well, the family was formidable indeed.

As mentioned earlier, Flo at one time often wandered about together with the mother Olly, but their relationship was very different from that between Mike and J.B. or David and Goliath. For one thing, Flo was frequently aggressive toward Olly, and for another, neither would go to the assistance of the other in times of trouble. The only time I did see them united was when they ganged up on a young stranger female. This female had first appeared in camp boasting a pink swelling and surrounded by a retinue of males. She had come in every day for ten days and had become quite used to the strange place where bananas grew in boxes on the ground. Although she often had been in camp at the same time as Flo and Olly, the two older females had seemed to ignore her completely.

One day when a small group of chimps including Flo and Olly were grooming in camp, Hugo and I saw the young stranger female, her swelling quite gone, sitting in a tree at the edge of the clearing and looking nervously toward us. We were pleased, for at that time only a very few young females visited the feeding area. Just as we were getting some bananas ready for her we noticed Flo and Olly staring fixedly at the stranger, every hair on their bodies bristling.

It was Flo who took the first step forward, and Olly followed. They went quietly and slowly toward the tree, and their victim failed to notice them until they were quite close. Then, with pants and squeaks of fear, she climbed higher in the branches. Flo and Olly stood for a moment looking up before Flo shot up the tree, seized the branch to which the now screaming female was clinging, and, her lips bunched in fury, shook it violently with both hands. Soon the youngster, half shaken, half leaping, scrambled into a neighboring tree with Flo hot on her heels and Olly uttering loud *waa* barks on the ground below. The chase went on until Flo forced the female to the ground, caught up with her, slammed down on her with both fists, and then, stamping her feet and slapping the ground with her hands, chased her victim from the vicinity. Olly, still barking, ran along behind.

When the stranger had vanished along the forest track Flo

Eventually the chimpanzees let me follow them into the forest

Chimpanzees can undoubtedly recognize each other from their voices alone

Fifi
*Copyright National
Geographic Society*

Fifi continually wanted to touch her young brother. Ultimately Flo allowed her to carry Flint

Flint reached from Fifi to Figan. When Flo approached, Figan raised his
arms as if to show he was not harming the infant

Faben, Fifi, and Figan play around Flo and Flint

Flo became increasingly playful after Flint's birth. *Copyright National Geographic Society*

Flo

Flo resting on the ground

Fifi sees her reflection in Hugo's lens. *Copyright National Geographic Society*

Sometimes we hid bananas
under our shirts

Flo grooming Flint

Charging displays can
help a male's rise to
dominance

Mike bows to
the dominant Goliath

The dominant Goliath reassures Figan by touching him. Figan gradually relaxes

Mike uses noisy kerosene cans to help him take over as dominant male
Copyright National Geographic Society

Flint and Goblin interfere when Faben mates

Olly, followed by Gilka, responds to Leakey's courtship. *Below:* Fifi presses her bottom to the bottom of a mating male

That's one way of looking at it

stopped. Her face was spattered with liquid dung—product of the young female's terror—her hair was still bristling. Olly stood beside her, and the two old females listened as the sounds of screaming gradually receded up the valley. Then Flo turned, wiped off the dung with a handful of leaves, and slowly returned to camp—where throughout this incident Fifi had been looking after the eight-month-old Flint.

This was not the only occasion when we witnessed sudden alliances between two or more adult females which resulted in driving young newcomers of the same sex away from the feeding area. We have not seen them gang up in this way on stranger adolescent males; nor have we seen adult males of our group driving away strangers of either sex from the feeding area. What, then, motivates the aggressive behavior of these females? Is it perhaps the fact that older females, who normally have a smaller range than males, are more territorial? Or could it be due to some more complex emotion—do old females, perhaps, resent the attention paid to young stranger females by "their" adult males? Are they, in other words, motivated by the emotion that in human beings we call jealousy? We cannot be sure—but sometimes it certainly seems like it.

One day when Flo was socially grooming with four adult males, a young pregnant female arrived; she had recently joined our group from the north. Pregnant females often continue to show monthly swellings, and this one had a very pink posterior. The males on this occasion did not mate her, but they were nevertheless interested. They left Flo, hastened over to the newcomer, inspected her bottom, and began to groom her vigorously. It was only a few minutes later that I noticed Flo. She had moved several yards toward the young female and was standing staring at her with every hair on end. Had she dared, without doubt she would have attacked the newcomer. As it was, she presently walked slowly over to the group and herself inspected the swelling carefully. Then she moved away and sat down to groom Flint.

We could scarcely believe it when the following day Flo showed the beginnings of a swelling. Flint was less than two years old, and whereas young females may start swelling again when their infants are only fourteen months, old females like Flo do not normally become pink again for four or five years after giving birth. However, Flo's sex skin was swollen enough to arouse instant attention from Rodolf, who feverishly pushed her to her feet and intently inspected her bottom. So did two other males. Then they sat around grooming *her*. The next day that extraordinary swelling had gone—nor did Flo show any signs of swelling again for the next four years. I cannot believe that it was pure coincidence.

The female chimpanzee is indeed very different from the male, although, as in the case of humans, some females show masculine characteristics, and vice versa. When they are trying to get their own way with a social superior, adult females typically resort to pleading with many of the gestures and calls made by infants. Melissa when begging from a male reaches out her hand repeatedly, touches him ingratiatingly, and, if this behavior fails, may start to whimper or even scream like a child in a tantrum. Like other females, she can be very persistent in her begging, so that often she is eventually rewarded with a scrap of banana or cardboard or whatever it is she wants. Once when Mr. McGregor was grooming her, he turned to groom a higher-ranking male who had joined the group. Melissa stared at his back and then began rocking back and forth and whimpering. He ignored her. Her whimpers grew louder, and every so often she reached out and gave him a quick poke with her finger. Still Mr. McGregor continued to groom the other male. Finally, almost screaming in her frustration, Melissa reached out and gave him a hard shove with one foot—and at this the old male finally turned and began to groom the importunate female again.

It appears that females are more likely than males to harbor grudges. At one time Melissa, if she was threatened by a superior, nearly always hurried over to a higher-ranking individual, and while reaching out to touch him directed loud screams toward her aggressor. Obviously she was trying to incite her chosen champion to retaliate on her behalf. The fact that the males she approached seldom responded, except perhaps to reassure the noisy female, in no way dampened her ardor; she did exactly the same the next time she was threatened. On a day when she was lightly cuffed by Rodolf, he happened to be the highest-ranking male in the group. To our astonishment, when Mike arrived some ten minutes later,

Melissa rushed up to him, pressed her mouth to his neck, and then, with one hand on Mike's back, started screaming, all the while staring at Rodolf and making small flapping movements toward him with her other hand. As usual, her stratagem was ignored, but we saw her behaving in exactly the same way on other occasions.

Melissa was by no means the only female to nurse a grievance over a length of time. Pooch almost certainly lost her mother when she was between five and six years old, and she struck up a strange relationship with an old male, Huxley. For the most part they paid little attention to each other, although sometimes they sat grooming together; but whenever Huxley got up to leave, Pooch followed like a shadow. One day, when a large group of chimps had visited camp, Pooch, who was about six years old at the time, stayed behind with Evered, a year her senior, after the others had left. Neither had managed to get any bananas. As soon as the group was out of sight we gave them some fruit; a squabble broke out, and Evered cuffed Pooch, who screamed. Then she turned her rump, presenting submissively, he patted her, and they sat peacefully side by side feeding. We were astounded when Pooch, a few minutes later, suddenly dropped her bananas and attacked Evered, biting him and pulling at his hair. Evered was probably startled too, for it is unusual certainly for a female to attack a male older than herself.

Then we realized what had prompted Pooch's behavior. We saw old Huxley, his hair on end, standing a short way along the track and staring toward us. His glance moved from Hugo and me to the youngsters. Probably he had associated Pooch's earlier scream with us and for that reason had hurried back to her rescue. A moment longer he stood before charging down toward the squabbling chimps. It looked as though he cuffed them both; then he turned and plodded away again. Evered screamed until he got cramps in his throat and sat doubled up as though in pain. Pooch immediately started after her protector, and as she passed Evered she glanced at him with an expression I have never seen before or since in a chimpanzee. It looked exactly like the smirk a young human girl might be expected to give under similar circumstances.

What Pooch did to Fifi, a couple of years her junior and a playmate of long standing, was completely against chimp etiquette. It happened when the two were romping together and Fifi, probably accidentally, hurt Pooch, who screamed and hit at Fifi. Fifi grinned in fear and then turned her rump submissively and presented to Pooch. Pooch should have reached out and touched Fifi's bottom; instead she leaned forward and, very deliberately and rather hard, bit Fifi's little pointed clitoris.

Fifi, with all her mother's staunchness of spirit, turned and flew at the larger female. The two rolled and grappled on the ground, pulling out handfuls of each other's hair until Flo finally arrived, her hair on end, and Pooch retreated, screaming. Fifi, her screeches cramping in her throat, presented again—this time to her mother and Flo reassured her, patting her rump again and again until the child quieted. Her bottom swelled up and bled a good deal and obviously it was very painful. She made herself a soft leafy nest on the ground, where she reclined, gently dabbing at her wound with a handful of leaves.

There is a great deal in chimpanzee social relations to remind us of some of our own behavior; more, perhaps, than many of us would care to admit. Only by carrying on our research for years to come and studying the social structure in a group where blood relationships between the different individuals are known shall we succeed in understanding the whole complex and intricate pattern.

11

THE GROWTH OF
THE RESEARCH CENTER

WHEN I FIRST SET FOOT on the sandy beach of the Gombe Stream
Chimpanzee Reserve I never imagined that I was taking the first
step toward the establishment of the Gombe Stream Research
Centre: that, nine years later, there would be ten or more students
not only studying different aspects of chimpanzee behavior but
also observing baboons and red colobus monkeys.

We took on our first research assistant, Edna Koning, soon after
Flint's birth. Edna wrote begging us to take her on in some capacity, and, since there had been too much work for me alone even
before Flo had produced a son, we felt it was an excellent idea.
Edna typed out my notes and also learned to make accurate observations herself. Then, when I followed Flo and Flint into the
mountains, I knew that if anything exciting happened in camp
Edna would record the events.

In those days we worked all day and far into the night. I dic-
tated my observations onto tape, which meant that I didn't have
to take my eyes off the activity around me. Edna typed out the
tapes in the evening while I struggled with analysis for my Ph.D.
thesis. We started making an extra copy of my notes, three copies
in all, and I marked this copy into categories of behavior—grooming, submission, aggression, and so forth. Edna, Hugo, and I cut
these up and pasted them in their relevant sections into large note-
books. This of course was immensely helpful for my analysis. The
third copy was always sent off every month to Louis for safekeeping
in case of fire, flood, or some other catastrophe at the Gombe.

Then, too, there was dung-swirling. It was Hugo who first thought of washing the chimps' dung rather than examining dried samples for indications of what food had been eaten. Chimpanzees swallow many stones of fruits when they are feeding, so that we always had a good idea of what species were currently ripe. It is amazing how much of a chimpanzee's food seems to pass through the digestive tract only partially digested. Dung-swirling was an excellent method of finding out how often members of our group ate insects and meat, and data gathered in this way, together with information gleaned from watching chimpanzees eating, gave us a very good picture of their diet throughout the year. We swirled the dung down by the stream, putting each specimen in a large tin with holes in the bottom, pouring in water, and swirling it over a hole we had dug.

Hugo, in addition to helping me with my analysis, had a lot of his own work. He was still financed by the National Geographic Society and did all the accounts, both his own and mine. He had to write out a lot of descriptions for his movie film and 35mm photographs, and particularly in the rainy season he had a constant battle to keep his photographic equipment in working order.

We all worked so hard that Vanne, who came to visit us that year and was instantly roped in for her share of the chores, suggested taking off one evening a week from our toils. This was an excellent move; we looked forward to our "rest nights" as many people look forward to the weekends. On these precious evenings we played taped music, had a couple of drinks around a fire, and enjoyed a leisurely supper instead of swallowing down our food in one of the tents before rushing back to work. Sometimes we had hilarious sessions of liar dice.

Even on these nights our conversation was almost entirely "chimp"; if our work had not also been our pleasure it is doubtful whether we should have been able to keep up the pace. We all were totally immersed in the goings-on of our chimpanzee group. As Hugo so often said, it was like being spectators of life in some village. Endless fascination, endless enjoyment, endless work.

Toward the end of that year, try as we would we couldn't keep up with all the work, since new chimpanzees constantly were joining the regulars at the feeding area, and there was Melissa's baby,

Goblin, as well as Flint, demanding very detailed observation. So we took on a secretary, Sonia Ivey, and she, like Edna, became fascinated with the work and with the chimpanzees. Sonia typed out all my tapes, which gave Edna more time to make observations and me more time to pursue investigations in the forests. The chimps became more and more tolerant of my following them closely, so I was able to stay with them for increasingly longer stretches.

By this time we had a group of forty-five chimpanzees visiting camp, some of them regularly (like the Flo family) and others (from groups normally ranging to the south or north) only when their wanderings brought them close to our valley. Apart from some of the very infrequent visitors, these chimps were so accustomed to the setup at the feeding station that they showed no hesitation in wandering in and out of our tents, taking anything they fancied.

We had profited from Kris Pirozynski's experiences: we were careful to put away all clothing in tin trunks—including our bedclothes, which we laboriously had to fold up each morning. Once, just after dawn, I heard an anguished yell from Vanne. When I went to investigate I found that David Graybeard had caught her dressing. She was sitting half naked on her bed and clinging frantically to one pajama leg while David sat beside her, one hand on her knee, sucking the end of the other pajama leg. When I could stop laughing I fetched a banana and stood with it outside the tent. David, though he pulled his part of the pajamas quite hard, eventually let go and accepted the banana as a substitute while Vanne quickly zipped up the tent and bundled her pajamas to safety.

There was no one to offer Rodolf a banana when, far up in the mountains, he suddenly left off grooming his chimpanzee companions and approaching me with his hair on end seized hold of my shirt and pulled. He looked so ferocious that I was just about to strip, but his hair slowly flattened and he sat close to me and began to suck the cloth where he was. He stayed there fifteen minutes and then, with a tiny corner he had torn off, returned to his grooming.

In time we began to feel that nothing was sacred. Quite often we hid a few bananas in the pockets of our clothes, ready to smuggle them to Fifi or some other youngster who had been unable to get a share from the boxes; but since the adult males quickly realized what was going on we soon had to stop. The chimps remembered this hiding place for a long time. One morning Hugo, just dressed and half asleep, let out a yell when Leakey appeared in the tent doorway, stared hard at him, lifted up his shirt, and poked an inquiring finger right into his navel. It was Leakey also who noticed what seemed to him to be a most promising bulge in Edna's shirt and reached up and gently squeezed her breast.

One day, unthinkingly I put a tasty banana into my pocket for my own consumption. When Fifi tried to push her hand in I moved away. After staring very hard at the bump in my pocket Fifi picked a long thin grass, which she very gently inserted deep down into my pocket. She withdrew it and intently sniffed the end. This apparently told her all she wanted to know, and she followed me around, whimpering, until I finally had to give her the fruit.

We also had to keep our egg supply very carefully hidden. Mr. McGregor, Mr. Worzle, and Flo were the three chimps who most loved eggs. One day old McGregor managed to make off with four hard-boiled eggs that Edna had prepared for lunch—and it was well worth the loss for the laugh he gave us. The chimpanzee almost always eats an egg together with a large mouthful of leaves; only when sufficient leaves have been stuffed into his mouth along with an egg does he crack the shell. Then he sits savoring the egg-leaf wad for minutes on end.

Mr. McGregor looked startled when he put the first of the eggs into his mouth—no wonder, for it was hot. He took it out, looked at it carefully, sniffed it, and shoved it back in with copious handfuls of leaves. Then we heard him crack the shell. This obviously was even more puzzling: no delicious liquids ran into his mouth. He spat out the whole mass of leaves and egg and stared at it. He tried all four eggs, each time stuffing in more and more fresh leaves, until he was surrounded by fragments of white and yellow egg and mounds of crumpled greenery.

Another of our problems that year was to protect the tents. We fixed all the guy ropes high up onto trees or onto a thick wooden railing Hassan had built around the tent—for the chimps had found that to yank out tent pegs, one by one, as they charged past during an arrival display, produced spectacular results. Temporarily we had no further trouble. Then one day Goliath displayed straight through the middle of our tent, and as he did so snapped in two the thick wooden tent poles, one after the other, as though they had been matchsticks. In his wake he left a crumpled mass of canvas partially held up by those guy ropes that were attached to trees. Finally we got some sturdy tree trunks and with Hassan's help erected these, the bases sunk in cement. They made somewhat unconventional but very satisfactory tent poles.

During most of that year the chimps' banana supply was our worst headache. For one thing, there never seemed to be enough boxes. Hassan was making more almost nonstop, but every day two or three—or even more—were put out of commission by one of the chimps. Even when everything had been sunk into cement, a few of the adult males still managed to break something. J.B. was the worst offender. He kept breaking off the steel handles of the levers, so we could not close them. And he managed to snap even strong cables, though the only part showing was a length of about seven inches between the cemented end of the pipe and where it was attached to the lever. It was a rather terrifying indication of the tremendous strength of these chimpanzees.

It was all right if a group came in and left before the next group arrived; then we had a chance to refill the boxes from our small store. But we dared not open this cache with a group of chimps in the vicinity. As it was, we were often surprised during an attempt to replenish the boxes; and if J.B. or Goliath or one of the other big males swaggered up when we were holding a bucket full of bananas we simply had to give them the lot—they were too powerful to trifle with.

Worst of all was the problem of David Graybeard's banana supply. David remembered the good old days when he, Goliath, and William had been able to make off with any bananas that were available. In those days he didn't have to compete for a share with five to ten other hungry males. David never hurried when he arrived at camp: he liked to let the other males rush on ahead so that by the time he arrived most of the excitement would be over. Yet somehow we had to have bananas for him when he did come;

otherwise, with his lower lip pushed determinedly forward, he would plod into one tent after the other looking for them. He would pull everything apart, push everything over, even rip open mosquito-net windows if the tent was zipped shut. And so by some means we had to have twenty or thirty bananas hidden away for David. The problem was, of course, that the other chimps also looked through the tents for hidden fruit—though not so thoroughly and disastrously as David. They quickly learned our different hiding places and we constantly had to think of new ones.

When David's supply remained intact we still had the difficult task of getting it to him without the other more aggressive males noticing. And after we had with great trouble succeeded in getting a pile right into his arms, Flo or Melissa or some of the other females usually would cluster around and reach out, one after the other, to take fruits from David's pile. David seldom objected; after all, *he* would always be able to get more. Life became increasingly hectic and impossible, and increasingly I longed for those uncomplicated days when I roamed the mountains alone.

In 1965, however, things began to look up. The National Geographic Society, which was still supporting the research, granted us funds for the erection of some prefabricated aluminum buildings. We chose another site even farther up the valley which offered a superb view of the mountain opposite and a glimpse of the lake. Once again all the work had to be done at night, but apart from the preparation of the cement floors it did not take long to set up the buildings. When they were ready and covered on the sides and roofs with grass they blended in well with their forested surroundings. The largest one contained a fairly big room for working and for files of records, two very small rooms to serve as bedrooms for Edna and Sonia, and two even smaller ones as a kitchen and storage area. The other building was for Hugo and myself. In addition we put up a smaller hut as a banana storehouse down in the valley just below the new camp.

This time we had even less difficulty in acquainting the chimps with the new site. One morning, when Hugo and I were up at the completed new buildings checking to see that everything was ready, we looked over the valley and saw David Graybeard and Goliath feeding in a palm tree. What luck! Quickly we held up a large bunch of bananas. The two males screamed and hugged each other for fully a minute before rushing down and hastening across the valley. As it happened, fifteen other chimps were scattered about the valley, and upon hearing the excited calling of David and Goliath they too hurried toward us; the whole group converged upon the new feeding area. The only disappointment was that since the attempt was unplanned Hugo had no camera to record the wild excitement, the embracing and kissing and patting and screaming and barking that went on before the chimps had calmed down sufficiently to start feeding.

Within three days nearly all the chimps—all but the most irregular visitors—had discovered the new site and we were able to close down completely our other feeding area. The new buildings were so luxurious compared to anything Hugo and I had ever known at Gombe that it was heartbreaking for us to have to leave the place a few weeks after everything was finished. Hugo had to start another photographic assignment, for the National Geographic Society could not afford to maintain a photographer full time at the chimpanzee camp, and I had to spend nine months in England to finish writing up results for my Ph.D. dissertation.

Not until Hugo and I had actually left the Gombe Stream did we realize that during the year we had made one grave mistake. We had encouraged Flint to touch us and we had tickled him gently. It had been a delightful experience, and Flint had become more and more trusting. We had marveled that a wild chimpanzee mother could lose her fear of humans to the extent of allowing her infant to play with us. But Fifi had copied Flint's example, and so had Figan. At the time it had not seemed to matter; it proved, as my grooming of David had proved, that it is possible to establish a close and friendly relation with a creature who has lived the first years of his life in fear of man. Hugo and I were actually able to tickle Figan and wrestle with him, rolling on the ground, although even when only eight years old the young male was much stronger than either of us.

When we left—when the potential of the new research buildings dawned on us, when we began to receive letters from students asking if they could join our team—we realized the foolishness of our behavior. The adult male chimpanzee is at least three times stronger than a man; if Figan grew up and realized how much weaker humans really were, he would become dangerous. Moreover, repeated contact with a wild animal is bound to affect its behavior. We made a rule that in the future no student should purposefully make contact with any of the chimpanzees.

Edna and Sonia, who also had soon learned to make accurate observations, kept things going for almost a year on their own. Since then we have had a constant stream of research assistants working at Gombe. Gradually our research program has expanded so that for the past few years we have offered facilities to those wishing to study baboon and red colobus behavior. Some students have worked at the Gombe for one year as my research assistants, keeping up the all-important general record of the behavior of known chimpanzees; most of these young people had B.A. degrees, and all put in hours and hours of work and added considerably to our knowledge of chimpanzees. Some of them elected to stay on for a second year working as research students on some chosen aspect of chimpanzee behavior.

In 1967 there was a major change in the status of the Gombe Stream: it was taken over by Tanzania National Parks and became the Gombe National Park. Game Department scouts gave place to National Parks rangers with their own quarters down in the southern section of the park. Together with the National Parks authorities, we are slowly working our way toward opening a second feeding station, in the southern area, for the benefit of interested tourists and visitors. For two years students have been working in the proposed area, living on their own, trying to habituate the chimpanzees of the southern group, as in 1960 I struggled to get our own group accustomed to me.

The Gombe Stream Research Centre has gradually expanded. Today there are eight small sleeping houses up at the observation area, nestling out of sight in the surrounding trees. There are three larger buildings down on the beach, and three more huts for the students working on baboons and monkeys. The African staff alone have quite a "village" at the beach grouped around the house of old Iddi Matata. Dominic and Sadiki and Rashidi all are with us still, and there are many more. It cannot be said that conditions at the Gombe Stream Research Centre are in any sense luxurious, but the facilities are more than adequate for young people who love animals, exciting and fascinating research—and hard work.

The biggest challenge we have faced at any time has been the actual presentation of the bananas: how to offer them in a way most similar to a natural food supply, and so as to affect as little as possible the social behavior of the chimpanzees. There has been much trial and error throughout the years.

To start with we gave the chimps bananas whenever they came into camp. It was so exciting to Hugo and me to be able to film and watch individuals at close quarters and regularly that we didn't worry too much if they visited the valley more frequently than they might have done had the feeding station not existed. Also, in those early days, the idea of really long-term research had not been born, and we were anxious to record as much as we could before we had to leave for ever. After a few years, however, we realized that the constant feeding was having a marked effect on the behavior of the chimps. They were beginning to move about in large groups more often than they had ever done in the old days. They were sleeping near camp and arriving in noisy hordes early in the morning. Worst of all, the adult males were becoming increasingly aggressive. When we first offered the chimps bananas the males seldom fought over their food; they shared boxes or, at worst, chased off another individual, or threatened, without actually attacking.

Hugo and I returned to the Gombe in 1966, after I had completed my terms at Cambridge, and we were shocked by the change we saw in the chimps' behavior. Not only was there a great deal more fighting than ever before, but many of the chimps were hanging around camp for hours and hours every day. This was entirely due to Fifi and Figan and, to a lesser extent, Evered.

These three youngsters had discovered that in order to open a banana box all they had to do was to pull out the simple pin serving to keep the lever closed. Laboriously Hassan had worked at the fastening, cutting threads into both pin and handle so that it had to be unscrewed rather than simply pulled out. This had worked for a few months, but eventually the same three youngsters had solved that problem also. Then Hassan had fixed nuts onto the ends of the screws so that those had to be removed before the screws could be unscrewed. Just before Hugo and I had returned, Figan, Fifi, and Evered had mastered this. Things were chaotic.

Evered would go up to a handle, unscrew it, and then, with loud food barks, hurry to the box that he had thus opened. So, of course, did any other chimps in the vicinity, and it was rare for Evered to get more than one or two bananas, if that—unless he happened to be the only chimp, or the highest-ranking one, in camp. Usually he simply went around opening box after box until eventually he had "fed" all the others, and then if there was a box left he got that himself. His only attempt at guile was to arrive earlier and earlier in the morning—presumably in an endeavor to be first in camp and have the field to himself. But the others came earlier and earlier too.

Fifi and Figan were far more astute. Both of them learned quickly that however many boxes they opened they were unlikely to get any bananas when there were higher-ranking chimpanzees around. So they just lay around, together with Flo, waiting for the others to leave. Then when there were no adult males in camp they would quickly open a box each. Sometimes they could not resist going up to a handle and unscrewing the screw. But they did not then release the lever and hurry to the open box: they just sat casually grooming themselves and looking anywhere except at the box, with one foot keeping the lever closed. Once I timed Figan sitting thus for over half an hour. Of course, though the other chimps had not mastered the secret of the screws, they were bright enough to realize that, if they hung around, Fifi or Figan might eventually provide them with bananas. So they stayed in camp longer and longer. Sometimes they did manage to wear out Fifi's patience—particularly Mike—but not often. And so day in day out the Flo family remained in camp, and it amused us to see that it was Flo who occasionally tried to lead her offspring away, just as the year before they had tried to lead her away from termite heaps. Only Flo had no lure, and after plodding off down the path, repeatedly looking back over her shoulder, she nearly always returned and collapsed once more in the shade of a palm tree.

While we were impressed by the intelligence shown by Figan and Fifi, it meant that we had to devise a completely new system of banana-feeding. Our next attempt was to install a large number of Nairobi-made steel boxes. These were battery-operated and could be opened by pressing buttons inside the research building. One advantage of this system was that when a large chimpanzee group arrived we could offer each of the adult males their share at more or less the same time; they no longer had to stay around waiting and becoming more and more aggressive. Also, the chimps began to associate bananas more with boxes than people, for most of them never connected the pressing of a button with the opening of a box.

We decided, in addition, to feed bananas on an irregular schedule. For two or three days running there would be no bananas at all. We hoped in this way to prevent the chimps from hanging about in our valley for days at a time. The system worked well during 1967, but we had by no means achieved the final answer.

The next problem was one that had been ever present and steadily growing worse each year: competition at the feeding area between chimpanzees and baboons. In 1968 when Hugo and I again returned to the Gombe for a few months, we found that things were in chaos. One baboon troop—the Camp Troop, as it was known—had taken to lingering at the feeding station, either in nearby trees or on the other side of the valley, from where there was a good view of our buildings. As soon as a chimpanzee group arrived, the baboons rushed in to try to get a share in the bananas. Over and above this, a second troop—Beach Troop—had also started spending several hours each day in the vicinity of camp.

The adult male baboons had become very aggressive, not only to the chimpanzees but to humans as well. Some of our students were worried by the situation, especially the girls—and rightly so, for a male baboon can be quite as dangerous an adversary as a leopard.

For a time we tried to discourage the baboons by refusing to open laden boxes while they were around, but this merely built up tremendous tensions and frustrations in the chimpanzees who were there. Baboons and chimps alike knew that there were bananas in the closed boxes, and the longer we delayed opening the worse the situation became. Aggressive interactions multiplied, and when the boxes were finally opened there was bedlam. Something had to be done, and done quickly.

First we stopped feeding altogether. As Hugo and I had anticipated, the chimps, when they arrived day after day and found all the boxes open and empty, began visiting camp less frequently. Within a week it was very quiet. Small groups occasionally wandered through, peering at the boxes and trailing off again. The baboons stopped waiting around also.

After three weeks we began feeding again, very irregularly and filling the boxes only when it was certain that the baboons were sleeping far away and would not be around early in the morning. Meanwhile work was going on for the construction of an underground bunker stretching some ten yards from the main observation building.

The finished bunker is about four feet wide and high enough for a person to walk upright. There is room for storing inside enough bananas for any one day, so the boxes, dug up from the slopes, were placed along either side of the bunker—or the Trench, as it came to be called. The boxes open both outward and inward. At long last we have complete control of when and whom we feed. If some boxes have been filled and baboons come in before the chimps have eaten, we merely remove the bananas through the inner side of the box, open the outward side, and so far as chimps and baboons are concerned there are no bananas that day. If a small group of chimps arrive they can be fed the appropriate boxfuls of bananas with no difficulty at all.

Since the construction of the Trench we have had almost no problems—only when the inner side of one box broke and Goblin discovered that he could squeeze through into the tunnel. He would emerge from the box with an armful of bananas purloined from the supply within.

It is now possible to regulate quite carefully the frequency with which individual chimps are fed, and we make certain that none has bananas more than once in ten days or two weeks. So the chimpanzees have almost completely resumed their old nomadic habits, and wander through camp for the most part only when they happen to be in the vicinity. Consequently this means that we cannot get as much information as when they all came more frequently, but they pass through often enough for the students to make fairly regular records on most individuals.

For the past few years we have collected information on the

chimpanzees' behavior both at the feeding area—where it is possible to learn a great deal about changes in dominance and other relationships between individuals as well as to collect a wealth of data on infant development—and in the forests, under more normal conditions. The chimpanzees themselves have become amazingly tolerant of humans wandering along the mountain tracks behind them, almost part of their group. And, if they do become annoyed, it is the easiest thing in the world for them to shake off their followers in that rugged terrain.

How long the current feeding system will continue to operate smoothly we cannot say. At present it seems as though at long last we have hit upon the ultimate solution. When I look back through the records on the different individuals, the quickly accumulating life histories of chimps such as Flint and little Goblin, how worthwhile have been the struggles and heartaches and near despair.

12

THE INFANT

THE BIRTH OF A BABY is something of an event in many animal and human societies. In the chimpanzee community, where mothers only have an infant about once every three and a half to five years, births are relatively few—not more than one or two a year in our group of thirty to forty individuals. So the appearance of a mother with a brand-new baby often stimulates much interest among the other chimps.

When Goblin was first introduced to a large group, he was two days old. He could only grip on for a couple of steps without support from his mother, Melissa, and he was still attached by the umbilical cord to the placenta. The group was peacefully grooming, but when Melissa approached the tree and began to climb it I sensed the tension as first one and then another chimpanzee stared toward the new mother. Fifi instantly swung over toward her. Melissa, moving carefully, went to greet Mike, pant-grunting submissively and reaching to touch his side. She presented and he patted her rump, but when he moved forward, staring at Goblin, she hastily moved away. It was the same when she greeted Goliath. He too wanted to see the baby more closely. So did David and so did Rodolf.

After five minutes Mike began to display, leaping through the tree and swaying the branches. Melissa, screaming, jumped away from him. As she did so the placenta almost caught in some twigs. I was suddenly concerned that the newborn might be torn from his mother's breast, but Melissa gathered up the cord just as Goliath displayed toward her. Soon the entire group was in confusion—all the adult males leaping around and swaying branches, Melissa and also the other females and youngsters rushing out of the way and screaming. It looked for all the world like a wild greeting ceremony for the new baby, though in reality it was undoubtedly provoked by a sense of frustrated curiosity: Melissa simply would not let the males get close enough to examine the baby properly.

Eventually things calmed down and the males began to groom each other again. Then Fifi and the other young females in the group gathered around the mother and baby to stare long at Goblin. If they moved too close, Melissa threatened them with a soft bark or upraised arm, but she did not move away and they were able to look their fill.

Since that day we have seen similar displays when new mothers first appeared with their babies, though normally only when the mothers themselves were young. There is usually far less commotion when an old female, such as Flo, appears with yet another infant. Since the experienced female does not run away from them, the other chimpanzees are able to satisfy their curiosity. We have seen a group of four males sitting calmly very close to an old mother and staring fixedly at her newborn. When the mother runs away the situation is potentially very dangerous for a newborn baby, since for the first few days of its life the chimpanzee infant often does not seem able to grip well to its mother's hair. Usually there is the added danger of a dangling placenta, for, so far as we know, the chimpanzee mother in the wild makes no attempt to break the umbilical cord herself. We have never actually seen an infant dropped or hurt during these wild displays. On the other hand, we know of several babies that have mysteriously disappeared during the first few days of life.

During the six years since Flint and Goblin were born, twelve healthy infants have been born to our group, and although several died before they were a year old our observations on them and their mothers have taught us much. Babies less than five months of age are normally protected by their mothers from all contact with other chimpanzees except their own siblings. Infants from the age of three months onward often reach out to other chimps sitting nearby, but usually their mothers pull their hands quickly away. It was, however, very different for Pom, one of the first female infants born into our group. Her mother, Passion, actually laid the baby on the ground the very first day of her life and allowed two young females to touch and even groom her as she lay there. But then, in all respects, Passion was a somewhat unnatural mother.

She was no youngster, this Passion. She had been fully mature when I first came to know her back in 1961, and I know she lost one infant before Pom's birth in 1965. If her treatment of Pom was anything to go by, I suspect Passion had lost other infants, too, for Pom had to fight for her survival right from the start. When she was a mere two months old, she began to ride on her mother's back—three or four months earlier than other infants. It started when Pom hurt her foot badly. She could not grip properly, and Passion, rather than constantly support the infant with one hand as most mothers would have done, probably pushed Pom up onto her back. The very first day that Pom adopted this new riding position, Passion hurried for about thirty yards in order to greet a group of adult males, seemingly quite without concern for her infant. Pom, clinging on frantically, managed to stay aboard—though much older infants, when they start riding on their mother's back, usually slide down if their mothers make sudden movements.

We expected that when her foot was better Pom would revert to clinging underneath Passion. Nothing of the sort happened. It is probably more comfortable for the mother when the child rides on her back, and having achieved this happy state of affairs three months early, Passion had no intention of letting things change. Even when it poured with rain and Pom whimpered as she tried to wriggle under her mother's warm body for protection, Passion seldom relented, instead again and again pushing her infant back on top.

Most of the mother chimpanzees we have watched were helpful when their small babies nuzzled about searching for a nipple. Flo had normally supported Flint so that suckling was easy for him throughout a feed, even when he was six months old. Melissa also had tried, though often she had bungled things and held Goblin too high so that his searching lips nuzzled through the hair of her shoulders or neck. But Passion usually ignored Pom's whimpers completely; if she couldn't find the nipple by herself it was just bad luck. If Pom happened to be suckling when Passion wanted to move off, she seldom waited until the infant had finished her meal; she just got up and went, and Pom, clinging for once under her mother, struggled to keep the nipple in her mouth as long as she could before she was relentlessly pushed up onto Passion's back. As a result of her mother's lack of solicitude, Pom seldom managed to suckle for more than two minutes at a time before she was interrupted by Passion, and often it was much less. Most infants during their first years suckle for about three minutes once an hour. Pom probably made up for her shorter feeds by suckling more frequently.

It was the same story when Pom started to walk. Flo, it will be remembered, was very solicitous when Flint was finding his feet, gathering him up if he fell and often supporting him with one hand as he wobbled along. Melissa was less concerned, and if Goblin fell and cried merely reached her hand toward him while he struggled to his feet. Passion was positively callous. One day, previous to which Pom had never been seen to totter on her own for more than two yards, Passion suddenly got up and walked away from her infant. Pom, struggling to follow and falling continually, whimpered louder each time, and finally her mother returned and shoved the infant onto her back. This happened repeatedly. As Pom learned to walk better, Passion did not even bother to return when the infant cried—she just waited for her to catch up by herself.

When Pom was a year old it was a common sight to see Passion walking along followed by a whimpering infant who was frantically trying to catch up and climb aboard her moving transport. It was not really surprising that, during her second year, when most infants wander about happily quite far away from their mothers, Pom usually sat or played very close to Passion. For months on end she actually held tightly on to Passion with one hand during her games with Flint and Goblin and the other infants. Obviously she was terrified of being left behind.

Like human children, chimpanzee children are dependent on their mothers for several years. Most chimp youngsters continue to suckle and sleep with their mothers for over four years, and though they ride less and less often on their mothers, they are quick to jump aboard at any sign of excitement in the group or some other danger until they are four or even five years old. During this period of dependence the infant gradually masters his physical environment: he learns to move easily and rapidly over the ground and through the trees, and he becomes increasingly skillful in his manipulation of objects—such as branches and twigs while he is feeding and nest-making.

Flint first attempted to make a nest when he was ten months old. He bent a small twig and sat on it on the ground in the approved manner. Then he bent a handful of grass stems onto his lap. After this I sometimes saw him trying to make nests as he dangled in midair, bending down twigs and attempting to hold them under him with his feet as he reached for more. During the next few months Flint became more and more proficient and, like other year-old infants, he often made a nest while he was playing around by himself in a tree. Sometimes he lay in it for a short while, but more typically he just bounced around in it, frequently breaking it apart and then after a few minutes making another. This constant practicing means that when a youngster is four or five years old and ready to sleep on his own he is skilled in nest-making techniques. It is the same with the use of twigs and sticks for insect-eating: infants play with and poke about with such materials long before they are interested in using them for the serious business of feeding.

Human infants, by and large, learn to toddle and climb the stairs and feed themselves with a spoon much more readily than they learn to behave in the well-mannered way required of them by most grownups. Quite often a small child shows a remarkable lack of perception of the mood of his elders; when he has been banging on the table with a tin plate for minutes on end, his mother may have to tell him repeatedly to stop, or snatch the plate away, or smack him before he recognizes her irritation. When his father is engrossed in a book, the child may persistently try to attract his attention, in spite of the fact that his only rewards are stern glances and angry demands for him to keep quiet.

Such behavior is sometimes labeled deliberate naughtiness, yet we see the same sort of thing occurring in chimpanzee society. Chimpanzee infants can walk and climb before they start to use most of the submissive gestures of the adult communicatory system during interactions with their elders, and they too, during the first year of life, show a surprising lack of perception as to the mood of their elders. At this time it is the chimpanzee mother who must keep a watchful eye not only on her child but also on the other individuals of the group around them.

One day I followed a small group up the mountainside. Presently they settled down to groom and rest, and I sat down near them. Goblin, still tottery on his legs at ten months, wobbled over to Mike, who was sitting in the shade of a palm tree chewing on a wad of fig seeds and skin. As Goblin looked up at him, the dominant male reached out and patted the infant's back very gently many times. Goblin stumbled away, tripped over a length of vine, and fell flat on his face. Almost at once Fifi hurried over and gathered him up, holding him close for a moment. She began to groom him, but he pulled away and wandered off again. A small tree stump lay in his way and, fixing this with the intense concentrated gaze of the young infant, Goblin went up to it and tried to climb onto the top. Halfway up he lost his grip with one hand and nearly fell. David Graybeard, who was sitting nearby, quickly reached out and put his hand under the infant's elbow until he was safely up.

Just then Flint, six months older than Goblin, came bouncing up and the two children began to play, both showing their lower teeth in the chimpanzee's playful smile. Flo was reclining nearby grooming Figan; Goblin's mother, Melissa, was a little farther away, also grooming. It was so peaceful, this scene in the deep forest, high up on the side of a mountain with the gleam of the lake just visible through a gap in the trees. All at once a series of pant-hoots announced the arrival of more chimpanzees, and there was instant commotion in the group. Flint pulled away from the game and hurried to jump onto Flo's back as she moved for safety halfway up a palm tree. I saw Mike with his hair on end beginning to hoot; I knew he was about to display. So did the other chimpanzees of his group—all were alert, prepared to dash out of the way or to join in the displaying. All, that is, save Goblin.

He seemed totally unconcerned and, incredibly, began to totter toward Mike. Melissa, squeaking with fear, was hurrying toward her son, but she was too late. Mike began his charge, and as he passed Goblin seized him up as though he were a branch and dragged him along the ground.

And then the normally fearful, cautious Melissa, frantic for her child, hurled herself at Mike. It was unprecedented behavior, and she got severely beaten up for her interference; but she did succeed in rescuing Goblin—the infant lay, pressed close to the ground and screaming, where the dominant male had dropped him. Even before Mike had ceased his attack on Melissa the old male Huxley had seized Goblin from the ground. I felt sure he too was going to display with the infant, but he remained quite still, holding the child and staring down at him almost, it seemed, in bewilderment. Then as Melissa, screaming and bleeding, escaped from Mike, Huxley set the infant on the ground. As his mother hurried up to him Goblin leaped into her arms and she rushed off into the undergrowth. Their screams gradually receded as Melissa hurried away from the group.

It is difficult to understand Mike's behavior. Normally, small infants are shown almost unlimited tolerance from all other members of the community; it almost seems as though the adult male may lose many of his social inhibitions during his charging display. Possibly Mike, in the frenzy of the moment, considered any object lying in his path a suitable prop to enhance his display. Once I watched Rodolf pound and drag an old female during one of his displays while her screaming infant clung beneath her; then, almost before he had stopped attacking her, he turned around to embrace, pat, and kiss her.

It was only a week or two after Mike had displayed with him that Goblin was involved in another dramatic sequence of events. This started while Goblin was playing with a female infant quite close to their two mothers, who were grooming each other. Suddenly there was a commotion. A male charged toward the group and one of the mothers was briefly attacked. Instantly both females rushed to their infants, and Melissa, who arrived first, seized the wrong one and rushed with her up the slope. The second mother grabbed Goblin and almost at once pushed him from her to race after her own screaming child. Goblin was left alone, his face almost split in two by his huge grin of fear. At this moment Mike ran up, but now his behavior was completely different. He gathered up the terrified Goblin in the gentlest manner and carried him for some way pressed to his breast. When the infant struggled to escape, Mike put him down, though he stayed with him for ten minutes, threatening or chasing off other chimpanzees who approached too closely. When Melissa finally arrived on the scene, Mike watched benignly as Goblin raced to join his mother.

Goblin, like some other first infants of young and inexperienced mothers, got into more scrapes than youngsters like Flint, who had a mother to whom child-raising was no novel experience. Of course when Flint was small there also was Fifi to look after him; several times it was Fifi who was closest when danger threatened, and she who seized him and ran with him to safety.

Some mothers appear to be overcautious and repeatedly "rescue" their infants from situations that do not seem to be dangerous at all. When Gilka was just a two-year-old, she always became excited on the rare occasions when her mother remained for a while in a large group with a number of adult males. Like a little human girl showing off in front of a circle of grownups, Gilka would stand upright, swinging her arms and stamping her feet or pirouetting interminably. If she approached one of the males he usually responded by reaching out to pat her or to tickle her in the most tolerant way possible. Yet Olly nearly always hurried up, pant-grunting nervously, touched the male submissively, and took Gilka away. Once, when Gilka kept pirouetting over to a peaceful group of adult males, Olly four times followed and quite literally dragged her daughter away by the hand.

It was even worse, so far as Olly was concerned, when Gilka tried to initiate play with a mature male. Most males responded readily enough to the advances of the gay infant, but as soon as Olly noticed she hurried up and either took Gilka away or began to groom the male, so that quite often his attention was distracted from her child. Yet on none of these occasions were any of the males showing a sign of aggressive behavior.

Once Olly, noticing that Gilka was having a tickling game with Rodolf, quickly approached and with worried pant-grunts laid her hand placatingly on the big male's back. Rodolf, who did not need placating, continued to play, lying on his side and heaving with quiet chimpanzee laughter as Gilka clambered up his large frame and play-bit into his ticklish neck. After watching the two for a moment Olly started to groom Rodolf, nervously pulling away her hand every time he waved an arm or leg during the game. Suddenly Rodolf turned to Olly and began to tickle her in the neck with one hand while with his foot he continued to tickle Gilka. Olly's face was a study. Her lips wobbled in agitation, her eyes stared, and her pant-grunts became positively hysterical. She pulled back, but Rodolf followed and tickled her again. For a few moments her long lips bunched themselves into the semblance of a play-face, and I detected a note of laughter in her frenzied grunts; but after a moment she could endure it no longer, and moved away from such alarming physical contact with an adult male.

In fact some of the big males do without warning attack a female during a game. I am not sure why, but I think it is because as they grow rougher, and perhaps hurt the female, she draws away from them. This seems to make them irritated. Olly, I am sure, need not have worried: I never saw Rodolf end any play session aggressively.

Young chimpanzees spend a great deal of time in playing. Indeed, when they are two or three years old it often seems that they do little else. Play is a much argued about category of behavior in scientific circles. What is it? What is its function? How should it be defined? And yet, despite all the discussions and speculations, most people, whether they be trained scientists or casual observers, readily agree as to when animals are playing, be they watching a litter of puppies tumbling about or a young chimpanzee turning somersaults.

Perhaps some of the arguments have arisen because in *human* children two entirely different types of activity are labeled "play." The two-year-old who with intense concentration builds ten blocks into a tower is said to be "playing" with his bricks. It is a completely different sort of behavior from that shown by the same child when he toddles around the sofa shrieking with laughter while his father crawls after him, patting at his legs. The infant chimpanzee who tries over and over to bend a branch under him for a nest or attempts to catch a termite with a minute and totally inadequate piece of grass is probably performing a behavior that is equivalent to tower-building in the human child. But most of the behavior that in chimpanzees we refer to as playful is of the romping, laughing type shown by the human child when he is chased or tickled.

Young chimps often play by themselves when no playmates are available, swinging about in a tree, jumping continually over the same gap onto the same springy branch, somersaulting or gamboling on the ground. Mostly, however, they like to play with each other, chasing round a tree trunk, leaping one after the other through the treetops, dangling, each from one hand, while they spar and hit at each other, playfully biting or hitting or tickling each other as they wrestle on the ground.

Whether or not scientists will ever agree as to the function of play, it does serve to make the growing youngster familiar with his environment. He learns during play which type of branch is safe to jump onto and which will break, and he practices gymnastic skills, such as leaping down from one branch and catching another far below, which when he is older will serve him in good stead—during an aggressive encounter with a higher-ranking individual in the treetops, for instance. It is not true, as some people have suggested, that he would learn these facts just as well during the feeding and normal locomotion, and so on, because these routine activities seldom necessitate wild leaps.

Over and above these considerations, social play certainly offers the young chimp the opportunity to become familiar with other youngsters. He learns which of them are physically stronger than he is and which ones have mothers higher-ranking than his own who may retaliate, if a squabble breaks out, with unpleasant consequences to himself. He discovers which of his playmates can be intimidated by a show of strength and which of them will in a similar context turn around and call his bluff. In other words, he learns something of the complex structure of chimpanzee society.

While play may be a type of schooling for the young chimp, it is obviously most enjoyable. Many mothers have great difficulty in persuading their offspring to leave a game when they themselves are ready to move on. Passion, of course, seldom had any difficulty in persuading Pom to follow her—at least until the infant was three years old and less terrified of being left behind. At one time Pom was so anxious lest Passion should go without her that she would sometimes rush away from her playmates if her mother merely moved a few yards to a new resting place. Other infants, on the contrary, often showed great reluctance to leave a game.

Flo sometimes coped with the task of wresting Flint from his playmates by playing with him herself. Then, when she dragged him away by one foot, he apparently continued to regard it as a game, for he often laughed as his back went bump, bump, bump over the uneven ground. I was reminded of Christopher Robin dragging Pooh Bear downstairs. It was Melissa who really amused us. One day when Goblin was playing with Flint, Pom, and a few others, Melissa wanted to leave. She pulled Goblin from the group, pressed him to her tummy, and set off. She had gone only ten yards or so when Goblin detached himself and came cantering back to dive into the wrestling youngsters once more. Melissa, uttering soft whimpers, followed him. For a few moments she stood looking at her son and then once more gathered him up and set off. This time she went farther, but when she had gone thirty yards Goblin again came romping back. Melissa followed, whimpering louder this time. She was still whimpering when she pulled him from the group and set off for the third time. Melissa took Goblin away, and followed him back, whimpering, no less than fifteen times before she finally succeeded in leaving.

When one watches the gradual development of male and female infants there are not many obvious differences in the behavior of the two sexes. Male infants tend to indulge in more rough-and-tumble play than do females, and they practice aggressive display patterns more often during their games, such as dragging branches and swaggering about. Also, male infants usually start to threaten and attack others at an earlier age than do females. In addition there is one major difference and that lies in the precocious sexual development of the male infant. From a very early age the male shows great interest in the pink swellings of females. I remember Flint struggling to reach a female in this state almost before he could walk. Once he did get to her, he made repeated attempts to mount her as she reclined on the ground. At that time I was astonished; subsequently it became clear that this was normal behavior for a male infant, although, to be sure, Flint was somewhat forward.

Between the ages of one and four or five years, male infants spend a great deal of time, when a pink female is in the group, hurrying up to her, mounting her, and making all the movements shown by an adult male during mating. I remember Goblin, when he was two years old, approaching one female fifteen times in half an hour. Usually she crouched for him so that he could mount her easily; once or twice she stood up before he had finished with her so that he was suddenly lifted from the ground and ended by scrambling onto her back, where he sat looking rather surprised. When his approach did not cause the female to crouch down, Goblin tried to reach her by climbing twigs or by balancing on the tips of his toes as he "mated" her.

Flint, when he was three years old, began to show some of the courtship displays of the adult male. One day when he had "mated" young Pooch about twenty times during a play session, she appeared to get tired of the infant and climbed away from him into a small tree. Flint sat below, staring up at her with all his hair on end, and waved twigs violently until, whimpering, she climbed down and once more crouched low for her small but demanding suitor.

When it comes to real sex, male and female infants behave in exactly the same way. Nearly always, as soon as they notice a mature male mating a female, they rush up and try to interfere. At no time does the male demonstrate more clearly his amazing tolerance toward infants. Sometimes he may be almost lost to view as up to four youngsters converge upon him, pushing at him or putting their hands to his face as he mates. For the most part he simply turns his head away and appears to try to ignore their very existence. Only occasionally does he hit out at an infant—and then the victim is usually a male three or four years old.

Why infants should behave thus we do not know. When Fifi pushed at Flo's suitors during her infancy it seemed that something akin to jealousy might be motivating her, but since then we have seen males pushed and mobbed by infants whether the female happened to be the mother of one of them or not. For the time being it must remain one of the many mysteries.

During the chimpanzee youngster's fourth year the very tolerant atmosphere in which up to this time he has been nurtured gradually begins to change. His play sessions become rougher and wilder, and older chimpanzees are quicker to threaten him if he behaves incautiously. This is the time, too, when most youngsters are actually weaned, and weaning can be a very trying business, lasting in some cases more than a year. For Gilka, whose weaning period coincided with so many other adverse circumstances, the transition from infancy to the juvenile stage was a particularly unhappy time.

13

THE CHILD

LISTLESSLY GILKA DANGLED from the branch of a tree above me, one leg bent at the knee and the foot pressed into the opposite groin. For a full minute she remained thus, almost motionless. Then, her movements slow, she climbed to the ground and hobbled forward on three limbs, still keeping her foot tucked into the opposite groin. When she was some four feet from Olly, who was working with a grass tool fishing for termites, Gilka stopped and began to utter a series of low whimpers. For a brief time Olly ignored the child, then she reached out, drew Gilka close, and began to tickle her. Soon Gilka was uttering the panting chuckles of chimpanzee laughter. The game had lasted for less than a minute when Olly pushed her daughter away and resumed her endless termite-fishing. Nevertheless, just as Fifi had been temporarily distracted from her early attempts to touch or pull away Flint by similar playful behavior on Flo's part, so it was with Gilka. She looked around, picked up one of Olly's discarded tools, and idly pushed it into an opened-up termite passage. No insect clung to the end when she withdrew the grass; she tried once more, abandoned the attempt, and sat grooming herself.

A few minutes later Gilka again approached Olly and stood uttering her soft, pleading whimpers. Again at first Olly ignored her completely; then suddenly she reached out and drew her daughter close, allowing her to suckle for about half a minute before pushing her away. Gilka stood staring at Olly for a moment, turned away, and climbed back into her tree. There she sat, slumped, and picked little pieces of bark from the trunk. She broke them in her fingers, scarcely looking at what she was doing, and dropped them to the ground.

At this time Gilka was about four and a half years old, and for the past seven months she had been going through an increasingly difficult period. First of all, her elder brother, Evered, who had been her constant playmate, had reached adolescence and in consequence moved about with his family less and less frequently. Secondly, Fifi's attitude toward Gilka had undergone an abrupt change. When Flint was three months old Fifi had not only ignored all Gilka's invitations to play but also threatened and sometimes attacked the younger chimp whenever she went too close to Flint. And finally, just as Fifi became less possessive of her small brother, more willing to play with Gilka, more tolerant of Gilka's playing with Flint, Olly began to shun the Flo family. This was almost certainly due to the fact that at the time Faben and Figan were both spending a great deal of time with Flo and the rest of the family. Olly was nervous when in the company of these two physically splendid and vigorous young males.

So, often for days at a stretch Gilka wandered through the forests with only her old mother for companionship—a mother who was weaning her child and rejecting Gilka's attempts to suckle ever more frequently. Also, it was the termiting season, and Gilka, like all youngsters, became bored when her mother sat fishing for the insects three or more hours at a time.

Small wonder that this combination of circumstances resulted in Gilka's becoming increasingly lethargic—she who formerly had been such a gay and lively little chimp. Small wonder that she began to show strange idiosyncrasies such as putting one foot in the opposite groin, sometimes for long intervals, or senselessly doodling with pieces of bark. Almost certainly it was because of her boredom, her lack of chimpanzee playmates, that Gilka during that period formed a very strange friendship indeed.

One day when Gilka was again waiting while Olly fished for termites, I heard a baboon bark farther down the valley. At the sound Gilka's whole attitude underwent an immediate change. She stood upright, looking toward the sound, then climbed higher in the tree and peered toward a clearing about one hundred yards himpanzees resting in a tree. *Copyright National Geographic Society*

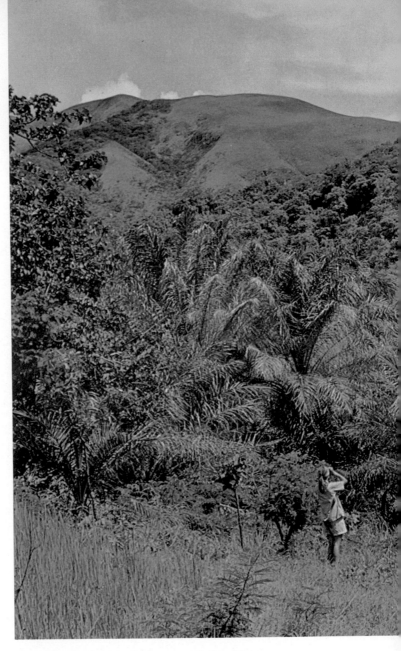
It was a vast, rugged country in which to search for chimpanzees
Copyright National Geographic Society

David Graybeard
Copyright National Geographic Society

The fishermen attract *dagaa* to their boats with lights
National Geographic Society

A thunderstorm over Lake Tanganyika is dramatic
Copyright National Geographic Society

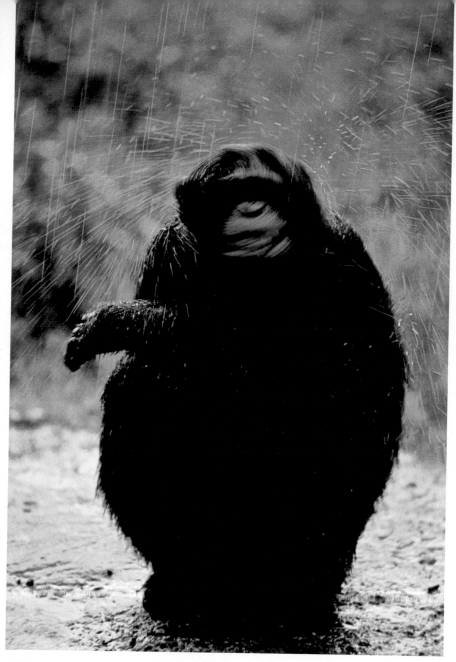

Chimpanzees do not shelter from the rain
Copyright National Geographic Society

Before Flint was born Gilka and Fifi often played together. *Copyright National Geographic Society*

Flo and Flint in a day nest. Nests are usually 30 feet or more from the ground *Copyright National Geographic Society*

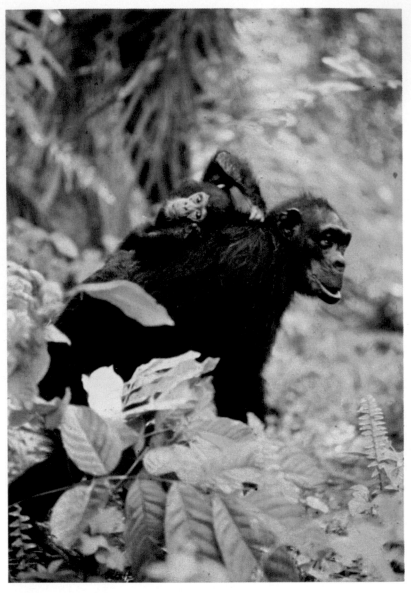

Eight-month-old Flint feels at home on Flo's back
Copyright National Geographic Society

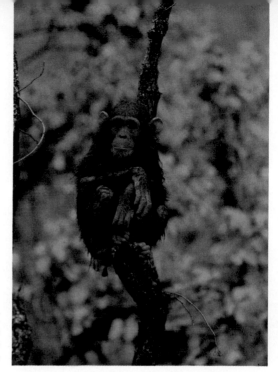

The orphan Merlin remained stunted and grew neurotic *Copyright National Geographic Society*

Humphrey and two other males pant-hoot as they see other chimpanzees arriving. *Copyright National Geographic Society*

Ultimately they became accustomed to my presence
Copyright National Geographic Society

...ugo I found a kindred spirit
...yright *National Geographic Society*

Hugo records laughter as Flint plays with an adolescent. Flo lies
unconcerned. *Copyright National Geographic Society*

Hugo and I could communicate by walkie-talkie
Copyright National Geographic Society

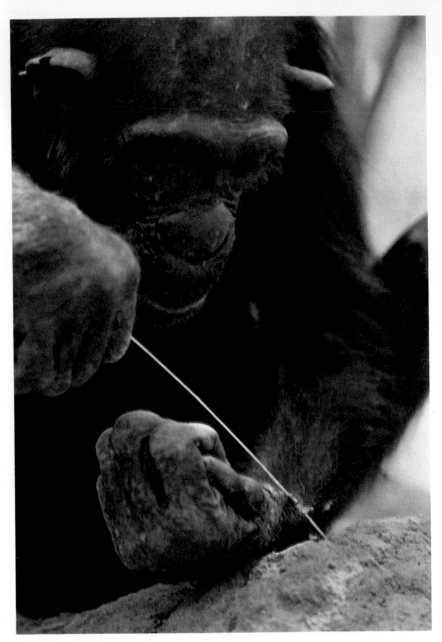

Flo using a grass tool to catch termites
Copyright National Geographic Society

down the valley. When I too looked in that direction I could just make out some baboons moving through the trees. After a few moments Gilka swung rapidly from the tree and set off toward the clearing. Olly merely glanced after her daughter and then went on with her endless termite-eating.

I followed Gilka for a short distance and when I could see fairly well into the clearing stopped to watch what would happen. A moment later I saw Gilka move out from the trees, and at almost the same time a small baboon detached itself from the troop and cantered toward her. I did not need binoculars to identify Goblina, a female of about the same age as Gilka. As I watched, the two ran up to each other, and for a moment I saw their faces very close together. Each had one arm around the other. Then next moment they were playing, wrestling, and patting each other. Goblina went around behind Gilka and, reaching forward, seemed to tickle the chimpanzee in the ribs. Gilka, leaning back, pushed at Goblina's hands, her mouth open in a wide smile.

It is fairly common for young chimpanzees and young baboons to play together, but the games usually consist of wild chasing around, either on the ground or through the trees, or sparring when each hits out quickly toward the other and then draws away. Often, too, such games end with aggressive behavior from one or the other. Gilka's friendship with Goblina was quite different: the contact between the two youngsters was nearly always gentle, and they often deliberately sought each other's company—as they had done on this occasion. No one was studying baboons at this period, but Hugo and I had known Goblina for a long time, and it was evident that at quite a young age she had lost her mother. When I watched the troop settle down for sleep one night I saw Goblina run from one adult female to another and finally huddle close to an old and childless female. Unlike Gilka, she had baboon playmates galore in her troop.

I watched Gilka and Goblina playing for ten minutes, and all the time they were amazingly gentle. Then the baboon troop started to move on and Goblina scampered after it. Gilka stood looking after her before turning and slowly walking back toward Olly. She swung into a tree as she passed me and, still playful, stamped along a branch just above my head, showering me with twigs. Then she approached Olly and began her soft whimpers. This time Olly continued to ignore her daughter, and after a while Gilka climbed into a tree. The playful mood had gone; she began picking off pieces of bark, crumbling them in her fingers, and dropping them to the ground.

The strange friendship between Gilka and Goblina lasted for nearly a year, after which Olly and Gilka disappeared. We thought something must have happened to them, but later they were seen some three miles to the north. When they returned to our valley six months later, Goblina was already adolescent and less playful, for baboons mature faster than chimpanzees; the friendship between the two youngsters was not revived.

We soon realized that during those six months Gilka had been weaned, and although she still accompanied her mother constantly, we saw few friendly interactions between the two. Actually, Olly, whom we soon discovered was pregnant, sometimes seemed to be unnecessarily aggressive toward her daughter. Often, for instance, she would mildly threaten Gilka if the child approached within ten feet or so as she was feeding—even when the two were eating in a tree that was producing more than sufficient food for their needs.

I was interested to find out whether Gilka was still sharing her mother's nest at night, and so at the first opportunity I followed the pair as they left the feeding area after a late afternoon visit. In the past I had spent many hours roaming the forests with these two chimpanzees, so they paid me scant attention as we walked briskly along one of the well-worn tracks leading into the mountains. Occasionally Olly or Gilka paused to pluck a ripe fruit or a tempting handful of vine leaves from the side of the path, but obviously they had a definite goal in view.

Presently we left the forest and moved on to one of the ridges overlooking the lake. There the grass was high—on a level with my head. Often I feared I had lost Olly and Gilka, but luckily the faint rustle they made as they proceeded along gave away their whereabouts, and so I managed to keep behind them. Just before dusk Olly, closely followed by Gilka, climbed into a tall tree. For twenty minutes the two fed on the yellow blossoms that grew in profusion. Finding a comfortable rock, still warm from the sun, I settled down to wait until their meal was over. I had a view over the evening lake and watched as the reflected crimson and brick-red of the sunset gradually gave place to bluish-purple and steel-gray while the sun sank lower behind the dark mountains of the Congo on the far side of the lake. The high-pitched shrilling of the cicadas gave way to the night symphony of the crickets. Slowly the colors drained from the trees and grass and the thin sickle of the new moon and her attendant evening star became visible above the lake. Would Olly and Gilka never finish their evening meal?

There was just enough light for me to see the tree ahead when Olly and Gilka climbed down and set off along a narrow track toward a small pocket of forest about one hundred yards away. Hastily I followed. As they entered the trees the blackness of their coats merged with the darkness and I could no longer see them. I knew that it would be only a matter of moments before they went to bed, so I walked a short distance along the track and then stopped to listen. Sure enough, I soon heard the loud report of a snapping branch and, moving my position a bit, saw the dark shape of a chimp outlined against a sky from which the last vestiges of daylight were rapidly fading. Two minutes later the nest was completed and the chimp lay down.

A few moments afterward I saw movement in another part of the same tree as a smaller chimp began to construct a nest. Eventually Gilka also lay still. I waited another ten minutes, since it is not uncommon for a chimpanzee child to construct a small nest near that of its mother in the evening and then leave it to join her. Gilka, though, did not move, so I set off for camp, grateful in the darkness for the torch which is regularly a part of my equipment at night. I have always found walking through tall grass rather unnerving. It is actually easier to find one's way about without a torch; even when there is no moon, the light from the stars is usually sufficient to outline the salient features of the landscape, and these are no longer clear once a torch is switched on. In my early days at Gombe Stream, however, I had learned that the small circle of light provided by a torch gave me a tremendous feeling of security. Beyond in the outer darkness the leopard could prowl and the buffalo stamp and all to no avail, for within my own magic light spot, where the grass regained its color and the rocks on the ground their shape, I was safe. What a difference the discovery of fire must have made to the life of primitive man.

I followed Olly and Gilka one other evening, and again Gilka settled down for the night in her own separate nest. Returning before dawn, I saw that Gilka was still in the same nest when she woke up in the morning.

Earlier I described how Fifi went through a period of dependence just after Flo's milk dried up and for some time clung to her mother like an infant. Her problems, however, had been of short duration compared to Gilka's, and once she had lost her almost fanatical obsession for Flint, she became a relaxed and particularly playful juvenile. She enjoyed games with many of the adolescent and mature males as well as with all the members of her own family. Once she romped with old J.B. for twenty minutes, chasing him around a palm tree. The large, fat, and often bad-tempered male was soon laughing out loud as he ran, seemingly in expectation of the tickling that would come when he stopped and Fifi flung herself onto him. Most other juveniles we have known, both male and female, were too afraid of the big males to play with them except on rare occasions.

Possibly Fifi's relaxed behavior with her elders stemmed from the fact that she enjoyed a particularly friendly relationship with her mother. Flo was more tolerant of her juvenile daughter than Olly was of hers, and far more so than old Marina of her juvenile daughter Miff. Miff was a contemporary of Fifi's; she had one elder brother and one younger. Their mother appeared to have a very cold disposition indeed. I never saw her playing with Miff, and she seldom played with two-year-old Merlin unless he pestered her to tickle him by continually pulling her hand toward him.

I never saw any friendly interaction between Miff and her mother except for their sessions of social grooming. Miff, in fact, was afraid of her mother. She never ran up to share a box of bananas with Marina as Fifi always did with Flo. Nor did Miff beg for fruit from her mother if she herself had none, whereas Fifi not only begged persistently in such a situation, but was likely to fly into a tantrum if Flo withheld the food—screaming, hurling herself to the ground, flailing her arms. This often resulted in Flo's relenting and handing her daughter a banana, at least until Fifi was an adolescent about eight years old.

There are especially vivid recollections of the behavior of Marina and Flo toward their respective daughters during the termiting season. Once when Marina and Miff were working at the same heap I noticed that Marina was having little success at her hole, while a few yards away Miff's hole was working well. Marina walked over to her daughter and deliberately pushed her aside. Miff moved, whimpering slightly, and watched as Marina extracted a grassful of juicy termites. Then the child moved some yards from the heap, selected another long grass stem, and went to try her luck at a new hole. Just then Marina's own grass tool bent in the middle, and without hesitation she reached over and pulled the fine new stem from Miff's hand.

What a contrast was Flo's treatment of Fifi. Once, near the beginning of the season, Flo chose to work a termite heap that was largely covered with dead leaves. The openings of the nest passage were buried, so it took moments before Flo, scratching around, found a good place to work. Fifi wandered around also looking, but she could not find a good hole and finally she went to Flo and sat close, peering intently. Soon Fifi began to whimper, rocking slightly back and forth and inching her hand, in which she held a grass stem, toward her mother's hole. Presently, as Flo withdrew a stem, Fifi, after briefly looking up at her mother's face, cautiously poked her own tool into the hole. Patiently Flo waited until her daughter had pulled the stem out before once more poking her own down. This continued awhile and then Flo moved off and found another place to work. It was not long before Fifi's hole stopped yielding a good supply of insects and she again approached her mother and tried to share her hole. This time Flo gently pushed the child's hand away twice, but when Fifi began to whimper and rock to and fro her mother gave in and once more went off in search of a new place to work.

The young juvenile, particularly if her mother has a new infant, has to learn that it is now up to her to keep an eye on her mother and that it is not the other way around as in the past. If she does become accidentally separated, she usually is very upset. Even after Flint's birth old Flo nearly always waited for Fifi, but once when

Fifi was about five and a half she was so busy playing with an infant that she didn't notice Flo getting up to go. Flo, after looking around many times, gave up and wandered away with Flint.

As soon as Fifi realized her mother was no longer in the group she became agitated. Whimpering softly to herself, she rushed up a tall tree and ran from one side to the other, staring across the valley in different directions. Her soft calls of distress became loud grating screams. All at once she swung down and, still crying, hurried along a track. She chose the direction exactly opposite to the one her mother had taken. I followed Fifi. Every so often she climbed a tree and stared all about, and then, with her hair on end, started along the track again, crying and whimpering.

Just before dusk she came upon Olly and Gilka, but though Gilka kept approaching Fifi, grooming her, trying to play, Fifi ignored her friendly advances, and instead of remaining to sleep near Olly hurried off by herself again. She made a lonely nest at the top of a tall tree. I spent the night nearby; three times during the darkness I heard her calling out, screaming and whimpering.

Very early the next morning before it was light Fifi, whimpering, left her nest and ran off into the forest. It was not light enough for me to follow, so I returned to camp. Hugo told me Fifi had appeared, still whimpering and staring around, at about seven o'clock that morning and had then hurried off up the valley.

Two hours later Fifi arrived back in camp with Faben. Normally Faben paid scant attention to his sister, except to join her occasionally for a game; nevertheless, Fifi now seemed calm and relaxed in his company. They were still in camp when Flo arrived. We had expected a rapturous reunion, but instead Fifi merely hurried over to her mother and the two settled down to groom each other intently and vigorously. Since then we have seen other reunions between mothers and their lost children and each time the greeting has been unspectacular: the two merely have groomed one another, which is a further indication of the importance of social grooming in chimpanzee society.

One thing puzzling us is that whereas a mother will hurry toward the sound if she hears her lost child crying, she herself makes no loud call to indicate her whereabouts to the child. If when she reaches the determined location of the crying the child has moved out of earshot, it may be hours or even days before the two are reunited. Marina, as might be expected, seldom looked to see whether Miff was following when she left, so Miff's sad whimpering and crying as she searched for her mother were very common sounds when she was a five-year-old.

The male juvenile, although he also gets upset when he accidentally loses his mother, nevertheless may initiate his independence at a much earlier age than a female. Some juvenile males may move about with other chimps for several days at a time when they are only six years old.

Figan, however, spent most of his childhood roaming the mountains with Flo and Fifi. One day, when he was about six years old, he was with Flo and Fifi feeding in a large fig tree. A loud burst of pant-hooting and drumming announced the arrival of a large chimpanzee group in the valley. From the sounds it was obvious that they were climbing into some more fig trees farther up the stream. Flo and her family looked toward the sounds and hooted, and Figan swung through his tree, stamping on the branches, and so to the ground. He ran along the track toward the others, again breaking into pant-hoots and then drumming on the buttress of a tree. After this he paused and looked back toward Flo, obviously expecting that she would follow, but the old female was quite content where she was.

Eventually Figan turned and went on, but where the track wound out of sight he again stopped and looked back at Flo. After a moment he began to walk back toward his mother; then he stopped, looked once more toward the big group, turned around, and set off resolutely away from Flo and Fifi. This time he vanished from sight, and I heard his high-pitched pant-hoots farther along the track. Within four minutes he was back, walking in a nonchalant manner and hitting out at me as he passed, half playfully, half aggressively—the sort of gesture by which a human might try to cover a feeling of embarrassment.

Later on in the day Flo did join the big group. When she left to make her nest farther away, Figan quite deliberately chose to stay behind. He was away from his mother for two days, and they met again in camp. Fifi, who had missed her playmate, rushed up and embraced him, but Figan ignored her. Then, to complete the picture of the undemonstrative elder brother, he walked over to Flo and merely brushed the side of her face with his lips. Soon, though, he was tumbling about with his sister in evident enjoyment.

Male juveniles show much caution when interacting with their elders. It is probably their increasing respect for the adult males that leads to a reduction of or complete abstinence from the mounting of pink females which occurs so frequently in male infants. Although I have never seen a juvenile son who was frightened of his mother, as Miff was of Marina, nevertheless the male juvenile normally shows a good deal of respect for his mother.

One day I came across Figan with the freshly killed body of a colobus monkey. He climbed a tree with the tail of the monkey in one hand and the body slung over his shoulder. He was closely pursued by Fifi. When he reached a comfortable branch he sat and began eating, and Fifi, who was about three years old at the time, begged persistently. Several times Figan gave her small fragments of meat.

A few minutes later I saw Flo climbing toward Figan. Instantly he slung the carcass over his shoulder and climbed to a higher branch. Flo remained in a low fork, gazing around, not once looking at her son. He relaxed and began feeding again, though constantly he glanced somewhat apprehensively toward his mother. The old female sat there for a full ten minutes. Then, with only a preliminary fleeting glance at Figan, she very slowly climbed slightly higher, looking oh so nonchalant, and sat on the next branch up. Figan, glancing down even more frequently, continued to feed. The next time Flo casually climbed a little higher, Figan, feeling perhaps that she was getting too close, climbed higher too.

And so it went on. Flo's intentions were obvious to her son as well as to me. When he reached a very high position in the tree Flo could keep up her pretense no longer—without warning she rushed toward him. Figan with a scream leaped down into the foliage and vanished from sight, Fifi and Flo swinging in pursuit. I could not find them again.

14

THE ADOLESCENT

ADOLESCENCE IS A DIFFICULT and frustrating time for some chimpanzees just as it is for some humans. Possibly it is worse for males, in both species. The male chimpanzee becomes physically mature at puberty, when he is between seven and eight years old, but he still is nowhere near being full-grown—he weighs about forty pounds as compared to the hundred pounds of the fully mature male. And he still is far from socially mature; he will not be ranked among the mature males for another six or seven years. Although he is increasingly able to dominate, even terrorize females, in his interactions with the big males he must become ever more cautious in order to avoid arousing their aggression.

One of the most stabilizing factors for the adolescent male may well be his relationship with his mother. Old Flo, affectionate and tolerant with all her offspring, was frequently accompanied by Faben and Figan during their adolescence. Olly and Marina, both of whom were less relaxed and tolerant of their youngsters than Flo, were joined less often by their adolescent sons; nevertheless, we saw them together on many occasions. For the most part these adolescent males, even when they were ten or eleven years old, continued to show respect for their old mothers. If we offered a banana the son usually stood back and waited for his mother to take the fruit. Once I held a banana between Evered and Olly: both hesitated, and then both reached forward. Evered at once drew back his hand—but so did Olly, her lip wobbling as she turned quickly to glance at her son. Very gradually Evered's hair began to stand on end, but he made no further move, and Olly, with a series of nervous pant-grunts, finally reached for the banana.

On many occasions a mother will hurry to try to help her adolescent son. Once when Mr. Worzle attacked Faben, who was then about twelve, Flo, with hair on end and Flint clinging to her, rushed toward the scene of strife. As she approached, Faben's frightened screams instantly turned to angry *waa* barks and he began to display, standing upright and swaggering from foot to foot. Then mother and son, side by side, charged along the track toward old Mr. Worzle, Flo uttering loud barks in her hoarse voice and stamping on the ground in her fury. Mr. Worzle turned and fled.

When an adolescent is attacked by a high-ranking male there is little the mother can do, but she usually hurries up to see what is going on, and may utter *waa* barks in the background. Even timid Olly once hung about barking while Mike attacked Evered, and afterward, when her son had run off screaming, she crept submissively up to Mike, pant-grunting hysterically, and laid her hand on his back—as though to propitiate him for whatever rash act on the part of her son had led to the fight.

Of course, the relationship between mother and son does change somewhat as the young male grows older. When Figan rushed past Flo in a charging display at the age of seven, she completely ignored him—though other adult females normally fled. A year later, in contrast, Flo rushed out of Figan's way when he careened toward her, dragging a branch and with his hair on end looking twice his normal size. Nevertheless, in that same year we once saw Flo, during the excitement of banana-feeding, pound aggressively on Figan's back with her fists so that he ran off screaming.

As the adolescent male grows older he becomes increasingly likely to hurry to his mother's aid when *she* is threatened or attacked. One day the old mother Marina threatened Fifi. Fifi screamed, Flo ran to her daughter's assistance, and the two old females tumbled over in the dust. At this moment Marina's nine-year-old son Pepe, who had been feeding in a palm tree, noticed what was going on. He climbed rapidly from his tree and charged toward his mother. Flo, seeing him coming, turned and fled. Then Marina and Pepe chased Flo and Fifi away, and Flo, who had been able to make mincemeat out of Pepe only two years before, screamed in her hoarse voice until she choked with rage.

In his dealings with the higher-ranking males the adolescent must be cautious, because now, more than when he was a mere juvenile, an act of insubordination tends to bring severe retribution. Once when Leakey was enjoying a particularly large pile of bananas, we saw Pepe moving very cautiously toward him. Pepe obviously was half expecting some threatening gesture as a warning to keep his distance, for each time the mature male made a sudden movement Pepe jumped. Gradually, though, he got closer, and finally sat only a few feet away, with a huge grin of fear on his face. He reached hesitantly toward a banana, but his fear of Leakey caused him to withdraw his hand with sudden nervous squeaks. Again he reached out, and again caution got the better of him and he pulled back, screaming louder. Then Leakey leaned reassuringly toward Pepe and touched the young male on his mouth and in his groin. Pepe, however, still continued to make small fear-squeaks, until Leakey once more reached toward him and repeatedly patted the youngster's head and face. At last Pepe was calmed and gathered a small pile of bananas to take away and eat at a more comfortable distance from the mature male.

Many adult males are less tolerant than Leakey. In fact, on other occasions, in a different mood, Leakey might well have threatened rather than reassured Pepe, no matter how submissive the adolescent's approach had been. And there are times when, as a youngster sits at a distance watching a high-ranking male stuffing himself with food, the tension appears to build up to such a point that the adolescent has to give vent to his frustration in a charging display. Off he goes, crashing through the undergrowth and dragging branches. Even this may provoke a reprimand from one of the big males, since it appears that adult chimpanzees are often irritated by a lot of noise and commotion from a youngster. The adolescent may well be chased and even attacked for his ill-advised display. Figan learned this lesson quickly. Twice during the same week we saw Mike attack him after such displays. The following week, after rocking slightly in frustration as he watched Mike feeding, Figan, who had been unable to get any bananas for himself, suddenly got up and half walked, half ran away from the group.

As he went he gave loud whimpering calls like a child, until he
neared a huge buttressed tree that grew some hundred yards along
the main track. His whimpers became a series of high-pitched
adolescent pant-hoots as he leaped up at the buttresses of the tree
and drummed with his feet *de-dum, de-dum, de-dum.* Then he
came walking back along the path in that jaunty manner of his
and sat down again, seemingly quite relaxed and calm. Subsequently, Figan went off on his own to display and drum on the
tree on many occasions when he was frustrated in the presence of
his elders.

However, even Figan with all his skill in avoiding punishment
was often attacked as an adolescent; and others of his age seemed
to be attacked still oftener. Why then does the adolescent male so
frequently associate with mature males? Part of the answer probably lies in the fact that on most occasions aggressive incidents are,
as it were, "made up" very quickly—particularly those involving
young adolescent males. To many youngsters the need for friendly
physical contact from a male who has just threatened or attacked
them appears to be imperative.

One time Evered was attacked savagely by Goliath, simply because he got in his path during a charging display. At the end of
the incident Evered was bleeding and had lost great handfuls of
hair. Yet even so he followed Goliath as the big male walked away,
and when Goliath sat he crept cautiously toward him. Evered was
screaming loudly, and his fear of Goliath was such that he kept
turning and starting to move away. His desire for a reassuring touch
would prevail, though, and eventually, still screaming, he got close
enough to present his rump and crouch flat to the ground. After a
moment Goliath reached out and began to pat Evered's back, until
after fully one and a half minutes Evered's screams became whimpers, and he finally quieted altogether. Only then did Goliath stop
patting him.

Away from the artificial conditions of the feeding area, the aggression of the high-ranking males toward their subordinates is
much decreased, and the young adolescent male often appears more
relaxed in the company of adult males when in the forest. Usually
he does not join in the long sessions of social grooming so beloved
by his elders: he sits a few yards away from the mature males

grooming himself. When the group climbs into a tree to feed, the adolescent male often sits at a discreet distance from his superiors—at times he even feeds in a neighboring tree. When the mature males start their displays on arrival at some food source, the adolescent male sometimes keeps well out of the way until things have calmed down. Nevertheless, he is a part of the adult male group and therefore able to learn from his superiors; young chimpanzees almost certainly do learn a good deal simply from watching others of their kind. The growing female can learn much from her mother that will benefit her in later life, particularly when a new sibling is born. Since the young male has no father as such—no male, that is, who is attached permanently to the family group—he must leave his mother and deliberately seek out adult male company.

When the frustrations of being with individuals so dominant to him become too great, the adolescent male either travels with his mother for a while or, frequently, by himself. As they grew older nearly all the adolescent males we have known have spent long periods—hours or even days—completely out of sight and often out of earshot of other chimpanzees. This aloneness, on some occasions anyway, is quite definitely deliberate. I once followed Figan when as an eight-year-old he set off with a large group of adult males and females. For an hour he remained with the others, but when they climbed into a tree to feed he moved on by himself. Soon he too climbed to eat figs, and twenty minutes later swung to the ground and traveled on, continuing to head away from the group. The following day he visited the feeding area, still on his own, and he was alone when he left. That evening, however, he joined up with Flo and Fifi.

We have watched several splendid young males aged between thirteen and fifteen gradually leaving adolescence behind them as they entered the dominance hierarchy of the socially mature males. Faben and Pepe, who were about the same age, not only displayed frequently and vigorously at each other in their competition for dominance, but also began to display at the lower-ranking mature males. It may well be that the charging display is particularly adaptive in this respect. Earlier I discussed the possibility that during such a display the male chimpanzee might lose many of his social inhibitions. This could explain why a young male may actually charge toward a chimpanzee to whom during less frenzied moments he would show great respect. Even a high-ranking male may on occasions move out of the way of a vigorously displaying adolescent. If an adolescent is able to displace low-ranking adult males frequently enough, this will undoubtedly increase his self-confidence; and possibly the pattern of dominance will be permanently disrupted. Certainly it seems that the more spectacular and violent his charging display, the more likely the youngster is to break into the hierarchy of his elders. After a while both Faben and Pepe began to hold their ground and even retaliate when lower-ranking adults threatened them. They started to join in grooming sessions with Rodolf and Leakey and David Graybeard, the more tolerant of the high-ranking males. They charged into camp along with the other big males and took their turn at courting attractive females during the frenzy of excitement after arriving at a food source, instead of waiting until things were calm and their elders less worked up. Their period of apprenticeship was over. From then on, their rise in the dominance ladder would depend on individual intelligence and determination rather than on slow maturing of their physical selves.

The female chimpanzee also becomes adolescent at about seven years. She starts to show very small and irregularly occurring swellings of her sex skin, although she will not menstruate or become sexually attractive to the mature males for another two years or so. She, too, must be cautious in her dealings with her social superiors; in her case, the adult females and adolescent males as well as the adult males. And she may be threatened by the precocious juvenile offspring of high-ranking mothers.

When Fifi became an adolescent there was no discernible change in her relations with her mother, except that gradually Flo became less tolerant of her daughter's sharing her food. Fifi continued to follow Flo through the forests, to nest near her mother at night, and to help look after the four-year-old Flint. When Fifi was threatened or attacked Flo usually hurried to help her and Fifi would sometimes back up her mother. We have only been able to observe interactions between one other mother with her adolescent daughter. Like Flo and Fifi, these two usually traveled around together, but otherwise their relationship seemed very different: in feeding situations she was obviously afraid of her mother, and we never saw either of them show concern if the other was threatened or attacked. There was, in fact, little of the relaxed and friendly comradeship that existed between Flo and Fifi, although in both cases mother and daughter spent much time grooming each other.

At this age the young female is, if anything, even more fascinated by infants than she was as a juvenile. Not only does she frequently carry an infant short distances, play with and groom it, but she also shows concern for its welfare. When Pooch was about eight years old she once carried a six-month-old infant up a tree and began to groom him. It so happened that the tip of a palm frond, swaying gently in the breeze, occasionally brushed past Pooch's shoulders as she sat there. I noticed that the infant was watching this frond as though fascinated. All at once he grabbed hold of it, wriggling off Pooch's lap, and the frond swung with his weight back toward the trunk of the palm tree. For a moment Pooch stared after the infant as if she couldn't believe her eyes; her face contorted in a huge grin of fear. Frantically she climbed down her tree and rushed up another, from a branch of which she was just able to reach the frond as it swung like a pendulum back toward her. Then she seized the infant, who was not at all frightened and probably thoroughly enjoying the swing, and hugged him tight. The grin of fright only slowly left her face.

After about a year of adolescence the sexual swelling of the female gradually becomes larger, but it does not yet equal the proportions of the fully adult swelling. Even at this stage the mature males show no interest, though male infants constantly mount these young females when they are pink; at this stage the female seems to welcome such attention from her tiny suitors, and is usually quick to present, crouching very low when they approach. One young female actually pulled Flint away when he was mating another, then crouched to the ground as she solicited his attention herself.

Finally, however, the day comes when a female develops a swelling that attracts the mature males—usually when she is about nine years old. I remember well the day when Pooch showed her first grownup pinkness. First one, then another of the adult males approached her with their hair erect, shook branches at her, swag-

gered from foot to foot, or hunched their shoulders. Almost all of
the gestures of courtship are also part of threatening behavior.
Pooch screamed continuously and fled, but the males followed her
and their courtship became increasingly aggressive. Eventually
Pooch turned and rushed toward them, crouching close to the
ground and screaming as at last the males mounted her. After the
sexual act she rushed away, still screaming. Her fright and bewilderment on that first day were only too obvious. By the second day
she had calmed down somewhat, and though she still screamed
when a male approached her she appeared far less terrified.

Fifi's sexual development was quite different from Pooch's and
also different from that of any other young female we have watched
to date. In fact she was probably the chimpanzee equivalent of a
nymphomaniac. About six months before she developed her first
truly adult swelling, Fifi showed an almost fanatical interest in the
sexual behavior of older females. Sometimes she would trail after
Pooch or Gigi or one of the others when they were pink and was
thus close at hand when they mated. And when such moments
came, Fifi either jumped onto the pink female's back, pushing her
own little bottom as close to the male as she could, or she rushed
around behind the pair and pressed her bottom against the male's
as he mated.

When Fifi finally achieved a full swelling of her own she showed
none of Pooch's terror, but responded instantly to the slightest
sign of sexual interest in any of the males. Indeed, she often fore-
stalled them, hurrying up and presenting before they had even
looked in her direction. When these first pink days at last ended,
Fifi, it seemed, could not believe it. The first morning we saw her
hurry up to Mike, turn and present her rump, and crouch, solicit-
ing mating. For a few moments she remained motionless, then
she looked at him over her shoulder as though wondering why he
did not respond. She backed an inch toward him, still watching.
Ultimately Mike reached out, made a few grooming movements
on her rump, and moved away. Slowly Fifi sat up, staring after
him as if in amazement. Not long afterward Evered came into
camp. Fifi rushed over to him and repeated her solicitation. Again
and again she backed toward him, again and again he inched out
of the way. The last time she backed, he had just turned to look

elsewhere and Fifi caught him off balance. Evered all but toppled over backward before scrambling to his feet and making haste to increase the distance between himself and this importunate young female.

Fifi continued to present in this way for two more days and then evidently resigned herself to the fact that she was no longer attractive. We couldn't help laughing when during her next period of pinkness we constantly saw her reclining on her side with one hand draped as though protectively over her pink swelling—for all the world as if she was determined that *this* time it would not vanish so mysteriously.

For the next year Fifi evidenced a keen desire for sexual contact during her pink days. She took to hanging about, either in camp or somewhere in the valley, where she could observe the chimpanzees who arrived for bananas. If a male arrived she would often rush over and solicit mating. Although the adult males did not show quite the enthusiasm for the daughter as they had for the mother, they usually responded to her invitations.

We were interested to discover that Fifi was extremely reluctant to be mated by her brothers. She even prevented little Flint from mounting her—though in the days before her first true swelling she had shown no objection whatsoever. Moreover, though Faben and Figan were observed to mate with their sister—after much screaming on her part—subsequent sexual interactions between the siblings occurred rarely.

There was one chaotic period when Flo and Fifi went pink together. The males had an exhausting eight days or so, and the chimps moved about in a huge group of more than twenty individuals. Every time that Flo was mated Fifi and Flint rushed over to interfere by pushing at the male's face, and afterward Fifi would solicit mating herself. And every time that Fifi was mated Flo and Flint would rush up and interfere, after which the male would usually mate with Flo. Added to this usually there were two or more infants other than Flint also rushing up to interfere, so that sometimes the mating couple would be almost invisible beneath the cluster of chimpanzees that were all getting in the way. It was one of the rare occasions when chimpanzees other than infants were observed interfering with mating.

It seems significant that during this flurry of sexual activity we never observed copulation between Flo and either of her socially mature sons. Indeed, one day Flo was mated by every physically mature male of the group with the exceptions of Faben and Figan. Nor did we ever see Evered copulate with his mother when she was pink.

Of the nine females whose progress during adolescence we have been able to watch, not one has given birth until at least two years after her first adult swelling. The same is often true of captive individuals. Exactly what physiological processes are at work we do not yet understand. Certainly, though, the time lag is beneficial to a wild chimpanzee female: at nine years of age she is not socially mature, nor is she completely full-grown, and she has quite enough to cope with without the added burden and responsibility of a baby.

15

ADULT RELATIONSHIPS

IN HUMAN SOCIETIES there is no definite point in time at which the pimples and awkwardness of youth give place to the assurance of young woman- or manhood. The change gradually takes place over a period of many months; one day, to their surprise, the parents of a child realize that he is a child no longer. It is the same with the chimpanzee.

It was one hot day in the summer of 1966, as I watched the old mother Marina and her children, that I suddenly knew Pepe was indeed a splendidly mature male, an adolescent no longer. I could see the muscles taut beneath his sleek coat as with both hands he pushed a short thick length of stick backward and forward in the entrance of an underground bees' nest to enlarge the opening. Clustered around him were two females, his old mother Marina and his sibling, the juvenile female Miff. All three seemed insensitive to the swarm of infuriated bees buzzing around them, but the infant of the family, little Merlin, had rushed up a tree some distance away when the others had begun raiding the nest for honey and grubs.

After a few moments Pepe put his stick aside and waited while Marina reached down with her hand and withdrew a section of honeycomb. Then he reached in and took out some crushed waxen cells for himself. Miff did not dare take any of the treat but she watched intently as the other two ate, her face only an inch or two from Pepe's mouth.

Fifteen minutes later Pepe wandered away from the empty nest.

Marina felt inside once more before following him, and Miff finally got her hand down into the hole and time and again licked from her fingers the slightly sweet earth. Then she too followed her brother into the shade of a large tree. Merlin swung from his branch and made a generous detour through the trees to join the rest of his family.

Pepe began to groom with Marina, Miff climbed into a tree to feed on the leaves of a vine, and Merlin swung to and fro above his mother and brother, hitting toward Pepe's head with one hand. Presently he dropped down, landing on his brother's shoulder, and with a wide play-face pulled at Pepe's hand. Idly Pepe tickled the infant while he continued to groom Marina with the other hand. Encouraged, Merlin became more vigorous, standing upright and pulling at the hair on Pepe's shoulders, crawling onto him, pushing between Pepe and his mother.

A casual observer passing by would without doubt have fancied that he saw a typical family group—a mother with her two young children and her mate. Because we had watched these chimpanzees over a number of years, we knew Pepe was her son. In chimpanzee communities, of course, family groups comprise only a mother and some or all of her offspring; the father, apart from his necessary contribution to the conception of a child, plays no further part in its development. In fact, neither we nor the chimpanzees normally have any idea as to which male was responsible for siring which child.

This exclusion of the male from familial responsibilities is perhaps one of the major differences between human and chimpanzee societies, for most human family groups look upon the father not only as the begetter of the children but as the protector, and usually as the provider of food, or land, or money. Admittedly things are changing today in certain parts of the world where women are demanding equality and where free love results in large numbers of unmarried mothers—but these things are only happening in a very small minority of cultures if the peoples of the world are considered as a whole.

Obviously, human families vary enormously in structure. The smallest unit—the husband, wife, and children—can be extended to include two or two hundred wives and any number of blood relations and relations by marriage. As yet we do not know whether the chimpanzee family group ever expands to include grandchildren as an integral part of the unit. Certainly, though, it can never include the "wife" or children of a male offspring or the "husband" of a female offspring.

Despite this basic difference in the structure of the human and the chimpanzee family group, the behavior of some human males is not so different from chimpanzee males as might be expected. In the Western world at any rate, many fathers, even though they may be materially responsible for their families' welfare, spend much time away from their wives and children—often in the company of other men. All-male groups are popular in many cultures: they range from clubs and stag parties in the Western world to initiation and warrior groups in primitive societies. In short, a vast number of human males, although they may be only too anxious at times for feminine company, are equally keen for much of the time to "get away from women" and relax in the ease of male companionship. Chimpanzee males seem to feel rather the same. Naturally they cluster around pink females when these are available, but often they travel about and feed in all-male groups and are more likely to groom each other than they are to groom females or youngsters.

Never, however, have we seen anything that could be regarded as homosexuality in chimpanzees. Admittedly a male may mount another in moments of stress or excitement, clasping the other around the waist, and he may even make thrusting movements of the pelvis, but there is no intromission. It is true, also, that a male may try to calm himself or another male by reaching out to touch or pat the other's genitals; while we still have much to learn about this type of behavior, it certainly does not imply homosexuality. He only does this in moments of stress, and he will touch or pat a female on her genitals in exactly the same contexts. Figan, in fact, frequently touches his own scrotum in moments of sudden apprehension.

What about the normal heterosexual relationships that may develop between human beings and those that may be observed between chimpanzees? The obvious difference between the two species lies in the fact that men and women are capable of establishing and maintaining monogamous relationships both physical and spiritual of long duration, and this sort of bond is not known in the chimpanzee. Monogamy, however, is far from being the only relationship found between men and women. Actually, human males the world over tend to be promiscuous. In some cultures this is acceptable and men are permitted or even expected to have more than one wife. In other societies, where monogamy is the rule, it is nevertheless an acknowledged fact that unmarried and even married males will indulge in love affairs, or pick up women for a night, or visit brothels. Many young girls too will show promiscuous sexual behavior if given the chance. It may, in fact, be that what we think of as true love—an emotion that encompasses both the body and the mind of the beloved, that mellows with time and brings about harmony of living, that removes any need in the man or the woman concerned for another sexual partner—is, indeed, one of the rarest of human heterosexual relationships.

Sexual relationships between male and female chimpanzees are in large part similar to those that can be observed among many young people in England and America today. In other words, chimpanzees are very promiscuous, but this does not mean that every female will accept every male who courts her.

One young female, slightly older than Fifi, showed a marked objection to the advances of the aggressive male Humphrey. Gigi invariably had a large male retinue when she went pink—from the first time she had shown a true adult swelling it seemed that she had as much sexual appeal as Flo; but she simply could not bear Humphrey. When all the other males were satisfied, there would be Humphrey, his hair on end, glaring at Gigi, shaking branches, hunching his shoulders, stamping with his foot on the ground, moving cautiously toward her. All the while Gigi would be screaming and moving away from him. Sometimes Humphrey gave chase, but though he once shook her out of the tree in which she had sought refuge we never saw him actually "rape" her. Nonetheless, quite often he managed to get his way through dogged persistence. He went on courting her every time she went pink. His persistence was certainly rewarded eventually, for two years later Gigi seemed almost to prefer Humphrey to any other male.

Fifi also avoided Humphrey, though she was less frightened of him than Gigi had been and merely walked calmly away when he began to court her. Once we watched Fifi walking and cantering around a tree no less than fifteen times with Humphrey pursuing her, all his hair bristling. He could easily have caught her; instead, he finally charged away in a wild display of frustration, hurling huge rocks, stamping his feet, and vanishing completely from the scene. Similarly, other females avoid other males.

Sometimes a male chimpanzee will actually insist on an unwilling female accompanying him on his travels until he is no longer interested in her, or until she manages to escape. This sort of masculine assertion of power led to a number of "new" females being introduced to the feeding area in the old days. Hugo and I once saw J.B. bustling down the slope, while behind him, peering nervously in our direction, was one of the old mothers with her three-year-old infant. She had never been to camp before, so we two humans speedily hid in one of the tents. As the pair came closer the female stopped, staring. Suddenly J.B. looked around and saw that she was not following. Standing upright he seized a sapling and swayed it from side to side until, with a whimper, the female hurried toward him and reached to touch his side submissively. Her infant climbed a tree, where he remained throughout most of the proceedings.

J.B. set off again, but once more, after a few steps, the newcomer stopped, terrified by our tents. Just as J.B. looked back she turned to flee; quickly the big male pounded in pursuit, leaped onto her back, and attacked her by stamping with his feet. The female, screaming loudly, escaped, but she only ran a short way and then turned, hurried back to J.B., and crouched in submission until he reached out and repeatedly patted her on the head. Once more he moved on. This time she followed—but only for a few yards. J.B. again swayed a sapling, and her fear of him overcame her fear of the strange place to which he was leading her, so she hurried to his side. Finally she followed him right into the feeding clearing. To our surprise (for J.B. was normally possessive of his food), she was permitted to take a large share of his bananas.

The strangest part of the story lies in the fact that this female showed no sign of a sexual swelling. For three days J.B. forced her to accompany him into camp, and then he appeared without her. When some twelve days later I saw the same female, fully pink, together with a whole retinue of male suitors, J.B. showed no more interest in her than did any of the others. This sort of thing happens over and over, although some males only force sexually attractive females to follow them.

Leakey and Mr. Worzle, more than any other males, have constantly forced different females to accompany them for days on end. For a long time both of them picked on nervous Olly—again, often when she had no sign of a swelling. We never saw both of them with her at the same time; it was either one or the other.

When Fifi had been going pink regularly for about a year and most of the adult males were less interested in her than they had been at first, Leakey picked on her. Sometimes it was evident that Fifi was not at all loath to follow the old male. When she wanted to escape she usually edged away cautiously while Leakey's attention was elsewhere, but hurried back to him instantly if he spotted her maneuver—before he had time, as it were, to get angry with her.

One day we shall never forget. Leakey at that time had become most peculiarly preoccupied with females. Constantly he forced first one and then another to accompany him. On this occasion he had just lost his current victim and was sitting eating bananas in camp when Fifi arrived on the scene. She was pink, and instantly, his bananas forgotten, Leakey stood up, hair bristling, and shook branches at her. And then she ran quickly up to him and presented. He mated her and then the two sat grooming each other. Suddenly Leakey looked up and saw Olly approaching camp. Immediately all his hair stood on end again and he began waving branches at *her*. Olly hurried up and Leakey began to groom her. Fifi, looking innocent, walked very slowly away; but Leakey noticed, his hair rose once more, and Fifi ran back pant-grunting in submission. Next, Leakey tried to get both his females to follow, but neither wanted to go with him. He glared and shook branches at one until she ran up, and then at the other.

And so it went on until the strain and tension seemed abruptly to overwhelm Leakey. Even as Fifi obediently approached him he ran at her and attacked her, rolling her over and over on the ground. At this Olly made a silent and rapid getaway and was soon lost to sight. The attack over, Leakey stood puffing from the exertion, hair still on end, while Fifi, crouching to the ground, screamed without letup.

When Leakey noticed that Olly had gone he rushed some distance up the slope, peered in all directions, ran to the other side of the clearing, and looked around from there. And thus Fifi escaped. Not for ten minutes or more did Leakey's hair slowly sink, as he gave up the search and eventually settled down to eat some bananas.

The relationship that the large Rodolf struck up with Flo, described earlier, was of course rather different. Rodolf showed none of the bullying aggressive behavior toward Flo which characterized the relationships of Leakey and the others with the females of their choice. Rodolf followed Flo wherever she went, and it was to him that she most often turned for comfort when she was hurt or upset. Also, Rodolf remained with Flo and her family for two weeks after her swelling had vanished.

It is obviously fruitless to speculate as to the sort of heterosexual relationships that might develop if chimpanzee physiology were different: if, for example, Flo had been able to offer Rodolf continuing sexual satisfaction, if the female reproductive cycle of the chimp were the same as the human cycle. The fact remains: female chimpanzees have evolved in such a way that they are only sexually receptive to males for a mere ten days per month—provided they are neither pregnant nor lactating, which in older females means they may be denied sexual activity for up to five years. Along with this limited quota of sexual opportunities, evolution has landed them with ungainly sexual swellings.

Many times, as I have watched a hugely swollen female chimpanzee adjusting her position time and time again, trying to get comfortable on some branch or hard rock, I have thanked evolution for sparing human females a similar periodic disfigurement—though the designers and manufacturers of bustles would, I suppose, have been in clover. Why, in heaven's name, has the female chimpanzee been so encumbered? At times the answer seems simple. One day I was sitting with Goliath and David Graybeard, who were peacefully grooming each other. All of a sudden Goliath stared fixedly across the valley, and seconds later David followed suit. Even I with my naked eye soon spotted what looked like a large pink flower gleaming in a thickly foliaged tree. Already both males were off, moving fast through the undergrowth. I knew I could not keep up with them, so I stayed where I was and in time watched both Goliath and David swing up into the tree, swagger around in the branches, and mate with the female.

In cases such as this the swelling without doubt acts as a signal; and this, of course, can be important in a community where the members split up so freely and even females often wander about on their own. This is especially so if one realizes that all chimp females are not so forward as Fifi. Olly, to cite one, sometimes seemed to try to hide completely away from males during her pink days. But there is a snag in this theory. If female chimpanzees developed conspicuous pink bottoms in order to signal to prospective suitors over a distance, then why did female baboons develop swellings? They show enlargements quite as obvious as those of chimpanzees, and most baboons live in close groups where females are seldom out of sight of the males. There are other arguments that could be put forward, but since none of them can be applied equally to chimps, baboons, and the few other monkeys who show sexual swellings, there is little point in discussing them. To confuse the issue further, orangutans, which live in even more widely scattered units and thicker forests than most chimps, do not develop swellings at all. The reason for swellings must for the moment, perhaps for ever, remain something of a mystery.

Young female chimpanzees (even those with small infants) cycle much more regularly than old females. Flo and Olly, for instance, did not develop swellings for five years after the respective births of Flint and Gilka; nor did they show swellings during the early months of pregnancy. Melissa and other young females, in contrast, not only cycled throughout four or more months of their eight-month pregnancies, but also started to show swellings again when their infants were barely more than one year old. And it is primarily in young females that we see indications of quite stable preferences for individual males, and vice versa.

Figan was faithful to Pooch for over half a year—by which I mean not that he ignored other pink females, but that every time Pooch went pink during a six-month period the two went off together. So far as we know they were on their own at such times; certainly they did not visit camp, where without question Pooch would have met other males.

Once I saw them going off together on the third day of Pooch's swelling. I followed. When they were about a quarter of a mile from camp they climbed into a tree and groomed each other for over an hour. Then they wandered on, fed for a while, and as dusk fell climbed into another tree and made nests quite close to each other. I did not see them mating at all during that time. The next morning, when I arrived at their sleeping tree at dawn, they mated once before wandering off peacefully together to feed.

Six days later Pooch, her swelling shriveled, arrived at the feeding area on her own. About half an hour later Figan appeared, coming from the same direction, but they went off on their separate ways. We noticed that they never returned from such "honeymoons" together—it was as though they didn't want to be found out. The reason for the separate return probably lay in the fact that they only started to travel toward camp when Figan was no longer sexually interested in Pooch, and so on the way they had gradually drifted apart.

We shall never know how that relationship would have matured because unfortunately Pooch died when she was about ten years old. Since then Figan has often gone off in the same way with Melissa. They wander the forests together, Goblin accompanying them, and actual mating, as opposed to grooming and just being near each other, has only been observed rather infrequently. Interestingly enough, Faben also shows the same preference for Melissa, and recently Melissa and Goblin spent most of their time first with one brother and then with the other.

However, although such relationships may be shadowy forerunners of human love affairs, I cannot conceive of chimpanzees developing emotions, one for the other, comparable in any way to the tenderness, the protectiveness, tolerance, and spiritual exhilaration that are the hallmarks of human love in its truest and deepest sense. Chimpanzees usually show a lack of consideration for each other's feelings which in some ways may represent the deepest part of the gulf between them and us. For the male and female chimpanzee there can be no exquisite awareness of each other's body—let alone each other's mind. The most the female can expect of her suitor is a brief courtship display, a sexual contact lasting at most half a minute, and, sometimes, a session of social grooming afterward. Not for them the romance, the mystery, the boundless joys of human love.

When I first began studying chimpanzees I often wondered

whether a male and a female ever slept together at night. One evening I watched as a young female carefully tucked in the small leafy twigs that stuck out around her nest. Then she lay down. It was just light enough for me to see her lying there, about fifty yards away. A few moments later she sat up, and then, to my surprise, left her nest, climbed higher up the tree, and presently appeared at the edge of Mr. McGregor's nest. The old male sat up and began to groom her. Five minutes later, though, he turned away and lay down, and she left him to return to her own bed. When she finally settled down it was almost pitch-dark—but soon the moon would be up.

As I hastened down the mountain to camp, I determined to return later on and spend the night with the chimps. I had supper, wrote out my notes for the day, and then, at about eleven o'clock, set off once more. The mountains and valleys were very quiet and still under the full moon; in the coolness of night I always felt that I could run up the steep slopes. After reaching the Peak I decided to have some coffee before the start of my vigil, so I gathered a few twigs, lit a small fire, and hung my kettle on its waiting chain. Then I took my mug of coffee to the rocky perch overlooking the home valley. Below me the moonlight was reflected from the myriads of leaves forming the upper canopy of the forest, glistening brightly on the smooth shiny green of the palm fronds. Somewhere down there a baboon barked twice and then was silent. Behind me the darkness of the forest was closer; it was easy to imagine a leopard slinking through the trees, a herd of buffalo browsing the dank undergrowth.

I drank my coffee slowly, awed by the beauty around me. The moonlight was so bright that only the most brilliant stars were shining, and the gray mist of the sky clung around the mountain peaks and spilled down into the valley below. It was a perfect night for love—for human love. When I clambered down to the place from where I had watched the chimpanzees earlier, I could see, through my binoculars, that the two chimps were still respectfully separate. Mr. McGregor was flat on his back. The female was lying on her side, facing away from me, and I could just make out the pale gleam of her shell-pink swelling.

At about four o'clock the moon sank behind the mountains of

the Congo on the far side of the lake, and gradually even its lingering glow in the sky had faded. Then the night seemed very different—inky black and sinister with rustlings and crackling twigs everywhere. About an hour later the baboon troop in the valley below began to bark loudly, and after a few moments the chimpanzees joined in with their fierce *waa* barks and loud pant-hoots. I guessed there was a leopard prowling along the valley and pulled the blanket closer around me. Now the night seemed less romantic, but I would have been glad to have Hugo's masculinity close beside me just the same.

Eventually the grayness of dawn filtered through the sky and the everyday world began to emerge. There was no movement from the chimpanzees' tree. As it grew lighter I saw that the female and Mr. McGregor were still in their separate nests. At about six-fifteen the old male turned over, sat up, and then suddenly swung from his nest, and, moving rapidly through the tree, leaped right into the female's bed. She, almost certainly wakened from a deep sleep, uttered a piercing shriek and jumped out of her nest. Mr. McGregor rushed after her, down through the wildly swaying branches to the ground. Gradually her screams grew fainter as she fled through the forest, her impetuous suitor in hot pursuit. Not a very romantic ending to the night, perhaps, but it certainly showed that the female was very much in old McGregor's mind when he woke up that morning.

It was some years later—when Figan and Melissa were off on one of their trips—that just before darkness fell Figan moved from the branch where he had been sitting, chewing some food, and went toward Melissa's nest. The foliage was too thick to watch his progress, but there were no further sounds: none of the snappings of branches and twigs and the rustling of leaves that usually accompany the making of a nest. In the morning, after the chimpanzees had left, we peered from as many vantage points as possible to try to determine how many nests there were. The tangle of branches and palm fronds was very thick, and it is quite possible that we missed something, but none of us saw more than one nest. We all saw the same one—in the place where Melissa had made her bed the evening before. Had Figan and Melissa, perhaps, slept curled up together, with little Goblin to keep them company?

16

BABOONS AND PREDATION

FIGAN SAT IN THE SHADE and groomed himself, and about ten other chimps groomed or lay resting in small groups that were scattered around the camp clearing. One adult male baboon was in camp also, cracking open palm-nut kernels with his powerful teeth, and a juvenile baboon fed on the ripe fruit in one of the camp palm trees.

When Figan got up and began to walk in the tree's direction something in his gait, some tenseness in his posture caused Mike to look toward him intently. Briefly Figan glanced up at the young baboon and then, very slowly, began to climb the trunk. As he climbed higher, the baboon peered down at him and started to make little shrill sounds, showing its teeth in a frightened grin. Then it jumped across to the crown of a neighboring palm. Figan paused for a moment when he was at the top of his tree and very slowly moved after the baboon. Screeching louder now, the youngster jumped back to its original tree. Figan followed. Twice more, still moving slowly, Figan went after his quarry from the original to the second tree and back again. And then, quite suddenly, he rushed toward the baboon, which, terrified, took a huge leap into a tree some twenty feet below.

By this time all the chimpanzees on the ground were intensely interested in the chase and stood gazing up, many of them with their hair on end. As the baboon leaped so Mike rushed up the tree toward it—at the same moment when the adult male baboon came racing to the scene uttering loud roaring sounds. The quarry, screaming loudly, took a second leap to the ground. Mike jumped down and chased after it, the male baboon chased Mike, and, in the ensuing confusion from the milling around of other chimpanzees, the intended victim escaped.

Four years earlier, when Figan had been a young adolescent, Hugo and I had watched him creeping toward another juvenile baboon in a large fig tree. It had been Rodolf, so far as we could tell, who had actually initiated that hunt; he had walked toward the tree and stood, his hair very slightly on end; if he had looked at the baboon at all, we had not noticed. Yet, as though at a signal, the chimpanzees who had been resting and grooming peacefully on the ground had got up and stationed themselves close to trees that would act as escape routes for the intended victim. And Figan, the youngest adolescent male of the group, had crept toward the baboon.

On that occasion too the prey had escaped; in response to its calls the whole baboon troop had rushed some hundred yards to the scene, and chimps and baboons had engaged in fierce conflict. Despite the fact that they had leaped at each other and called loudly, so far as we could see no physical damage had been inflicted on members of either side, and the young baboon had made its getaway in the confusion.

During the ten years that have passed since I began work at the Gombe Stream we have recorded chimpanzees feeding on the young of bushbucks, bushpigs, and baboons, as well as both young and small adult red colobus monkeys, redtail monkeys, and blue monkeys. And there are two cases on record of chimpanzees in the area actually taking off African babies—presumably as prey, since when recovered from an adult male chimpanzee one infant had had its limbs partially eaten. Luckily these incidents occurred before I ever set foot at the Gombe Stream in other words, before I had "tamed" the chimpanzees.

Many people are horrified when they hear that a chimpanzee might eat a human baby, but after all, so far as the chimpanzee is concerned, men are only another kind of primate, not so very different from baboons in *their* eyes. Surely it should be equally horrifying to reflect on the fact that in a great many places throughout their range chimpanzees are considered a delicacy by humans?

Until recently, although we saw chimpanzees eating meat fairly frequently, those occasions when we were able to watch their hunting techniques were few and far between. During the past two years, however, with more people working at the Gombe and with the chimpanzees so tolerant of their human observers, we have been able to learn a good deal about their way of hunting. Sometimes it appears that the capture of a prey is almost accidental; the chimpanzee, as he wanders along, stumbles across a baby bushpig, grabs it, and the kill is made. On other occasions the hunting seems to be a much more deliberate, purposeful activity, and often at such times the different individuals of a chimpanzee group show quite remarkable cooperation—as when different chimpanzees station themselves at the bases of trees offering escape routes to a cornered victim.

I myself have only seen the actual killing of a prey animal on two occasions: once on that far-off day when Hugo and I watched a red colobus monkey seized and torn to pieces; and once, four years later, when a juvenile baboon was caught on the outskirts of camp. That was much more spectacular.

It happened one morning when Rodolf, Mr. McGregor, Humphrey, and an adolescent male were sitting replete with bananas and the baboon troop was passing through the camp area. All at once Rodolf got up and moved rapidly behind one of the buildings, followed by the other three. They all walked with the same silent, purposeful, almost stealthy pace that Figan had shown as he approached the palm tree harboring his intended prey. I followed, but even so I was too late to observe the actual capture. As I rounded the building I heard the sudden screaming of a baboon and a few seconds afterward the roaring of male baboons and the screaming and barking of chimpanzees. Running the last few yards, through some thick bushes I glimpsed Rodolf standing upright as he swung the body of a juvenile baboon above him by one of its legs and slammed its head down onto some rocks. Whether or not that was the actual death blow I could not tell. Certainly the victim was dead as Rodolf, carrying it in one hand, set off rapidly up the slope.

The other chimps followed him closely, still screaming, and a number of adult male baboons continued to harass Rodolf, lunging at him and roaring. This lasted only for a few minutes. Then, to my surprise, they gave up. Presently the four chimpanzees appeared from the undergrowth and climbed into the higher branches of a tall tree, where Rodolf settled down and began to feed, tearing into the tender flesh of the belly and groin of his prey.

Other chimpanzees in the valley, attracted by the loud screaming and calling that typifies a hunt and kill, soon appeared in the tree, and a group of high-ranking males clustered around Rodolf, begging for a share of his kill. Often I have watched chimpanzees begging for meat, and usually a male who has a reasonably large portion permits at least some of the group to share with him. Rodolf, on the contrary, protected his kill jealously that day. When Mike stretched out his hand, palm upward in the begging gesture, Rodolf pushed it away. When Goliath reached a hand to his mouth, begging for the wad of meat and leaves Rodolf was chewing, Rodolf turned his back. When J.B. gingerly took hold of part of the carcass, Rodolf gave soft threat barks, raised his arm, and jerked the meat away. And when old Mr. McGregor reached up and tentatively took hold of the end of a dangling piece of gut, it was only by pure luck that yards of intestine fell into his eager hands and festooned his bald crown and shoulders. Rodolf looked down and pulled at his lost food; the gut broke, and Gregor hurried to a distant part of the tree, where a group of females and youngsters quickly gathered around to beg tidbits from him.

Chimpanzees nearly always eat meat slowly, usually chewing leaves with each new mouthful as though to savor the taste for as long as possible. All in all, Rodolf kept almost the entire carcass to himself for nine hours that day, although from time to time he spat a wad of meat and leaves into a begging hand, or one of the other males managed to grab a piece from the carcass and make off with it. Sometimes small scraps fell, and then the youngsters were down the tree like a flash to search for the fragments in the undergrowth below. Often, too, I saw them actually licking the branches of the tree where the kill had touched them or where drops of blood presumably had fallen.

At this time, the third year of Mike's supremacy, Rodolf was no longer the very high-ranking male he had been when first we knew him. How was it, then, that he dared push away Mike's hand, he who normally went into a frenzy of submission when Mike approached him? How dared he threaten Goliath and J.B., who were normally dominant to him? Even more puzzling—why did not these higher-ranking males snatch at least a part of the kill away from Rodolf? I had seen this sort of apparent inconsistency before during meat-eating episodes and I often wondered whether the chimps perhaps were showing the crude beginnings of a sense of moral values. Rodolf killed the baboon; the meat, therefore, was Rodolf's. More serious consideration of the behavior has led me to suspect that something rather different may be involved.

Mike would have attacked Rodolf without hesitation had the prize been a pile of bananas, yet if Rodolf had gathered the fruits from a box for himself they would have been his property quite as legitimately as was the meat. I wonder, then, if the principle involved may be similar to the one governing a territorial animal within his own territory, when he is more aggressive, more likely to fight off an intruder, than if he met the same animal outside his territorial boundary. Meat is a much liked, much prized food item. An adult male in possession of such a prize may become more willing to fight for it, and, therefore, be less apprehensive of his superiors than if he has a pile of everyday fruits like bananas. In support of this theory, I should emphasize that in the early days of feeding, when bananas themselves were something of a novelty, the chimps very seldom did fight over the fruits.

And what of the lack of aggression in the more dominant males? Possibly, when they fail to detect those signals of apprehension that normally characterize their interactions with subordinates and instead meet very definite aggressive signals, they may feel hesitant in asserting their normal prerogatives.

This may be true of sexual behavior also; it may be the reason why adult males do not normally fight for the privilege of mating with an attractive female but, rather, await their turn. Perhaps the male about to mount may, likewise, be prepared to defend his sexual right to the act of reproduction. And it is quite possible that the human sense of moral values may in itself have originated from basic behavioral patterns of this sort.

Whatever the underlying reasons, we have seen Rodolf as well as others on many occasions guarding their meat from chimpanzees normally their social superiors. At such times the higher-ranking males, frustrated beyond endurance, frequently vent their aggression on lower-ranking individuals. And so, during the early part of a meat-eating session, before the big males have acquired portions for themselves, females and youngsters, as well as males of lower rank, are frequently chased quite violently through the branches, and particularly if they venture too close to the kill.

It was in this context, in the old days, that the male chimpanzees were often extremely aggressive toward me. One day when Rodolf was in possession of a kill and keeping everything to himself, J.B. hurried off to camp to snatch a few bananas. It was a journey of about two hundred yards, and on his return he must have thought that during his absence I had managed to get a share of the carcass. He bustled through the thick undergrowth toward the meat-eaters, suddenly noticed me, stopped, and stared. Slowly his hair began to bristle. All at once, with a loud bark, he charged straight toward me. I could not even try to get out of his way, since the tangle of vines around was too thick. As he stopped less than two feet from me and gave me a hard wham I think I closed my eyes. But he merely picked up first my sweater and then my haversack with quick frenzied movements, and sniffed them both intently. Then, setting them down, he turned and hurried off to try his luck with the real kill.

Another time it was worse. Hugo and I had been watching a large group of chimpanzees in a tree. Mike had a baboon kill, and while he was freely sharing with J.B. and a few others, five of the adult males had not succeeded in getting more than the odd scrap. These males kept displaying through the tree, chasing off any subordinates who happened to be in their way. The individual who appeared to us to be the most frustrated was David Graybeard. Soon Mike swung from the tree and sat feeding in some thick vegetation on the ground. The other chimps of course followed him. Hugo and I, as we crept closer to watch what was going on, made the mistake of moving too quietly: as we suddenly came into their view, one of the young females, a relative newcomer to our group, took fright and rushed off. This startled all the others and there was a brief stampede. Then the chimps realized that it was a false alarm, and after glaring at us for a few moments the five frustrated males charged toward us, running upright, waving their arms, and uttering loud fierce-sounding threat barks. Just before they reached us they stopped—all except David.

David Graybeard, as I have indicated earlier, could be a very aggressive chimpanzee if sufficiently aroused, and on that occasion he most certainly was. Hugo and I turned and fled at the same moment. When we looked around, David was still coming. Unfortunately Hugo, who was protecting me from the rear and struggling with his camera equipment, got caught in some vicious thorns. As he struggled to get free the enraged David still ran on, by now only a couple of yards from Hugo. Then, at the very last minute, he stopped, and with a final *waa* and an upward jerk of his arm turned and rushed back toward the other chimps.

Even to this day I feel sure that this episode was the closest shave we have had with any chimp. David, in spite of his normal gentle disposition, was in a way the most dangerous so far as we were concerned because of his total lack of fear of humans. Many people have evidenced surprise that Hugo and I ran, but this should not really be surprising. After all, the most submissive thing that a subordinate chimpanzee can do is to remove himself from the aggressor's presence—in other words, to run away. A social inferior who shows submissive behavior such as crouching, presenting, or holding out a hand toward an angry superior is quite likely to be attacked, whereas for the most part adult males do not persist in an aggressive incident if their intended victim runs off.

These days it seems that the chimpanzees not only have a far greater tolerance for the proximity of human beings, but they seem to realize that when they have meat their human watchers are unlikely to try to steal a share. Aggressive behavior during meat-eating directed toward researchers at Gombe is becoming increasingly rare.

Just as hunting behavior is interesting in that the chimpanzees show the beginning of cooperative endeavor—so characteristic of human hunting societies—the consumption of meat is similarly fascinating, because normally the possessor of the carcass is willing to share the meat with others, a characteristic not recorded for other nonhuman primate species in the wild. Often we have seen chimpanzees actually break off portions of their meat and hand them to begging individuals. One such incident was especially remarkable.

It was an outburst of chimpanzee and baboon calling that attracted us to the spot, and there we found Goliath with the freshly killed body of a baboon infant. Old Mr. Worzle was up in the tree too, begging for a share and whimpering like an infant as he did so. Every few minutes Goliath got up and leaped away from him, but Worzle followed crying, and, when Goliath stopped, reached out to beg again. As Goliath pushed his hand away for at least the tenth time, Worzle abruptly threw a tantrum worthy of an infant, hurling himself backward off the branch, screaming and hitting the surrounding vegetation. Then, to our astonishment, Goliath, with a mighty tearing of the victim's skin and sinews, pulled the body of his prey in two and handed Mr. Worzle the entire hind quarters. It was as though he could no longer endure the screaming and commotion when he wanted to enjoy his prize. And Goliath also shared with Flo when she shortly arrived on the scene.

Mike, once he had become well established in his top-ranking position, became increasingly tolerant and benign during interactions with his subordinates. When he was in possession of a carcass he usually permitted the other males to share at least some parts of it with him. One time when Mike had the remains of a baboon, I watched as he and Rodolf chewed together, each at an end of the carcass. Then the dominant male began to pull on his half. I had the impression that he was not trying to take away Rodolf's share but simply wanted to tear the carcass in two. Never have I been more impressed by Rodolf's strength than on that occasion. No matter how hard Mike pulled by standing up and heaving, Rodolf, as he held on to his end, simply remained almost motionless in his original position. He might have been solid rock for all the impression Mike's tugging and jerking made on his large frame. While Mike continued to pull, Rodolf leaned forward and gnawed away at the skin until the carcass split in two, leaving Mike with the head.

The brain appears to be a special delicacy, and Mike very often ends up with the head of the prey. I have watched him gradually enlarging the foramen magnum, where the vertebral column joins the skull, biting away fragments of bone with his teeth. When the opening was large enough he scooped out the brain with a crooked index finger. Sometimes the chimps open the brain by breaking away the frontal bones.

Another time, when David was watching Mike eating brain and was begging very persistently, Mike started to tickle him, as a mother will do with her child to distract it from some desired objective. After a few moments the two adult males were both uttering loud chuckles of chimp laughter as they tickled each other. And it worked; when David could endure the tickling no more he moved away and Mike continued to eat brain undisturbed.

Only in one instance did we see Mike lose the prized head with brain intact to another chimp. It was evening, and Mike had eaten well. As the last lurid rays of the sinking sun penetrated the forest canopy he held up the head of his victim, a juvenile baboon, and began to groom the fur. It was a gruesome sight, for one eye socket was empty and from the other the eye dangled on its optic nerve. Just then there was a rustling in the undergrowth and J.B. emerged at a fast run, seized the head, and vanished with it into the undergrowth. Mike, it appeared, was too full to care, for he did not pursue his friend. J.B. climbed into a nearby tree, made a nest, and sat there in his bed eating mouthfuls of brain and leaf until darkness fell.

The picture emerging from the years of information we have collected at Gombe suggests that meat-eating behavior in the chimpanzees occurs in cycles. It may be that a chance hunting success —when a chimpanzee accidentally comes across a baby bushpig in the undergrowth, for example—starts off a craze for meat in the group as a whole. While this craze lasts, for one or even two months, the adult and adolescent males may set out to hunt deliberately. Then, either because their craving is satisfied or because a succession of hunts results in failure and they lose interest, the chimpanzees return to a diet of fruit, vegetables, and insects, until a few months later something else triggers another meat-eating craze.

I remember when Humphrey came into camp with the skin of a red colobus monkey. As he left he was still clutching his trophy. About an hour later old Gregor arrived, from the same direction as had Humphrey. Whether or not he had been able to get a share of that kill, he certainly had a craving for meat. About fifteen minutes after his arrival he stared with concentration over the valley. Following his gaze we saw a small troop of red colobus monkeys. Almost at once Gregor set off with that fast, silent, purposeful walk, and the other chimps in camp followed him. We took out the telescope and waited to see what would happen.

Presently there was a violent swaying of branches. Monkeys began to chatter, and we glimpsed old Gregor, as well as a few other chimps and a number of colobus, leaping through the trees. I saw a colobus chase a small chimp who leaped, screaming, toward the ground. Then, to our astonishment, we saw Gregor pounding down an open grassy slope with a single male colobus bounding after him. This illustrates how, when an animal is sufficiently enraged, it can appear far more terrifying than it really is; that monkey would have come off very much the worse if Gregor had turned and attacked.

This observation makes more surprising the fact that adult male baboons, many times heavier and normally far more aggressive than male red colobus, are not more efficient as protectors when chimpanzees hunt their young. They do usually rush up and mob the chimpanzees, lunging at them, roaring, and generally making a commotion, when they notice that a hunt is going on, but so far, though the aggression looks fierce, we have never seen a chimpanzee hurt as a result of such an encounter. Once a male baboon actually leaped onto Mike's back and clung there for a few moments during a hunt, but Mike appeared none the worse afterward. Even when the chimps have caught an infant baboon that is alive and screaming in their clutches, the adult males do not attack. It is one more of those unsolved problems that make the continuation of research a challenge.

In fact the whole question of the relation between chimpanzees and baboons at the Gombe Stream is complex and very fascinating. In the early days of my study I found that for the most part individuals of the two species tended to ignore one another except for the youngsters, who often played together. Sometimes adult chimps and adult baboons fed quite peacefully in the same tree; if there were only a couple of chimps, they usually became restless when baboon after baboon climbed up into the branches of their tree, and finally left. I also saw a number of aggressive incidents between groups of the two species. In the light of our knowledge today I suspect that these were attempts on the part of the chimps to catch young baboons.

Since 1963 when our feeding area came into being, interactions between chimpanzees and baboons have increased enormously in frequency: during the worst years, just before we built the feeding bunker, individuals of both species were staying around camp for hours at a time in proximity. At the beginning it seemed that often the baboons showed more respect for the chimpanzees than they do today. I think that this in fact was simply because the baboons were more afraid of humans then, so that only a few dared to move out into the camp clearing. Also, since we tried to discourage them by shining a mirror into their eyes, they were apprehensive anyway, and the sudden leaping, arm-waving threat of a chimpanzee was more likely to be effective. Even in those days, however, some male baboons were very aggressive and able to scare most of the chimps.

Subsequently, when students started following the baboons around, studying their behavior, they lost most of their apprehension of humans and invaded our feeding area in even larger numbers. Small wonder, then, that they seemed more aggressive and that most of the chimps showed increasing respect for them. Although we watched many fights when baboon and chimp came into contact, we never saw serious wounds inflicted. For the most part, battles over bananas were based on threat and bluff—the baboons roaring, lunging forward with open mouths, or hitting toward their opponents and the chimps leaping up, waving their arms, uttering loud *waa* barks or screaming.

Victory in such an aggressive conflict depends to a large extent on the individuals concerned. The chimps themselves quickly learned which of the male baboons could be chased off by bluff and which would stand their ground and should therefore be avoided. And the baboons likewise realized that female and young chimps were for the most part easy game; that males such as David Graybeard could easily be intimidated into dropping a whole armful of bananas; that others, such as Goliath and Mike, were tougher customers. The baboons showed, too, a good deal of respect for old Mr. Worzle—maybe they disliked his strange humanlike eyes. Principally, though, it was because Worzle was usually fearless and simply stood his ground. Also, he was the first chimpanzee we ever saw throwing stones and other objects at baboons that approached and threatened him. True, Worzle sometimes hurled leaves if no more suitable missile was close at hand, and once he threw a whole handful of bananas at an aggressive male baboon, to the obvious satisfaction of his opponent! As time went on, Worzle became more selective, usually picking up and throwing rather large rocks.

We were not surprised when first we saw Worzle throwing a stone at a baboon, for we had seen chimps throwing things aggressively before. Rodolf had hurled a large rock straight at Hugo and me the first time he ever visited camp. He had, it seemed, followed Goliath along without really looking where he was going. When he suddenly awoke to the fact that there was a tent ahead, with us inside, he uttered a strangled call, stood upright, and threw his missile before bolting back to the bushes.

Soon after we first saw Mr. Worzle throwing at baboons, a number of the other males started doing likewise. These days nearly all the adult males use objects as weapons in this way, but though they usually choose fairly large stones they seldom hit the baboons unless they are at very close quarters.

At this point I must emphasize that, except during the actual distribution of bananas, relations between chimpanzees and baboons, even at the feeding area, are normally peaceful and individuals of both species show a good deal of tolerance toward each other. Actually it has often surprised us that immediately after a frenzy of aggressive behavior chimpanzees and baboons, when all bananas are finished, will often sit close to each other as they relax and rest.

Since both chimpanzees and baboons are well known for their intelligence, it is not really surprising that to some extent individuals of the two species are able to communicate with each other. One day, for example, a female baboon passed very close to Mr. Worzle and seemed to startle him slightly. He raised his arm and gave a soft threat bark, at which she instantly crouched and presented submissively. Mr. Worzle then reached his hand toward her rump and almost certainly touched her in reassurance. At any rate her posture became relaxed and she sat quite close to him. We have seen many other incidents of this sort.

When Flint was about eight months old he frequently tottered toward female baboons with sexual swellings and, to our initial amazement, these females often turned and presented their rumps to the small infant—just as a female chimpanzee would do. Some of them actually allowed him to touch their pink bottoms. Later we found that the same thing happened when Goblin or any other chimpanzee infant approached female baboons, though some of them were more tolerant than others in this context.

Particularly fascinating was the relationship between an old male baboon known as Job and many of our chimpanzees. Perhaps because of his age, perhaps for some other reason, Job took to remaining in camp for hours on end, often leaning up against a tree trunk as though life was altogether too much for him. One day we were amazed to see him approach Fifi and, turning sideways, signal his desire to be groomed. We were even more surprised when Fifi complied. After working on him for a few moments she in turn presented her side to him, but Job did not respond, and after a short time Fifi groomed him again for a few moments before walking away. After this it became quite common to see Job going up to different young chimps, begging them, by his posture, to groom him and fairly often being briefly groomed in response.

On another occasion Figan walked up to the old male baboon with the jaunty, slightly swaggering walk that signified his intentions were playful. He reached out and gave Job a few prods and then started chucking him under the chin. Finally, when none of these activities called forth any sort of response from the old male, who simply sat looking somewhat bewildered, if anything, Figan tried a new tactic. He pressed his forehead against Job's and persistently butted him so that the baboon's whole body was shaken. After a moment or two of this treatment Job evidently could tolerate no more and he made a threatening movement, lunging slightly toward Figan with his old teeth showing. Figan did not appear to be unduly perturbed by this, but nevertheless after a second or two he walked away. We saw two other adolescent male chimps trying to play with Job, thumping him and seeming to tickle him with their fingers, though they never succeeded in sparking off any sign of playful behavior in the old male.

Despite all these friendly interactions—and the many times we have watched young chimps and baboons playing together—we have never observed a friendship such as the one that grew up between Gilka and the young female baboon Goblina, which I described in Chapter 13. True, there was one very playful juvenile male baboon who quite often indulged in wild games with Flint, and even a subadult male who for a while played frequently with Fifi when she was about six. But these relationships did not persist for more than a few weeks and the individuals concerned played only when chance threw them together. The friendship between Gilka and Goblina, as I have pointed out, lasted for nearly a year and the two definitely had sought each other's company.

One day, when chimpanzee screams and baboon roars took Hugo and me running toward a tall tree, we saw two adult male chimps with the newly killed body of an infant baboon. We were so busy watching the behavior of the chimps that for some time we paid no attention to the mother baboon, who was repeatedly running at the chimps and calling loudly. When we did see who it was we could hardly bear to watch any longer. It was Goblina—the chimps had killed her first infant.

After about thirty minutes Goblina moved away with the one male baboon who had remained with her at the scene of the kill. Later she returned, still with the same young male, and sat farther up the slope, staring toward the chimpanzees. Every so often she uttered a low-pitched grunt that to Hugo and me sounded like a call of distress. She stayed there for ten minutes or so, and once more went away. During the four hours that the chimps remained in the area, she returned three times more, by herself. Three hours later she went back yet again to the deserted scene of the crime, still alone. And every few minutes she uttered that desolate-sounding call.

A year later Gilka's old playmate had a second infant, which today is a juvenile and with luck will not fall victim to the predatory attack of a chimpanzee. The baby we hoped would become a proper playmate for Gilka, her own sibling, had a fate possibly worse than that of Goblina's first infant.

17

DEATH

OLLY'S NEW BABY was four weeks old when he suddenly became ill. I had been excited when I heard of his birth: would his elder sister Gilka show the same fascination for him as Fifi had for Flint? And how would Olly react if she did? Though I was not at the Gombe when the baby was born, I was there a month later when one evening Olly walked slowly into camp supporting him with one hand. Each time she made a sudden movement, he uttered a loud squawk as though in pain, and he was gripping badly. First one hand or foot and then another slipped from Olly's hair and dangled down.

While Olly sat eating her bananas, Gilka groomed her mother. Often I had watched Gilka working her way closer to her small sibling's hands just as Fifi had done two years earlier when Flint was tiny. This time, however, Olly permitted her daughter to groom the baby's head and back without attempting, as she usually did, to push Gilka's hands away.

Next morning it was obvious that the baby was very ill. All his four limbs hung limply down and he screamed almost every time his mother took a step. When Olly sat down, carefully arranging his legs so as not to crush them, Gilka went over and sat close to her mother and stared at the infant; but she did not attempt to touch him then.

Olly ate two bananas and then set off along the valley, with Gilka and me following. Olly only moved a few yards at a time, and then, as though worried by the screams of her infant, sat down to cradle him close. When he quieted, she moved again, but he instantly began to call out so that once more she sat to comfort him. After traveling about a hundred yards, which took her just over half an hour, Olly climbed into a tree. Again she carefully arranged her baby's limp arms and legs on her lap as she sat down. Gilka, who had followed her mother, stared again at her small sibling, and then mother and daughter began to groom each other. The baby stopped screaming and, apart from occasionally grooming his head briefly, Olly paid him no further attention.

When we had been there some fifteen minutes it began to pour, a blinding deluge that almost obscured the chimps from my sight. During the storm, which went on for thirty minutes, the baby must either have died or lost consciousness. When Olly left the tree afterward he made no sound and his head lolled back as limply as his arms and legs.

I was amazed at the sudden and complete change in Olly's handling of her baby. I had watched a young and inexperienced mother carrying her dead baby, and even the day after its death she had held the body as though it were still alive, cradling it against her breast. But Olly climbed down the tree with her infant carelessly in one hand, and when she reached the ground she flung the limp body over her shoulder. It was as though she knew he was dead. Perhaps it was because he no longer moved or cried that her maternal instincts were no longer roused.

The following day Olly arrived in camp, followed by Gilka, with the corpse of her infant slung over her shoulder. When she sat down the body sometimes dropped heavily to the ground. Occasionally Olly pushed it into her groin as she sat; when she stood she held it by an arm or even a leg. It was gruesome to watch, and several of the young female chimpanzees went over and stared. So also did a number of baboons. Olly ignored them all.

Finally Olly wandered away from camp and she and Gilka, with me following, went some way up the opposite mountain slope. Olly seemed dazed; she looked neither to right nor to left but plodded up the narrow trail through the forest, the body slung over her neck, until she reached a place halfway up the mountainside. Then she sat down. The dead infant slumped to the ground beside her, and other than to glance down briefly Olly ignored it. She just sat staring into space, hardly moving for the next half hour save to hit away the fast-gathering swarm of flies.

Now, at last, came Gilka's opportunity to play with her sibling. It was not easy to watch. Already the corpse had begun to smell; the face and belly showed a definite greenish tinge, and the eyes, which were wide open, stared glassily ahead. Inch by inch, glancing repeatedly at her mother's face, Gilka pulled the body toward her. Carefully she groomed it, and then she even tried to play, pulling one dead hand into the ticklish spot between her collarbone and neck, and actually showing the vestige of a play-face. We had been so glad for Gilka's sake when old Olly had given birth again—but it looked as if Gilka was always to be ill-fated. Presently, with another quick glance toward her mother, Gilka carefully lifted the dead body of her sibling and pressed it to her breast. Only then did Olly's lethargy leave her for a moment. She snatched the body away, and then once more let it fall to the ground.

When the old female moved on, it was merely to plod down the same track and so back to camp. She ate two bananas, sat staring into space, and wandered off up the valley.

For another three hours I managed to keep up with the little family. Every ten minutes or so Olly just sat or lay, and Gilka, as before, groomed or tried to play with the dead body of her sibling. Eventually Olly became worried by my presence and started to walk fast, glancing at me over her shoulder. She headed into a dense thicket, and though I continued after her a brief distance, I decided I should desist. In fact I was glad to get out of the tangled vines, since in the hot and humid air the smell of death was heavy where Olly had passed, and each twig had its own quota of bloated flies.

The following afternoon Olly and Gilka arrived in camp without the body. Somewhere in the valley Olly must have finally abandoned it.

Had we known at the time that Olly's infant was without doubt the first victim of the terrible paralytic disease that struck our chimpanzee community, I would never have followed the family—for at this time my own baby was on the way. But we had no suspicion, and the next victims did not appear for another two weeks.

Later we discovered that there had been a bad outbreak of polio-myelitis among the African population in the Kigoma district. Since chimpanzees are susceptible to almost every human infectious disease, and are known to contract polio, it seems almost certain that the epidemic afflicting our chimpanzees actually was polio. We traced two of the human victims to a village ten miles to the south of our feeding area—just outside the park but in a valley where chimpanzees had been seen on many occasions. Possibly it was there that the first chimpanzee had contracted polio and from that place the disease had spread northward to affect those in our group.

When we realized that the disease was probably polio, we panicked, for Hugo and I and our research assistant Alice Ford had not received a full course of polio vaccine. We got through to Nairobi on the radio telephone and spoke to Louis. He arranged for a plane to fly down to Kigoma bringing sufficient vaccine for ourselves, our African staff—and the chimpanzees. We did not know to what lengths the epidemic might ravage the chimp community and we felt it was worth at least trying to stop it by treating those that were healthy.

The Pfizer Laboratories in Nairobi generously supplied us with the oral vaccine, and we offered it to the chimps in bananas. Each individual was supposed to have three drops once a month for three months. Most of them took the doctored fruit unhesitatingly, but a few spat the banana out after one mouthful—in spite of the fact that to us the drops were quite tasteless. For these fussy individuals we had to prepare three bananas, each with one drop of vaccine instead of three drops in one fruit. We had to be careful, too, that a higher-ranking individual who had had his monthly dose was not around when we dosed a subordinate from whom he might have snatched the banana, and thus receive a double dose.

I think those few months were the darkest I have ever lived through: every time a chimp stopped visiting the feeding area, we started to wonder whether we would ever see him again or, worse, if he would reappear hideously crippled. Fifteen chimpanzees in our group were afflicted, of whom six lost their lives. Some of the victims were lucky and survived with only minor disabilities. Gilka lost partial use of one hand and Melissa was affected in her neck and shoulders. The magnificent young males Pepe and Faben both appeared after short absences trailing one useless arm. One adolescent male returned, after a long absence, shuffling along in a squatting position and with both arms paralyzed. He could only eat the bits and pieces he was able to reach with his lips, and he was nothing but a skeleton covered with dull staring hair. We had to shoot him. And there were other victims—like fat, bustling J.B., of whom we had all become so fond—who just disappeared, and we could only conjecture about their lonely deaths. However, it is the nightmare of Mr. McGregor's illness that still haunts us in the wakeful hours of the night.

It was fairly late in the evening when Hugo noticed Flo, Fifi, and Flint moving cautiously toward a low bush just below camp, staring hard and every so often uttering soft worried calls as they stood upright to peer over the long grass. We hurried down to see what was happening. We saw the flies first. Every leaf and twig near the bush bore its burden of metallic blue and green flies, buzzing angrily as our approach disturbed them. As we moved closer, we expected to see some dead creature—but it was Mr. McGregor, and he was still alive. He was sitting on the ground reaching for the tiny purple berries that grew on the bush above his head and stuffing them into his mouth. It was not until he wanted to reach another cluster of the fruit that we realized the horror of what had happened. Looking toward the berries the old male seized hold of a low branch and pulled himself along the ground. Both legs trailed uselessly after him. When next he wanted to shift his position he put both hands behind him on the ground and inched his body backward in a sitting position.

Flo and her family soon moved away, but Hugo and I stayed there until darkness fell. To our amazement Mr. McGregor was able to pull himself up into a low-branched tree, using only his powerful arms. He hauled himself quite high and then managed to build himself a small nest. As he climbed we saw the reason for the horde of flies: he had lost the use of the sphincter muscle of his bladder, and every time he strained to reach a higher branch a spurt of urine trickled down his paralyzed thighs. We also saw that his bottom was raw and bleeding and realized that he must have dragged himself a long way in his efforts to return to camp. The following morning we followed his trail; the narrow lane of flattened vegetation led us some fifty yards downhill to the stream and continued twice as far again on the opposite side before we lost it in a steep gully on the mountainside.

The next ten days—and they seemed more like ten years—had a nightmare quality. We kept hoping to notice some flicker of life return to his paralyzed legs, but he never twitched as much as a toe. During this time he did not move from the vicinity of our feeding area. In the mornings he usually remained in his nest until eleven o'clock or even later. Then, slowly, he lowered himself to the ground, where he sat for half an hour or so, merely looking around and occasionally grooming himself. After this he usually dragged himself a few yards to some low-growing food and ate.

We found that he had another way of moving from place to place—a clumsy kind of somersaulting, head over heels. When we first saw this we were overjoyed, because we felt sure that there must be some muscles still active in his thighs. Soon we realized that it was merely the incredible strength in his arms that enabled him to raise his body from the ground together with the dead weight of his paralyzed legs. He could only move in this way when there were tough grass tufts or tree roots that he could grip with his hands for leverage.

Ordinarily he was back in bed by half past four or so, and during his whole illness he only made use of three different nests, two of which were in one tree. Near the beginning of it all, we watched as he started to climb three different trees—each one proving impossible for him in his handicapped state. After the tremendous effort of lifting himself to the lower branches he had to lower himself laboriously to the ground again.

Naturally we tried to help him. At first he was apprehensive if we approached too closely and threatened us with a quick raising of one arm and a soft bark. However, it was only two days before he seemed to sense that we were trying to help, and after this he even lay back and allowed me to pour water from a sponge into his open mouth. We made a small basket of leaves which we filled with food—bananas, palm nuts, any wild foods we could collect— and pushed it up to him in his nest on the end of a long stick. When he vacated his nest in the mornings, we climbed up and cleaned it for him, because, of course, he could no longer move to defecate over the side.

We soon realized that Mr. McGregor was being driven to distraction by the huge swarm of flies, so we took an aerosol spray whenever we visited him and squirted all around—each time killing well over a thousand of the revolting bloated things. At first this too scared the old chimp, but shortly he seemed to understand what it was all about, and then he welcomed the operation.

One of the most tragic things about the whole tragic affair was the reaction of the chimps to the stricken paralyzed male. Initially, almost certainly, they were frightened by the strangeness of his condition. We had noticed the same thing when some of the other polio victims appeared in camp for the first time. When Pepe, for instance, shuffled up the slope to the feeding area, squatting on his haunches with his useless arm trailing behind him, the group of chimps already in camp stared for a moment and then, with wide grins of fear, rushed for reassurance to embrace and pat each other while staring at the unfortunate cripple. Pepe, who obviously had no idea that he himself was the object of their fear, showed an even wider grin of fright as he repeatedly turned to look over his shoulder along the path behind him—trying to find out, presumably, what it was that was making his companions so frightened. Eventually the others calmed down; but, though they continued to stare at him from time to time, none of them went near him, and eventually he shuffled off, once more on his own. Gradually the other chimps became accustomed to Pepe, and soon the muscles in his legs were strong enough to enable him to walk about upright, as had Faben from the start.

McGregor's condition was patently far worse. Not only was he forced to move about in an abnormal manner, but there was the smell of urine and the bleeding rump and the swarm of flies buzzing around him. The first morning of his return to camp, as he sat in the long grass below the feeding area, the adult males, one after the other, approached with their hair on end, and after staring began to display around him. Goliath actually attacked the stricken old male, who, powerless to flee or defend himself in any way, could only cower down, his face split by a hideous grin of terror, while Goliath pounded on his back. When another adult male bore down on McGregor, hair bristling, huge branch flailing the ground, Hugo and I went to stand in front of the cripple. To our relief, the displaying male turned aside.

After two or three days the others got used to McGregor's strange appearance and grotesque movements, but they kept well away from him. There was one afternoon that without doubt was from my point of view the most painful of the whole ten days. A group of eight chimps had gathered and were grooming each other in a tree about sixty yards from where McGregor lay in his nest. The sick male stared toward them, occasionally giving slight grunts. Mutual grooming normally takes up a good deal of a chimpanzee's time, and the old male had been drastically starved of this important social contact since his illness.

Finally he dragged himself from his nest, lowered himself to the ground, and in short stages began the long journey to join the others. When at last he reached the tree he rested briefly in the shade; then, making the final effort, he pulled himself up until he was close to two of the grooming males. With a loud grunt of pleasure he reached a hand toward them in greeting—but even before he made contact they both had swung quickly away and without a backward glance started grooming on the far side of the tree. For a full two minutes old Gregor sat motionless, staring after them. And then he laboriously lowered himself to the ground. As I watched him sitting there alone, my vision blurred, and when I looked up at the groomers in the tree I came nearer to hating a chimpanzee than I have ever been before or since.

For several years Hugo and I had suspected that the aggressive adult male Humphrey was Mr. McGregor's younger brother. The two traveled about together frequently and often the older male had hurried to Humphrey's assistance when he was being threatened or attacked by other chimps. It was during the last days of Mr. McGregor's life that we became convinced these two males were siblings: no bond other than that of a family could have accounted for Humphrey's behavior then—and afterward.

In the whole period Humphrey seldom moved farther than a few hundred yards away from the old male—although even he never actually groomed McGregor. Sometimes Humphrey went away across the valley to feed, but within an hour or so he was back, resting or grooming himself near his paralyzed friend. On the first day of his return to camp McGregor climbed quite high in a tree and made a nest. Suddenly Goliath began to display around him, swaying the branches more and more vigorously, slashing the old male on the head and back. Gregor's screams grew louder, and he clung to the rocking branches tightly. At last, as if in desperation, he let himself drop down through the tree, from branch to branch, until he landed on the ground. Then he started to drag himself slowly away. And Humphrey, who had always been extremely nervous of Goliath, actually leaped up into the tree, displaying wildly at the much higher-ranking male, and for a brief moment attacking him. I could hardly believe it.

One day Mr. McGregor managed to pull himself right up to the feeding area, up thirty yards of very steep slope, to join a large number of chimpanzees who were eating there. We were able to give him a whole box to himself so that for a while, at least, he was part of the group again. When the others moved away up the valley, Gregor tried to follow. But whether he dragged himself on his belly, or hitched himself backward, or laboriously somersaulted, he could move only very slowly, and the rest of the group were soon out of sight.

After about five minutes we saw Humphrey coming back. For a few moments he stood and watched Gregor's progress, then he turned and moved after the other chimps again. Once more he came back and stood waiting for the old male. This time he actually shook grasses at Mr. McGregor, as though he were trying to force a reluctant female to follow him. Eventually Humphrey abandoned his attempts to follow the big group and built his nest close to Gregor's, just below the observation area.

On the tenth evening, when we went down with his supper, Mr. McGregor was not in his nest, nor could we see him sitting in the grass. When we found him, after a short search, we soon realized that somehow he had dislocated one arm. And then we knew that in the morning we would have to shoot our old friend. We had known it secretly all along—yet we had waited, hoping for a miracle. I stayed with him awhile, and as dusk fell he looked up more and more often into the tree above him. I realized that he must have wanted to make a nest, so I cut and took to him a large pile of green vegetation. At once he maneuvered himself onto it, lay down, and with one hand and his chin tucked the twigs over to make a comfortable pillow.

I went down to see him later the same night, and it says much for the extent to which we had won his trust and confidence that, having heard my voice, he closed his eyes and went back to sleep three feet away and with his back to me and my bright pressure lamp. Next morning, while he was grunting in delight over his favorite food—two eggs we had given to him—we sent him, unsuspecting, to happier hunting grounds.

We did not allow any of the chimps to see his dead body, and for a long time it looked as if Humphrey did not realize he would never meet his old friend again. For nearly six months he kept returning to the place where Gregor had spent the last days of his life, and would sit up one tree or another staring around, waiting, listening. During this time he seldom joined the other chimps when they left together for a distant valley; he sometimes went a short way with such a group, but within a few hours he usually came back again and sat staring over the valley, waiting, surely to see old Gregor again, listening for the deep, almost braying voice, so similar to his own, that was silenced for ever.

18

MOTHER AND CHILD

FIVE-YEAR-OLD MERLIN had been among the first victims of the polio epidemic. Though he had been one of our favorite youngsters, playful and impish, we were almost glad when he died, for by that time he had become a pathetic wreck of a chimpanzee, emaciated, lethargic, and morose. But I must go back to the beginning and relate the whole story.

When Merlin was about three years old, still suckling, still riding about on his old mother Marina and sleeping with her at night, the two stopped visiting the feeding area. Merlin's six-year-old sister Miff continued to appear regularly. Since previously she had always traveled about with her mother and small brother, we assumed that Marina and Merlin had died. Just over three months later Merlin reappeared, following his eldest brother, thirteen-year-old Pepe, into camp. He looked thin, with a tight hard belly, and his eyes seemed enormous, as though he had not slept for a long time. Goodness knows what had happened to his mother, or how long she had been dead. She must have died, because we never saw her again.

It appeared that the chimpanzees who were at the feeding area when Merlin returned had not seen him for a long time; they hurried to greet him, embracing and kissing and patting the infant. He ate some bananas and then sat huddled up close to his big brother. Later on that morning Miff arrived. At once she hurried over to Merlin, and brother and sister began to groom each other. Merlin only groomed Miff briefly, but she groomed him rapidly

and intently for more than fifteen minutes. When Miff was ready
to go she looked back over her shoulder toward Merlin and waited
until he followed before going on—just like a mother waiting for
her child.

From that moment Miff, to all intents and purposes, adopted her
little brother. She waited for him when she went from place to
place; she allowed him to share her nest at night; she groomed
him as frequently as his mother would have done. For the first
few days after his return she even permitted him to ride occasionally on her back; but after that she pushed him off if he tried to
jump on—she was a thin, long-legged youngster and Merlin was
probably too heavy for her. It seemed that Pepe was with his
younger siblings more than when Marina had been alive; possibly
because Miff, deprived of a mother, followed him instead. And
when he was there, Pepe normally went to Merlin's assistance
during moments of social excitement.

Gradually, as the weeks passed, Merlin became more emaciated,
his eyes sank deeper into their sockets, and his hair grew dull and
staring. He became increasingly lethargic and played less and less
frequently with the other youngsters. Also in other ways his behavior began to change.

One day Merlin was sitting grooming with Miff when a group
of chimpanzees approached along the forest path. Miff instantly
got up and hurried partway up a tree as Humphrey, who was in
the forefront of the group, started the pant-hoots indicating im-
minence of an arrival display. Two other females nearby also hurried out of the way, but Merlin began moving fast toward
Humphrey, pant-grunting in submission. Humphrey, who had already started to display, ran straight at Merlin, seized him by one
arm, and dragged him for several yards along the ground. As the
big male charged away, Merlin, screaming, rushed to embrace Miff.
He had behaved like a small infant that does not yet appreciate
the signals of impending aggression in his elders. Yet before this
Merlin, like all normal three-year-olds, had always responded instantly and appropriately to signals of this sort.

This episode, in fact, was the start of a marked deterioration
of Merlin's social responses. Time and again he was dragged or
buffeted by displaying males because he ran toward them instead

of away. When he was four years old Merlin was far more submissive than other youngsters of that age: constantly he approached adults to ingratiate himself, turning repeatedly to present his rump, or crouching, pant-grunting, before them. At the other end of the scale, Merlin was extra-aggressive to other infants of his own age group. When Flint approached to try to play, Merlin, although he sometimes merely crouched or turned his back, was equally likely to hit out aggressively, so that Flint, a year younger than he, ran off with squeaks of fear. And matching this decline in playful behavior, Merlin began to groom older chimps, notably his sister, more frequently and for longer at a time than other youngsters of his age.

As Merlin entered his sixth year his behavior was becoming rapidly more abnormal. Sometimes he hung upside down like a bat, holding on to a branch by his feet and remaining suspended almost motionless for several minutes at a time. Hunched up with his arms around his knees, he sat often rocking from side to side with wide-open eyes that seemed to stare into the far distance. And he spent much time grooming himself during which he pulled out hair after hair, chewed at their roots, and dropped them.

One of the strangest observations concerned Merlin's tool-using behavior during the termite season. I had often watched him as a two-year-old, playing about near Marina while she fished for hours at a time after the manner of old females. Occasionally, Merlin went to observe his mother carefully, and once I saw him take up a thin twig and, holding it rather as a human infant first holds a spoon, prod with it at the surface of the termite heap.

The following year, just before his mother died, his tool-using ability had improved, though it was still far from efficient—as was only to be expected in a three-year-old. Nearly always he chose grasses or twigs that were too short, about two inches long as compared to the eight- to twelve-inch lengths favored by adults, and he manipulated his tiny tools clumsily and incompetently, pushing them somewhat carefully into termite passages but then almost instantly yanking them out—so that even if a termite had managed to cling on it would undoubtedly have been jerked off. Once he pushed a thick piece of straw firmly into a hole from which he was unable to extract it.

Unfortunately I was not at the Gombe Stream for the following termite season, and Merlin's tool-using behavior was not recorded. The next year, when he was five years old, I watched him on several occasions. Normally a youngster is efficient at this age, both in his choice and his manipulation of grass tools. I was amazed to find that Merlin's technique had hardly improved since I had watched him two years earlier. He still chose, for the most part, minute tools, and if he selected one that was of reasonable length, it was limp or bent. He still jerked his tools from the holes rather than withdrawing them with the care of an adult. It was indeed strange—particularly as Miff was a keen termite-fisher and Merlin must have spent many hours with her while she worked heap after heap.

Only in one respect had his behavior matured. Two- and three-year-old chimp youngsters seldom spend more than a couple of minutes at a time working at the job. After this they move away and play around for a while before making another brief attempt. But Merlin worked away with the concentration of a chimpanzee older than his five years; on one occasion he persisted, without interruption, for forty-five minutes. During that time he caught only one termite, and that was on the end of his finger when he was trying to enlarge a hole.

By this time Merlin was so thin that every bone showed. His hair was not only dull but there were great patches of it missing on his legs and arms where he had gradually pulled it out during self-grooming. Often he lay stretched flat on the ground while the other youngsters played, as though he was constantly exhausted. He was definitely smaller than the younger Flint.

Just before the start of the short rains we briefly wondered whether he was beginning to improve, for he began to play again. Some of his games with Flint, Goblin, and Pom were quite vigorous—but as soon as one of his playmates got rough Merlin still either crouched squealing in submission or else turned and hit out aggressively. In spite of this improvement, when the rains began we all felt convinced that he could not survive six months of cold and wet. At the slightest shower he started to shiver, and often his hands and feet and face actually went blue with cold. That is why we were in many ways relieved when polio put an end to his sufferings.

Merlin is not the only orphan we have known. Three other infants lost their mothers, and two of them, like Merlin, were adopted by their elder siblings. Beatle lost her mother when she was about the same age as Merlin had been when Marina died; but Beatle's sister was two or three years older than Miff and a much stronger female, bigger in build. Beatle not only traveled around with her big sister and slept with her at night but also was allowed to ride about on her broad back.

Beatle showed similar signs of depression to those shown by Merlin: she too became rather emaciated, she too played less and less frequently. At about the time when Merlin's behavior had begun to deteriorate even more, however, Beatle's began to improve. And during *her* sixth year Beatle behaved just like a normal child of that age—except that, as Merlin had been, she was still very dependent on her older sister. Unfortunately these two sisters did not visit camp frequently, and just after this they stopped coming altogether for months on end. Then the elder of the two appeared several times on her own. We do not know whether Beatle managed to survive.

In some ways Sorema was the most tragic orphan, for she was only just over a year old when her mother died and still almost completely dependent on her for transport, protection, and, most important, food. Solid foods do not start to play an important role in the diet of an infant chimpanzee until it is over two years of age. During the two weeks that Sorema survived her mother she was carried everywhere by her six-year-old brother Sniff. It was a touching sight to see the juvenile male moving about with his tiny sister, pressing her against his breast with one hand, cuddling and grooming her. When they were in camp Sorema ate a few bananas, but it was milk she needed, and each day she seemed weaker and her eyes looked bigger. Then, one morning, Sniff came into the feeding area cradling her dead body.

It seems strange that an orphaned infant should be adopted by an elder sibling rather than by an experienced female with a child of her own, who could perhaps provide the motherless infant with milk as well as adequate social protection. When Cindy's mother died we fully expected the three-year-old child to move about with the adult female who had been her mother's frequent companion, especially as we thought these two females had been sisters. This did not happen. Cindy was never seen traveling with her mother's friend but either moved about alone or trailed along with any group she happened to encounter. She showed signs of depression far quicker than the other three-year-old orphans, and less than two months after her mother's death she stopped visiting the feeding area and was never seen again.

Why does a three-year-old chimpanzee become so depressed when he loses his mother? True, he is still dependent to some extent on her milk—but he only suckles for a couple of minutes every two or three hours, and he is able to eat the same solid foods as an adult. We do not yet know the answer to this question, but we have a clue if we look at the differences in behavior shown by Merlin and Beatle after their mothers died. Both of these infants had been deprived of their mothers at a similar age, and deprived of the reassurance of the breast. Both initially showed gradually increasing depression. Then Merlin's condition declined, whereas Beatle's improved. Beatle was able to continue riding about on another chimpanzee after her mother's death. Her world had, indeed, been shattered by her loss; if her sister moved even a few yards without her she whimpered, screamed, and rushed after her. Nevertheless, once she had scrambled aboard she was again in close physical contact with a large chimpanzee—an individual who knew what to do in times of trouble, who would rush her to safety up a tree at the right time, who could run fast and swiftly and carry them both to safety.

Merlin, by contrast, had no haven of refuge after Marina's death. Miff was no more than a constant companion and was of little use to her brother in times of social excitement in the group. And so it seems possible that Merlin's troubles were principally psychological, that his terrible physical condition resulted more from a sense of social insecurity than from any nutritional deficiency caused by the absence of his mother's milk. This theory is to some extent supported by the fact that when his physical condition was at its worst, just before he died, he did seem to cheer up somewhat mentally, as though, very slowly, his mind might have been recovering. But by that time it was too late.

If one day we are able to study the development of a chimpanzee orphan to adulthood we may learn much. Will time heal the wound caused by the death of the mother? What abnormalities will persist as a result of his early traumatic experience? The answers may be beneficial to those studying orphaned or socially deprived human children, for, although chimpanzee society does impose certain rules of conduct, it imposes far fewer than even the most primitive human society. A human has amazing powers of self-control, and he learns early in life what are the accepted norms of behavior. This means that unless he is mentally unbalanced he is usually able to control, at least in public, any inclination he may have to behave in an unacceptable way. A chimpanzee, on the contrary, is not inhibited by any fear of "making a fool of himself."

We can of course learn much about the effect of an early traumatic experience in the subsequent adult life of a human; but not only is a man's behavior much more complex, it is also more difficult to make consistent, regular observations on an adult human. So, a real understanding of the less complicated behavior of a chimpanzee orphan during successive years may prove invaluable to our better understanding of some of the problems faced by human orphans.

We hope that we at least shall be able to make a thorough study of one particular chimpanzee whose behavior has been quite severely disturbed by a change in his mother's attitude toward him. This, together with some other circumstances, did produce symptoms in the child not unlike those characterizing the behavior of our orphans. I am referring to Flint.

Flint was just less than five years old when Flo became pink for the first time since his birth. On this occasion, unlike that marathon five-week swelling which had heralded Flint's arrival, Flo was fully pink for only four or five days, during which Flint was not permitted to suckle. Flo fended him off and often played with him vigorously every time he tried. When her swelling shriveled, though, he resumed suckling again—despite the fact that she was, as we subsequently discovered, pregnant. In addition, Flint continued to sleep with Flo at night and often to ride about on her back.

Flint's prolonged infancy was possibly due to Flo's extreme age, to the fact that she no longer had the strength to battle with her somewhat obstreperous child; for in point of fact she had initiated the slow process of weaning him when he was three years old. Flint, from the start, had shown remarkable persistence in getting access to the breast; on those occasions when Flo had not quickly given in to his gentle pushing and whimpering, Flint had flown into terrible tantrums, hurling himself about on the ground, flailing his arms, rushing down the slope screaming until Flo, after staring for a moment in the direction of his receding screams, had plodded in pursuit to reassure her son and suckle him. As Flint had grown older he had taken to hitting and biting his mother when she refused him the breast—and though Flo had sometimes retaliated, she had at the same time held the child very close, as if trying to reassure him even while she bit or cuffed him. After these violent episodes, she had always given in and allowed him to suckle in the end.

When Flo had been pregnant for six months her milk seemed suddenly to dry up. Deprived of this comfort at last, Flint had gone through the same stage of babyish behavior that had marked Fifi's weaning five years earlier: constantly he clung to his mother, whimpering if she set off only a few yards ahead of him, frequently pushing in when Flo was grooming one of her other offspring, and crying if she did not instantly turn her attention to him.

We felt really sorry for old Flo during the final months of her pregnancy. It was the height of the dry season and swelteringly hot. As she moved slowly along the mountain tracks, she had to support, in addition to the new baby within her hugely swollen belly, the half-grown male body of Flint, perched ridiculously on her frail old body. Sometimes, when I followed them, I feared that Flo would be unable to survive the birth of yet another infant. Every few yards she would stop to rest, and her eyes often looked vacant and faraway. Also, Flint was a bully to his old mother. When she had sat for a few minutes he was anxious to go on, keen to reach the fruit trees for which they were heading. He would push insistently at his mother's back, whimpering ever louder, until she got up and once more plodded on as Flint instantly climbed onto her. Sometimes he actually kicked her if she did not respond to his pushing by hand. And when he was not pestering her to move on he was bothering her to groom him, whimpering and pulling at her hands if she ignored him.

We saw the new baby, Flame, when she was only just dry, early in the morning. It is possible that Flo moved to a new nest during the moonlit night, or even climbed down to give birth on the ground, for at dawn she had not been in the nest she had made the evening before. Flame, even as a newborn baby, was pretty—unlike the ugly little Goblin. She had a pale face in which her eyes, misty with extreme youth, looked almost blue. We were amazed, though, at how little hair she had—her chest and belly and the insides of her arms and legs were completely pink and naked.

We followed Flo that morning as she wandered along, accompanied by Flint, supporting with one hand Flame and the placenta to which the baby was still attached. Somewhat to our surprise, Flint's behavior was exemplary—as it was for the first few weeks after Flame's birth. He stopped pestering Flo for grooming and he no longer tried to ride on her back. He often went up to touch Flame, but when Flo gently pushed his hand away he did not persist.

I shall never forget when, after his attempts to make contact with his little sibling had been repeatedly prevented, Flint deliberately picked a small twig and reached out to touch Flame with *that*. Then he withdrew it and intently sniffed the end. This happened for the first time when Flame was less than a day old; afterward we saw him do the same thing a number of times. He was, in fact, using the twig as a tool to aid in his attempt to find out about the new baby.

Flame rapidly developed into a healthy, alert, and somewhat precocious infant. Flint, however, after his initial good behavior, began to show signs of reverting to the dependent, clinging, and irritating child he had been before his sister's birth. Once more he demanded to climb onto Flo's back when the family was on the move; actually there were a few occasions when Flint was suddenly scared, when he clung underneath, embracing Flame's tiny body as well as his mother's with his arms and legs. Also, he threw the most terrible tantrums if Flo did not immediately permit him to climb with her and Flame into their communal bed.

As the weeks went by Flint's behavior began increasingly to resemble that of an orphaned youngster: he started to decline invitations to play with other youngsters; he spent longer periods of time grooming; he became noticeably listless and lethargic. He did not show any inclination to harm Flame, unlike some human children who are jealous of a new sister or brother. Indeed, when Flame was three months old and Flo less possessive of her, both Flint and Fifi spent much of their time playing with Flame, grooming and cuddling her. Sometimes these two took turns carrying Flame through the forest while Flo plodded along behind them, seemingly quite unconcerned.

When Flame was six months old Flo became very ill with the same flu-like disease that had claimed old William and has stricken the chimpanzees nearly every rainy season. For six days Flo, Flint, and Flame were missing, and all the students at the Research Center went out on search parties hunting for them. When she was finally found, Flo was so sick that she could hardly move—and Flame had gone. We expected that Flo would die because she could neither eat nor climb off the wet ground. Amazingly, the tough old female regained her health and strength.

From this time onward Flint, who had not been ill at all, began to show a change in his behavior. As the days went by he lost his lethargy and once more began to play frequently with his old playmates, to whirl and pirouette and somersault as in the days before Flame's birth. Nonetheless, he did not relinquish his babyish behavior—in fact, so far as dependency on Flo was concerned, Flint became more clinging than ever. For a while we thought that he might actually start to suckle again since he was constantly putting his lips to Flo's nipples; but it became evident that during her illness his mother's milk had dried up. In all other respects, Flint again became Flo's baby. She shared her food with him; she permitted him to climb onto her back or even on occasions cling to her belly. She groomed him constantly and, as of old, she welcomed him into her bed at night. This state of affairs persisted until Flint was more than six years old.

What went wrong with Flint's upbringing? Had he as a small

infant been "spoiled" by too much attention from his mother, sister, and two big brothers? With the backing of that close-knit family he certainly got his own way nearly all the time in his dealings with individuals outside the family group. Did Flo fail to wean her son at the proper time because she was so old that she could no longer cope with Flint's tantrums when she denied him access to the breast?

Whatever the reason for Flo's failure, there can be no doubt but that Flint, today, is a very abnormal juvenile. Will he gradually lose his peculiarities as he grows older, or will some traces of infantile behavior characterize him when he is mature? This question, like so many others, can only be answered by the continuation of our research at the Gombe Stream.

Already, however, we have been repeatedly impressed by the extent to which the growing child depends on his mother. Who would have thought that a three-year-old chimpanzee might die if he lost his mother? Who would have guessed that at five years of age a child might still be suckling and sleeping with his mother at night? Who would have dreamed that a socially mature male of about eighteen years of age would still spend much time in the company of his old mother?

It seems, so far, that most wild chimpanzee mothers are quite efficient at rearing youngsters. Nevertheless, we have learned too that occasional maternal inadequacies—such as Flo's inability to wean Flint at the proper time or the somewhat callous attitude of Passion to her infant Pom—may have marked consequences for the youngsters concerned.

I was at the Gombe Stream for several months during 1966 when my own child was on the way and also during the following year when he was with me as a tiny baby. I watched the chimpanzee mothers coping with their infants with a new perspective. From the start Hugo and I had been impressed with many of their techniques, and we made a deliberate resolve to apply some of these to the raising of our own child. First, we determined to give our baby a great deal of physical contact, affection, and play. He was breast-fed, more or less on demand, for a year. He was not left to scream in his crib. Wherever we went we took him with us so that though his environment was often changing, his relationship with

Adolescent males are usually nervous about joining in adult grooming sessions

An experienced mother allows other chimpanzees to inspect her newborn infant

Faben brandishes a stick
on seeing his reflection in a mirror

Figan tries to play with the old baboon Job

Faben has thrown a stone
at a baboon who approached a
banana box, and a fight ensues

Olly's infant was the first victim of the polio epidemic

Sniff adopted his sister
after their mother's
death

Mike, the dominant male, begs Leakey for a piece of meat. *Photograph by Geza Teleki*

With Grub in the forest

Flo with Flint and Flame. *Photograph by Patrick McGinnis*

Flo and Fifi startled by a sudden noise

Physical contact is reassuring, even when only between two hands. *Below:*
Submissively Melissa kisses J.B.'s reassuring hand

Gilka, eighteen months after contracting a fungus disease

Presenting is a sign of submission

Rodolf attacks a female, then immediately reassures her with an embrace

Two chimpanzees embrace in greeting

Flo and Flame

his parents remained stable. When we punished him we quickly gave him reassurance through physical contact and, when he was small, we tried to distract him rather than simply prevent him from doing something naughty.

As he grew older it became increasingly necessary, of course, to temper chimpanzee techniques with our own common sense—after all, we were dealing with a human, not a chimpanzee infant. We tried not to punish him for errors until he reached an age when he could understand the reason behind the reprimand, and we continued to keep him with us and to give him frequent physical and mental reassurance.

Has our method of bringing him up been successful? We cannot say as yet. We can only point out that today, at four years of age, he is obedient, extremely alert and lively, mixes well with other children and adults alike, is relatively fearless and is thoughtful of others. In addition, and quite contrary to the predictions of many of our friends, he is very independent. But then, of course, he might have been like this anyway, even if we had brought him up in a quite different way.

19

IN THE SHADOW OF MAN

THE AMAZING SUCCESS OF MAN as a species is the result of the evolutionary development of his brain which has led, among other things, to tool-using, toolmaking, the ability to solve problems by logical reasoning, thoughtful cooperation, and language. One of the most striking ways in which the chimpanzee biologically resembles man lies in the structure of his brain. The chimpanzee, with his capacity for primitive reasoning, exhibits a type of intelligence more like that of man than does any other mammal living today. The brain of the modern chimpanzee is probably not too dissimilar to the brain that so many millions of years ago directed the behavior of the first ape men.

Previous to that far off day when I first watched David Graybeard and Goliath modifying grass stems in order to use them to fish for termites, the fact that prehistoric man made tools was considered to be one of the major criteria distinguishing him from other creatures. As I pointed out earlier, the chimpanzee does not fashion his probes to "a regular and set pattern"—but then, prehistoric man, before his development of stone tools, undoubtedly poked around with sticks and straws, at which stage it seems unlikely that he made tools to a set pattern, either.

It is because of the close association in most people's minds of tools with man that special attention has always been focused upon any animal able to use an object as a tool; but it is important to realize that this ability, on its own, does not necessarily indicate any special intelligence in the creature concerned. The fact that the Galápagos woodpecker finch uses a cactus spine or twig to probe insects from crevices in the bark is indeed a fascinating phenomenon, but it does not make the bird more intelligent than a genuine woodpecker that uses its long beak and tongue for the same purpose.

The point at which tool-using and toolmaking, as such, acquire evolutionary significance is surely when an animal can adapt its ability to manipulate objects to a wide variety of purposes, and when it can use an object spontaneously to solve a brand-new problem that without the use of a tool would prove insoluble.

At the Gombe Stream alone we have seen chimpanzees use objects for many different purposes. They use stems and sticks to capture and eat insects and, if the material picked is not suitable, then it is modified. They use leaves to sop up water they cannot reach with their lips—and first they chew on the leaves and thus increase their absorbency. One individual used a similar sponge to clean out the last smears of brain from the inside of a baboon skull. We have seen them use handfuls of leaves to wipe dirt from their bodies or to dab at wounds. They sometimes use sticks as levers to enlarge underground bees' nests.

In captivity chimpanzees often use objects as tools quite spontaneously. One group that was studied intensively by Wolfgang Köhler used sticks to try to pry open box lids and to dig in the ground for roots. They wiped themselves with leaves or straw, scratched themselves with stones and poked straws into columns of ants in order to eat the insects rather as the Gombe Stream chimpanzees fish for termites. They often used sticks and stones as weapons during aggressive encounters. Sometimes they used bread to lure chickens close to their enclosure, whereupon they would suddenly prod the birds with sharp sticks, apparently for amusement. Extensive tests have been carried out in laboratory settings in order to find out more about the tool*making* ability of the chimpanzee. Results show that he can pile up to five boxes one on top of the other in order to climb to a hanging food lure, that he can fit up to three tubes together to reach food placed outside the bars of his cage, and that he can uncoil part of a length of wire for the same purpose. So far, however, no chimpanzee has succeeded in using one tool to make another. Even with tuition one chimpanzee, the subject of exhaustive tests, was not able to use a stone hand ax to break a piece of wood into splinters suitable for obtaining food from a narrow pipe. She could do this when the material was suitable for her to break off pieces with her teeth but, although she was shown how to use the hand ax on tougher wood many times, she never even attempted to make use of it when trying to solve the problem. However, many other chimpanzees must be tested before we say that the chimpanzee as a species is unable to perform this act. Some humans are mathematicians—others are not.

When the performance of the chimpanzee in the field is compared with his actual abilities in test situations, it would seem that, in time, he might develop a more sophisticated tool-culture. After all, primitive man continued to use his early stone tools for thousands of years, virtually without change. Then we find a more refined type of stone tool-culture suddenly appearing widespread across the continents. Possibly a stone-age genius invented the new culture and his fellows, who undoubtedly learned from and imitated each other, copied the new technique.

If the chimpanzee is allowed to continue living he, too, might suddenly produce a race of chimp superbrains and evolve an entirely new tool-culture. For it seems almost certain that, although the ability to manipulate objects is innate in a chimpanzee, the actual tool-using patterns practiced by the Gombe Stream chimpanzees are learned by the infants from their elders. We saw one very good example of this. It happened when a female had diarrhea: she picked a large handful of leaves and wiped her messy bottom. Her two-year-old infant watched her closely and then twice picked leaves and wiped his own clean bottom.

To Hugo and me, and assuredly to many scientists interested in human behavior and evolution, one significant aspect of chimpanzee behavior lies in the close similarity of many of their communicatory gestures and postures to those of man himself. Not only are the actual positions and movements similar to our own but also the contexts in which they often occur.

When a chimpanzee is suddenly frightened he frequently reaches to touch or embrace a chimpanzee nearby, rather as a girl watching a horror film may seize her companion's hand. Both chimpanzees and humans seem reassured in stressful situations by physical contact with another individual. Once David Gray-beard caught sight of his reflection in a mirror. Terrified, he seized Fifi, then only three years old. Even such contact with a very small chimp appeared to reassure him; gradually he relaxed and the grin of fear left his face. Humans may sometimes feel reassured by hold-ing or stroking a dog or some other pet in moments of emotional crisis.

This comfort, which chimpanzees and humans alike appear to derive from physical contact with another, probably originates dur-ing the years of infancy, when for so long the touch of the mother, or the contact with her body, serves to calm the frights and soothe the anxieties of both ape and human infants. So, when the child grows older and his mother is not always at hand, he seeks the next best thing—close physical contact with another individual. If his mother is around, however, he may deliberately pick her out as his comforter. Once when Figan was about eight years old he was threatened by Mike. He screamed loudly and hurried past six or seven other chimps nearby until he reached Flo; then he held his hand toward her and she held it with hers. Calmed, Figan stopped screaming almost at once. Young human beings, too, continue to unburden their hearts to their mothers long after the days of child-hood have passed—provided, of course, that an affectionate relation-ship exists between them.

There are some chimps who, far more than others, constantly seem to try to ingratiate themselves with their superiors. Melissa, for one, particularly when she was young, used to hurry toward and lay her hand on the back or head of an adult male almost every time one passed anywhere near her. If he turned toward her, she often drew her lips back into a submissive grin as well. Presumably Melissa, like the other chimps who constantly attempt to ingratiate themselves in this way, is simply ill at ease in the presence of a social superior, so that she constantly seeks reassurance through physical contact. If the dominant individual touches her in return, so much the better.

There are many human Melissas: the sort of people who when trying to be extra friendly reach out to touch the person concerned and smile very frequently and attentively. Usually they are, for some reason or other, people who are unsure of themselves and slightly ill at ease in social contexts. And what about smiling? There is much controversy as to how the human smile has evolved. It seems fairly certain, though, that we have two rather different kinds of smile, even if a long time ago they derived from the same facial gesture. We smile when we are amused and we smile when we are slightly nervous, on edge, apprehensive. Some people, when they are nervous at an interview, smile in this way at almost everything that is said to them. And this is the sort of smile that can probably be closely correlated with the grin of the submissive or frightened chimpanzee.

When chimpanzees are overjoyed by the sight of a large pile of bananas they pat and kiss and embrace one another rather as two Frenchmen may embrace when they hear good news, or as a child may leap to hug his mother when told of a special treat. We all know those feelings of intense excitement or happiness which cause people to shout and leap around, or to burst into tears. It is not surprising that chimpanzees, if they feel anything akin to this, should seek to calm themselves by embracing their companions.

I have already described how a chimpanzee, after being threatened or attacked by a superior, may follow the aggressor, screaming and crouching to the ground or holding out his hand. He is, in fact, begging a reassuring touch from the other. Sometimes he will not relax until he has been touched or patted, kissed or embraced. Figan several times flew into a tantrum when such contact was withheld, hurling himself about on the ground, his screams cramping in his throat until the aggressor finally calmed him with a touch. I have seen a human child behaving in the same sort of way, following his mother around the house after she has told him off, crying, holding on to her skirt, until finally she picked him up and kissed and cuddled him in forgiveness. A kiss or embrace or some other gesture of endearment is an almost inevitable outcome once a matrimonial dispute has been resolved, and in many cultures the clasping of hands occurs to denote renewal of friendship and mutual forgiveness after a quarrel.

When one human begs forgiveness from or gives forgiveness to another there are, however, moral issues involved; it is when we consider these that we get into difficulties in trying to draw parallels between chimpanzee and human behavior. In chimpanzee society the principle involved when a subordinate seeks reassurance from a superior, or when a high-ranking individual calms another, is in no way concerned with the right or wrong of the aggressive act. A female who is attacked for no reason other than that she happens to be standing too close to a charging male is quite as likely to approach the male and beg a reassuring touch as is the female who is bowled over by a male while she attempts to take a fruit from his pile of bananas.

Again, while we may make a direct comparison between the effect on anxious chimpanzee or human of a touch or embrace of reassurance, the issue becomes complicated if we probe into the motivation that directs the gesture of the ape or the human who is doing the reassuring. Human beings are capable of acting from purely unselfish motives; we can be genuinely sorry for someone and try to share in his troubles in an endeavor to offer comfort and solace. It is unlikely that a chimpanzee acts from feelings quite like these; I doubt whether even members of one family, united as they are by strong mutual affections, are ever motivated by pure altruism in their dealings one with another.

On the other hand, there may be parallels in some instances. Most of us have experienced sensations of extreme discomfort and unease in the presence of an abject, weeping person. We may feel compelled to try to calm him, not because we are sorry for him in the altruistic sense, but because his behavior disturbs our own feeling of well-being. Perhaps the sight—and especially the sound—of a crouching, screaming subordinate similarly makes a chimpanzee uneasy; the most efficient way of changing the situation is for him to calm the other with a touch.

There is one more aspect to consider in relation to the whole concept of reassurance behavior in chimpanzees, and that is the possible role played by social grooming in the evolution of the behavior. For the chimpanzee—and for many other animals too—social grooming is the most peaceful, most relaxing, most friendly form of physical contact. Infant chimpanzees are never starved for physical contact since they spend much time close to their mothers. Then, as they grow older, they spend more time away from their mothers and also more time playing with other youngsters; and play typically involves a good deal of physical contact. As the youngster matures he gradually plays less frequently; he does, however, spend increasingly more time socially grooming, either with his mother and siblings or, as he gets older, with other adults. Sometimes a grooming session between mature individuals may last for two hours. The obvious need for social grooming was well demonstrated when old Mr. McGregor, with his paralyzed legs, dragged himself those sixty long yards to try to join a group of grooming males.

When a chimpanzee solicits grooming he usually approaches the selected partner and stands squarely in front of him, either facing him with slightly bowed head or facing away and thus presenting his rump. Is it possible, then, that submissive presenting of the rump, and submissive bowing and crouching, may have derived from the postures used to solicit grooming? That in the mists of the past the subordinate approached his superior, after he had been threatened, to beg for the reassuring, calming touch of grooming fingers? If so, then the response of the chimpanzee thus approached, the touch or the pat, may equally have been derived from the grooming pattern. Indeed, on some occasions a few brief grooming movements do occur when a dominant individual reaches out in response to the submissive posture of a subordinate. It is quite reasonable to suppose that such a response may have become ritualized over the centuries so that today the chimpanzee usually gives a mere token touch or pat in place of grooming his submissive companion.

When two chimpanzees greet each other after a separation, their behavior often looks amazingly like that shown by two humans in the same context. Chimpanzees may bow or crouch to the ground, hold hands, kiss, embrace, touch, or pat each other on almost any part of the body, especially the head and face and genitals. A male may chuck a female or an infant under the chin. Humans, in many cultures, show one or more of these gestures. Even the touching or holding of another's genitals is a greeting in some societies; in fact, it is described in the Bible, only it has been translated as the placing of the hand under the companion's thigh.

In human societies much greeting behavior has become ritualized. A man who smiles when greeting a friend, or who inclines his head when passing an acquaintance in the street, is not necessarily acknowledging that the other has a superior social status. Yet the nod undoubtedly derives from submissive bowing or prostration and the smile from a nervous grin. Often, though, human greetings still do serve to clarify the relative social status of the individuals concerned, particularly on formal occasions.

A greeting between two chimpanzees nearly always serves such a purpose—it reestablishes the dominance status of the one relative to the other. When nervous Olly greets Mike she may hold out her hand toward him, or bow to the ground, crouching submissively with downbent head. She is, in effect, acknowledging Mike's superior rank. Mike may touch or pat or hold her hand, or touch her head, in response to her submission. A greeting between two chimps is usually more demonstrative when the individuals concerned are close friends, particularly when they have been separated for days rather than hours. Goliath often used to fling his arms around David, and the two would press their lips to each other's faces or necks when they met; whereas a greeting between Goliath and Mr. Worzle seldom involved more than a casual touch even when the two had not seen each other for some time.

It is not only the submissive and reassuring gestures of the chimpanzee that so closely resemble our own. Many of his games are like those played by human children. The tickling movements of chimpanzee fingers during play are almost identical with our own. The chimpanzee's aggressive displays are not dissimilar to some of ours. Like a man, an angry chimpanzee may fixedly stare at his opponent. He may raise his forearm rapidly, jerk back his head a little, run toward his adversary upright and waving his arms, throw stones, wield sticks, hit, kick, bite, scratch, and pull the hair of a victim.

In fact, if we survey the whole range of the postural and gestural communication signals of chimpanzees on the one hand and humans on the other, we find striking similarities in many instances. It would appear, then, that man and chimp either have evolved gestures and postures along a most remarkable parallel or that we share with the chimpanzees an ancestor in the dim and very distant past; an ancestor, moreover, who communicated with his kind by means of kissing and embracing, touching and patting and holding hands.

One of the major differences between man and his closest living relative is, of course, that the chimpanzee has not developed the power of speech. Even the most intensive efforts to teach young chimps to talk have met with virtually no success. Verbal language represents a truly gigantic stride forward in man's evolution.

Chimpanzees do have a wide range of calls, and these certainly serve to convey some types of information. When a chimp finds good food he utters loud barks; other chimps in the vicinity instantly become aware of the food source and hurry to join in. An attacked chimpanzee screams and this may alert his mother or a friend, either of whom may hurry to his aid. A chimpanzee confronted with an alarming and potentially dangerous situation utters his spine-chilling *wraaaa*—again, other chimps may hurry to the spot to see what is happening. A male chimpanzee, about to enter a valley or charge toward a food source, utters his pant-hoots —and other individuals realize that another member of the group is arriving and can identify which one. To our human ears each chimpanzee is characterized more by his pant-hoots than by any other type of call. This is significant since the pant-hoot in particular is the call that serves to maintain contact between the scattered groups of the community. Yet the chimps themselves can certainly recognize individuals by other calls; for instance, a mother knows the scream of her offspring. Probably a chimpanzee can recognize the calls of most of his acquaintances.

While chimpanzee calls do serve to convey basic information about some situations and individuals, they cannot for the most part be compared to a spoken language. Man by means of words can communicate abstract ideas; he can benefit from the experiences of others without having to be present at the time; he can make intelligent cooperative plans. All the same, when humans come to an exchange of emotional feelings, most people fall back on the old chimpanzee-type of gestural communication—the cheering pat, the embrace of exuberance, the clasp of hands. And when on these occasions we also use words, we often use them in rather the same way as a chimpanzee utters his calls—simply to convey the emotion we feel at that moment. "I love you. I love you," repeats the lover again and again as he strives to convey his overwhelming passion to his beloved—not by words but by his embraces and caresses. When we are surprised we utter inanities such as "Golly!" or "Gosh!" or "Gee whiz!" When we are angry we may express ourselves with swear words and other more or less meaningless phrases. This usage of words on the emotional level is as different from oratory, from literature, from intelligent conversation, as are the grunts and hoots of chimpanzees.

Recently it has been proved that the chimpanzee is capable of communicating with people in quite a sophisticated manner. There are two scientists in America, R. Allen and Beatrice Gardner, who have trained a young chimpanzee in the use of the approved sign language of the deaf. The Gardners felt that, since gesture and posture formed such a significant aspect of *chimpanzee* communication patterns, such a sign language might be more appropriate than trying to teach vocal words.

Washoe was brought up from infancy constantly surrounded by human companions. These people from the start communicated in sign language with Washoe and also with each other when in the chimp's presence. The only sounds they made were those approximating chimpanzee calls such as laughter, exclamations, and imitations of Washoe's own sounds.

Their experiment has been amazingly successful. At five years of age Washoe can understand some three hundred and fifty different symbols, many of which signify clusters of words rather than just a single word, and she can also use about one hundred and fifty of them correctly. The Gardners have been criticized for allowing Washoe to use "sloppy" signing. As a matter of fact, some signs were taught to Washoe in a slightly different form when this corresponded quite closely to one of her own gestures. Other signs Washoe changed of her own accord when she was small—and, interestingly, it came about that many of these adaptations were exactly the same as those used by small human children. In other words, they represent the "baby talk" of the deaf and dumb child. Many of these Washoe corrected as she grew older.

I have not seen Washoe, but I have seen some film demonstrating her level of performance and, strangely enough, I was most impressed by an error she made. She was required to name, one after the other, a series of objects as they were withdrawn from a sack. She signed off the correct names very fast—but even so, it could be argued that an intelligent dog would ultimately learn to associate the sight of a bowl with a correct response of one scratch on the floor, a shoe with two scratches, and so on. And then a brush was shown to Washoe, and she made the sign for a comb. That to me was very significant. It is the sort of mistake a small child might make, calling a shoe a slipper or a plate a saucer—but never calling a shoe a plate.

Perhaps one of the Gardners' most fascinating observations concerns the occasion when for the first time Washoe was asked (in sign language) "Who is that?" as she was looking into a mirror. Washoe, who was very familiar with mirrors by that time, signaled back, "Me, Washoe."

This is, in a way, a scientific proof of a fact we have long known—that, in a somewhat hazy way, perhaps, the chimpanzee has a primitive awareness of Self. Undoubtedly there are people who would prefer not to believe this, since even more firmly rooted than the old idea that man is the only toolmaking being is the concept that man alone in the animal kingdom is Self-conscious. Yet, this should not be disturbing. It has come to me, quite recently, that it is only through a real understanding of the ways in which chimpanzees and men show similarities in behavior that we can reflect with meaning on the ways in which men and chimpanzees *differ*. And only then can we really begin to appreciate, in a biological and spiritual manner, the full extent of man's uniqueness.

Man is aware of himself in a very different way from the dawning awareness of the chimpanzee. He is not just conscious that the body he sees in a mirror is "I," that his hair and his toes belong to *him*, that if a certain event occurs *he* will be afraid, or pleased or sad. Man's awareness of Self supersedes the primitive awareness of a fleshly body. Man demands an explanation of the mystery of his being and the wonder of the world around him and the cosmos above him. So man, for centuries, has worshiped a God, has dedicated himself to science, has tried to penetrate the mystery in the guise of the mystic. Man has an almost infinite capacity for preoccupation with things other than Self: he can sacrifice himself to an ideal, immerse himself in the joys or sorrows of another; love, deeply and unselfishly; create and appreciate beauty in many forms. It should not be surprising that a chimpanzee can recognize himself in a mirror. But what if a chimpanzee wept tears when he heard Bach thundering from a cathedral organ?

In his long quest for truth the scientist has never been able to provide a platform for man's ancient belief in God and the spirit. Yet, who in the silence of the night or alone in the sunrise has not experienced—just once perhaps—a flash of knowledge "that passeth all understanding"? And for those of us who believe in the immortality of the spirit, how much richer life must be.

Yes, man definitely overshadows the chimpanzee. The chimpanzee is, nevertheless, a creature of immense significance to the understanding of man. Just as he is overshadowed by us, so the chimpanzee overshadows all other animals. He has the ability to solve quite complex problems, he can use and make tools for a variety of purposes, his social structure and methods of communication with his fellows are elaborate, and he shows the beginnings of Self-awareness. Who knows what the chimpanzee will be like forty million years hence? It should be of concern to us all that we permit him to live, that we at least give him the chance to evolve.

20

MAN'S INHUMANITY

As the barbed arrow sank into her flesh, Flo lurched and staggered, clinging to the branch. Flint clung to her, screaming in fright, and the blood from his mother's wound slowly dropped down onto his face. As I watched, unable to move, unable to call out, Flo put a hand to her side and stared as if in disbelief at the blood. Then, in slow motion she fell—down, down, down . . . Flint, like a limpet, still clung to her dying body and they hit the ground together with a sickening thud.

As the grinning human mask approached, white teeth gleaming in ebony face, Flo gave one final convulsive heave and then was still. Screaming, fighting, biting, Flint was pushed into the dank, evil-smelling sack, down, down, down. Yet even in the darkness I could see the black shadow of the man . . .

I woke in a cold sweat with the blanket over my face. So vivid was the nightmare that I could not sleep again. Yes—a nightmare. But it does happen, over and over, in parts of West and Central Africa. In many areas chimpanzee flesh is a much prized delicacy and there are horrifying tales of infant chimps tied up beside the sliced-up bodies of their mothers in the meat market, on sale for fattening and future consumption by the protein-starved Africans. Also, chimpanzee infants are in great demand by the medical research laboratories of Europe and the United States and, God forgive us, this is the way we capture them, too—by shooting their mothers. How many mothers must creep away through the dense upper canopy of the forest mortally wounded and die later so that their doomed infants are orphaned? How many babies that survive both the shot and the crash to the ground must die within the first few days of capture, shattered and desolate? I estimate that for every live infant that arrives in the Western world an average of six others have lost their lives.

There is another shadow that is spreading over the chimpanzee today: with the spread of agriculture and forestry, the habitat as well as the life of the chimpanzee is threatened. Forests are cleared to make way for cultivation and food trees are poisoned to leave more space for better timber trees. Moreover, since chimps are susceptible to all the infectious diseases of man, wherever their populations are near new human settlements the apes are endangered by epidemics.

Fortunately, some people are waking to the dangers threatening chimpanzees in the wild. The enlightened governments of Uganda and Tanzania offer protection to their chimpanzee populations, and a recent international conservation meeting agreed to put these apes on their list of endangered species needing protection. Programs are being set up in order that chimpanzees needed for research can be bred in captivity, and if large and successful colonies can be established for this purpose it will do much to relieve the constant drain on wild populations. The chimpanzee is only one of the many species threatened with extinction in the wild; but he is, after all, our closest living relative and it would be tragic if when our grandchildren are grown the chimpanzee exists only in the zoo and the laboratory—a frightening thought, since for the most part the chimpanzee in captivity is very different from the magnificent creature we know so well in the wild.

Many zoos today are beginning to display their chimpanzees in groups in fairly spacious enclosures, although there are still many apes imprisoned in the old-fashioned concrete and barred cells. One summer I came to know two old zoo chimpanzees, a male and a female. They were housed in a very small cage with an indoor and an outdoor section separated by a steel door. It was very hot that summer, and though they were kept outside with the dividing door closed there was no awning when the sun was overhead and the concrete burned to the touch. The chimps had no branch to sit on, only a very small wooden shelf that held one of them at a time; it was always the male who sat on this shelf when the sun was hot. They were fed only twice a day—once in the early morning and once in the late afternoon. Their water supply was normally finished by ten o'clock in the morning but it was not replenished.

How long ago, I thought as I watched them, they must have forgotten the vines, the soft ground, the swinging in the branches, and the excitement of rushing through the forest clinging to their mothers' bodies. By now their only pleasure probably lay in their food, but they could not enjoy the fishing for juicy insects, or the flavor of fresh-caught meat and never again could they climb, with grunts of pleasure, to eat their fill of sun-ripened fruit in a cool forest tree. Also, how long the gap between meals must be for animals who by nature like to eat on and off throughout the day. Except for feeding, they had nothing to do save listlessly groom each other or themselves. They could not even escape from each other, these two, not even for one minute; the male could never relax in the comfort of male companionship and the female could never get away from male society.

A chimpanzee in such a zoo is probably somewhat similar to a human who has been in prison for many years and has no hope of release. Even in a better zoo, where the chimpanzee may be part of a slightly larger group and have a bigger concrete enclosure, he is a very different creature from the chimpanzee we know at the Gombe Stream. The zoo chimp has none of the calm dignity, the serenity of gaze, or the purposeful individuality of his wild counterpart. Typically, he develops odd stereotypes in his behavior. As he walks he may give one hand a slight rotation to the side, always the same hand, always to the same side. After shuffling across the confined space of his cage he may hit the iron frame of his door, always in the same place in the same way with the same rhythm. It is a pitiful vestige of the magnificent and impressive charging display of the wild male chimpanzee.

Most people are only familiar with the zoo or the laboratory chimpanzee. This means that even those who work closely with chimpanzees, such as zookeepers or research scientists, can have no concept or appreciation of what a chimpanzee *really* is. Which is, perhaps, why so many scientific laboratories maintain chimpanzees in conditions that are appalling, housed singly for the most part in small concrete cells with nothing to do day in and day out except to await some new, and often terrifying or painful, experiment.

I should make it clear that I am not trying to say we should never use the chimpanzee as an experimental animal. Recent work by physiologists and biochemists has shown that biologically—in the number and form of chromosomes, blood proteins, immune responses, DNA or genetic material, and so on—the chimpanzee is extremely close to man. He is as closely related to us in some respects as he is to the gorilla. Because of this, he is probably the only really effective substitute when for ethical reasons research cannot be carried out on humans. Kuru, a strange trembling illness of New Guinea, was a mystery of the medical world and claimed countless victims. Research with chimpanzees established it as a slow-acting virus disease and made the present dramatic cure possible. Also, because of the similarity of the chimpanzee brain to the human brain experiments carried out with chimpanzees will undoubtedly be of great value to those scientists who are grappling with the problems of human mental illness. Some people may not be aware of either the prevalence or the tragedy involved in disorders of the brain such as, for example, schizophrenia or severe depression. It is not only the victims themselves who are affected but also their families and friends. Chimpanzees may serve as experimental models for some of these disorders and thus assist science in its fight to alleviate human suffering.

On the other hand, while I agree that the chimpanzee should take part, if absolutely necessary, in some such experiments, I also feel strongly that laboratory chimpanzees in nearly all cases should be given much-improved living conditions. Surely if we want to use this ape as a guinea pig in medical research, whether it be in connection with kidney transplants, drug addiction, or long-term effects of the Pill, if we desire him to help man in his conquest of space—then we should make every effort to see that he is a well-treated and honored guest in our laboratories. His living space should be large, he should be provided with equipment to alleviate his boredom, tempting and tasty food, and when possible he should be housed with companions. Sometimes Hugo and I feel that the only way in which we might effect an improvement in the condition of most laboratory chimpanzees is to take those responsible for their upkeep to see our chimpanzees at the Gombe Stream.

21

FAMILY POSTSCRIPT

EVENTUALLY THE DETAILED UNDERSTANDING of chimpanzee behavior that will result from our long-term research at the Gombe will help man in his attempts to understand more of himself. Hugo and I are convinced of this. Yet it is not only for this reason that we continue our work year in, year out; we are also fascinated by the chimpanzees as individual beings. We want to know how Fifi, whom we first knew as a small infant, will look after her own children; whether Flo survives to be a grandmother, and if so how she will react to Fifi's infant; what happens to Flint when his mother finally dies; whether Figan one day may become top-ranking male. In effect, we want to continue observing the chimpanzees for similar reasons to those which impel one to read on to the end of an exciting novel.

These days we cannot spend too much time at the Gombe because we have a child of our own, and, as I mentioned earlier, chimpanzees have been known to prey on small human children. When our own son, little Hugo—better known as Grublin or Grub—was very small, we kept him inside a building in a cage up at the observation area. When Rodolf and Humphrey and young Evered looked in through the windows and rattled the bars, with their hair on end and their mouths tight-lipped and ferocious, we knew that if they had had the chance they would have seized Grub. We could not blame them for this; in captivity, where chimpanzees grow up in human rather than ape society, they are as tolerant and delighted with human as with chimpanzee babies. At the Gombe

Stream, the white-skinned apes that the chimpanzees have learned to tolerate, even to trust, are not normally associated with infants. Rodolf did not see Grub as my precious baby—merely as a tempting meal.

When Grub grew older we could no longer keep him in his babyhood cage, so we built a much larger one down on the beach, where the chimps seldom roam. This cage is attached to a prefab house, thatched with grass, and it is cool and airy. When Hugo and I are with him then Grub can run on the white sandy beach and splash in the sparkling lake, but if we are both up with the chimpanzees then Grub, together with the two Africans who look after him, stays in the safety of the cage. Grub is happy at Gombe —he repeatedly tells everybody that it is his "favorite place in all the world." This is lucky, since in the immediate future Hugo and I plan to return there on a more permanent basis.

For the past few years Hugo has been working on a study of the large African carnivores; just as Hugo has always involved himself in the chimpanzee research, so for a while I became involved in his project. From the time when we married, Hugo and I vowed to work together as much as we possibly could, for to our way of thinking two people with a harmony of interests and similar goals in life are most likely to enjoy to the full the richness marriage can offer. So, for a while I watched hyenas, and that experience has helped to broaden my outlook, has brought me back to contemplate chimpanzees with a fresh eye, and has been of value to my interpretations of their behavior.

Despite the fact that I have been away from Gombe for months at a stretch there has, of course, been no break in the records— thanks to our students. It is never quite the same to hear about something as actually to witness it, but it remains exciting, and most people who work at the Gombe Stream share our enthusiasm for the chimpanzees as individuals, so their accounts are vivid as well as accurate. Also, I have been lucky during my periodic visits. The chimps have seemed to stage exciting events almost as though they knew I was there. So each month brings in another installment, another chapter of the chimpanzee saga. Before ending my story I want to gather up some of the threads concerning those chimpanzee characters chosen to be covered in this book.

Let me first describe what has happened to Olly and her family. Almost exactly a year after losing her small infant during the polio epidemic, old Olly had yet another baby. It was two months premature and stillborn, and once again Gilka was deprived of a younger sibling. Six months after that Olly disappeared, and eventually we were forced to accept the fact that she must have died. Gilka, only seven years old, spent much time wandering around by herself, following the paths she had so often traveled with her mother.

Then, soon after Olly's death, Gilka developed a strange swelling on her nose. At first it seemed to be painful, for when another youngster approached to play, Gilka often pulled back abruptly, her eyes screwed shut as though in anticipation of being hurt. As the weeks went by it seemed to stop hurting her but it did not stop growing. Steadily it grew larger, until she could hardly breathe through her nose at all. A year after we first noticed the swelling Gilka's whole face was hideously deformed, her nose swollen into a gigantic and knobbly protuberance. Small bumps had appeared on either side of it, and another on her brow.

When Hugo and I paid one of our visits to the Gombe after a rather long absence, we were appalled by Gilka's appearance. She who had been one of the prettiest youngsters with her long silky hair, pale heart-shaped face, and small pointed white beard, looked like some nightmarish, grotesque gnome. We felt convinced the growth was cancerous and very soon Gilka would die.

We showed photographs of the condition to a variety of medical friends and finally, after much discussion, resolved to try at least to find out the nature of the growth, even though we feared there would be little we could do. This is not the place to describe the methods employed first to tranquilize and then to anesthetize Gilka. It is enough to say that, with the help of the well-known veterinarians Sue and Tony Harthoorn and Professor Douglas Roy and Dr. Bradley Nelson, we found Gilka's affliction to be a fungus disease, which at the present time we are treating with antibiotics. Gilka—the operation notwithstanding—has lost no confidence in humans, and our students have no difficulty in following her around in the mountains.

We all hope desperately that Gilka will recover. For one thing,

we are extremely fond of her. For another, she and Evered represent one of the very few sibling pairs whose relationship we have
been able to study in detail over a long period. For some three years
before Olly's death there had been little contact between her two
children, but during the years following the loss of their mother
Evered and his young sister seem to have grown closer. Quite often
the two wander around together. Moreover, they spend a good deal
of time grooming each other, whereas the other young males, Evered's contemporaries, very seldom groom Gilka; when they do, it
is normally a rather brief session.

Whether or not this friendship between Gilka and Evered will
persist for years to come, we cannot guess. Pepe and Miff, Marina's
offspring, also moved around together frequently during the year
following their mother's death; then gradually, however, they
seemed to drift apart. Unfortunately, Pepe only lived one year after
the death of his little sibling Merlin, leaving Miff the sole survivor
of Marina's family until, when she was between ten and eleven
years old, she had a daughter. We were amazed at the efficient way
in which she handled her infant. Each of the other new mothers
we have watched has been somewhat awkward and uncertain, at
least for the first few days after her infant's birth. Melissa definitely
had seemed quite dazed. Miff, however, accepted her baby as a
matter of course; she paid her about the same amount of attention
as old and experienced Flo had devoted to her last infant. We cannot help but wonder whether Miff's experience with her small
orphaned brother perhaps gave her this extra self-confidence.

For several years, as mentioned in previous chapters, we have
considered it a possibility that a sibling relationship lay behind
some of the close friendships between pairs of adult males. We
were therefore especially anxious to follow the development of the
relationship between Flo's elder sons Faben and Figan. When
they were both adolescent they often played together, though
Faben tended to be rather rough with his younger sibling. When
Faben became a socially mature male at about thirteen years of
age, he stopped interacting with Figan almost entirely. Hugo and
I began to question our theory concerning friendships between
males.

Faben has a magnificent physique, and during his first year as a mature male his charging displays, often performed in an upright posture, were splendid. Then he was stricken by polio and completely lost the use of his right arm and hand. Up to that time Figan, as the younger brother, had always been dominated by Faben, but it was typical of Figan's particular brand of intelligence that he took almost instant advantage of Faben's disability to better his own status. For the first few days after Faben appeared with his useless arm, Figan seemed to pay him no particular attention. Then he began deliberately to harass his elder brother.

The first time I witnessed this, Faben was sitting peacefully in a tree grooming himself. Figan stared toward him, slowly walked over, and climbed the tree. Commencing a wild display, he shook the branches and rocked the whole tree so violently that Faben, who at first had ignored his young brother's behavior, began to scream. Faben had not had a chance at that time to adjust to life with one paralyzed arm. Within a few moments he was shaken right out of the tree. Twice more during the next few days Figan displayed at Faben in the same sort of way. After this the elder brother's attitude underwent a remarkable change. The next time I saw the brothers meet, Faben, as he saw Figan approaching, hurried toward him with submissive pant-grunts. Figan just sat there and, as his elder brother crouched before him, patted him reassuringly on his head.

This state of affairs lasted awhile but gradually Faben became better adjusted to his handicapped state. He had been able to walk completely upright from the start, thus preventing his paralyzed arm from trailing on the ground; and slowly he became even more expert in this manlike method of locomotion. He was soon able to keep up with groups of adult males for rather long distances, and he began to regain something of his former agility when swinging through the trees. Also, little by little his charging displays regained their former magnificence. Figan must have noticed this physical improvement in his brother since he kept well out of Faben's way temporarily. Two years later there was no sign, when the two interacted, that Figan had ever been able to dominate his older brother.

It was when Figan himself was promoted to the rank of a socially mature male that for the first time since their adolescence we noticed a growing friendliness between the two brothers. They were frequently observed traveling about together, and lengthy sessions of social grooming between the two became commonplace. Perhaps, we thought, we had been right in our theorizing after all: perhaps this was the start of a friendship such as that between David Graybeard and Goliath, Mike and J.B., Mr. McGregor and Humphrey; a friendship that would persist, that would ensure one brother's running to help the other in times of trouble. We could only wait and watch.

During the next year the relationship between Figan and Evered (who was, it will be remembered, about a year older) became increasingly tense; these two young males often directed displays toward each other. These conflicts, however, were not seen to result in physical combat until one never to be forgotten day. The incident started when Evered arrived, hair bristling, to find Figan and Faben in camp together. When Evered advanced toward him, Figan hurried up to his brother Faben, embraced him briefly, and then turned back toward Evered. A moment later the two brothers, united, charged toward Evered, uttering loud *waa* barks, and chased him right out of the camp clearing. Screaming, Evered fled through the forest and took refuge up a tall tree. The brothers returned to camp. For the next few minutes first Faben and then Figan kept displaying across the clearing, uttering pant-hoots, dragging and flailing branches, and drumming. Once there were a few rather subdued hoots from Evered in his tree.

About half an hour after leaving camp, Evered moved back toward the clearing, but Faben at once charged in his direction and displayed. Figan hurried to join his brother and the two raced flat-out after Evered, who quickly retreated up his tree. This time the brothers followed him and sat about five yards from their victim, with their hair bristling. All three were silent, but Evered's lips were drawn way back in a grin of fear.

Presently Figan advanced a few steps toward Evered, who, with soft grunts, moved a few yards along his branch and then sat again. A few moments later, and still in silence, Faben moved toward Evered, who squeaked nervously, moved farther out along his branch, and then sat. Presently Figan also advanced on Evered, who gave low grunts but could retreat no farther. The brothers sat facing him, silent and still.

All at once, about five minutes after the three had climbed into the tree, the battle erupted as Faben and Figan together leaped with loud *waa* barks toward Evered. Screaming, Evered hurled himself into a neighboring tree, the brothers following close behind. There was a short chase and then Figan grabbed on to Evered at the extreme end of a thin branch, and as the two grappled Faben joined in the fight as well.

It was an incredible battle to watch as the three young males, in a screaming tangle, somehow managed to leap from one branch to another. Meanwhile, Flint had climbed into the tree and, keeping at a safe distance from the fight, stamped along the branches, and uttered high-pitched childish *waa* barks. Down below old Flo displayed on the ground, stamping and shaking vines and barking in her hoarse and ancient voice.

Suddenly Figan and Evered, still fighting, fell together. They almost drifted through the air to crash into a dense tangle of vines some thirty feet below. Faben instantly swung and leaped down after them. Evered, screaming loudly, fled away through the forest. Faben and Figan, followed by Flo and Flint, pursued him some distance and then one after the other displayed, uttering loud pant-hoots and drumming. A few hundred yards away, down near the stream, Evered was still screaming and whimpering.

During that encounter Figan hurt his arm, scraped some skin off his knuckles, and lost great patches of hair. Evered, however, came off much the worst: he split open one side of his face, from the corner of his lip right up his cheek. Everyone feared that he would remain with a permanent disfigurement, a sort of hideous grin that would leave his face as ghastly to look at as that of his sister, Gilka. To our surprise, however, it healed up with scarcely a mark to show.

Meanwhile our research team was gathering fascinating new information on the subject of male dominance. It was not so long after old McGregor's death that his presumed younger brother, Humphrey, developed into a truly massive male, and the larger he grew the more aggressive he became. By 1968, Humphrey had all the females and adolescent males very much in awe of him.

Often, when Humphrey and Mike were together in a group, new-comers would hurry to pay their respects to Humphrey before greeting Mike. During the following year, Humphrey gradually became dominant even over old Rodolf and Leakey and Goliath, but he still respected Mike as much as ever.

Figan was particularly in awe of Humphrey; at the same time, he began to show increasingly less respect for Mike. Mike began to be very worried about this young upstart. When Mike displayed, the other chimps, as before, rushed out of his way—all but Figan, who sat quite calmly with his back to Mike. This happened repeatedly, and Mike became increasingly uneasy. When Figan was near he displayed more frequently, and most of his displays were directed toward the young male. Indeed, he swayed the very branches on which Figan sat, his back still firmly turned toward Mike. Yet Mike, it seemed, dared not actually attack Figan.

There was one memorable occasion when Figan ventured to approach a pink female of whom Mike was being strangely possessive. When Mike began threatening Figan, shaking the branches of a tree, Figan actually displayed back, and in the resultant confusion both males rushed screaming from the tree. Then Mike, with a grin of fear, actually hastened to embrace Humphrey, seeking reassurance by this contact with the other male.

Shortly after this some incident occurred, unseen by human eyes, which put Figan firmly back in his place. After this Figan once again rushed out of the way when Mike displayed and hastened to greet him with submissive gestures. No sooner had Figan been subdued, however, than Evered, a year older than Figan, began to challenge Mike's supremacy. Just as Figan had done before him, Evered sat and ignored Mike's displays. And just as Mike had been worried by Figan's insubordination, so he was by Evered's. Mike remains the dominant male but he is very uneasy when he is on his own with Figan or Evered. Only when one of the old-timers such as Rodolf or Leakey is with him does Mike seem at all relaxed in the presence of these two young males. It is a strange situation. If either of the two did engage in battle with Mike, and dominate him, the old male would no longer occupy the top-ranking position; but neither would the youngster who had usurped his position—for both Figan and Evered continue to show tremendous respect for Humphrey. Soon then, we may have a situation where no single male is dominant in all situations. Certainly something is going to happen very soon.

Hugo and I suspect that eventually Figan will become the top-ranking male—possibly after Humphrey has had an inning. Figan is not only more intelligent than Evered, he also has the backing of a large family. The proximity of Faben will probably always give him that feeling of confidence that David Graybeard once gave to Goliath.

Goliath himself is a somewhat tragic figure these days. For four years after Mike had usurped his top-ranking position, Goliath remained a very dominant male. Then he became ill, his weight greatly diminished, and he lost his old friend David Graybeard, who died during an epidemic of the flu. Today Goliath is dominated not only by all the adult males but by most of the adolescent males too. He spends much time wandering about alone, or with old Rodolf or Leakey.

Soon, I suspect, Goliath will be no more. Nor can Flo, amazing though she is, be expected to survive much longer. We know so much about these chimpanzees, we have shared so much of their lives that it is always sad when they die. For me, of course, the saddest loss was when David Graybeard died. David had been the first chimpanzee to accept my presence and the first who permitted me to approach him closely. Besides providing me with my early exciting observations of meat-eating and tool-using and thus helping to ensure the availability of further funds for my research, he had been the first to visit my camp, the first to take a banana from my hand, the first who permitted a human hand to touch him. I have pointed out the mistake Hugo and I had made in allowing Flint to touch us, in encouraging Fifi and Figan to play with us. We endangered not only the validity of subsequent research but, worse, the safety of those students who would follow in our footsteps at the Gombe Stream. To this day Flint and Figan sometimes try to initiate play with their human observers.

I do not regret my early contact with David Graybeard; David, with his gentle disposition, who permitted a strange white ape to touch him. To me it represented a triumph of the sort of relationship man can establish with a wild creature, a creature who has never known captivity. In those early days I spent many days alone with David. Hour after hour I followed him through the forests, sitting and watching him while he fed or rested, struggling to keep up when he moved through a tangle of vines. Sometimes, I am sure, he waited for me—just as he would wait for Goliath or William—for when I emerged, panting and torn from a mass of thorny undergrowth, I often found him sitting, looking back in my direction; when I had appeared, he got up and plodded on again.

One day, as I sat near him at the bank of a tiny trickle of crystal-clear water, I saw a ripe red palm nut lying on the ground. I picked it up and held it out to him on my open palm. He turned his head away. When I moved my hand closer he looked at it, and then at me, and then he took the fruit, and at the same time held my hand firmly and gently with his own. As I sat motionless he released my hand, looked down at the nut, and dropped it to the ground.

At that moment there was no need of any scientific knowledge to understand his communication of reassurance. The soft pressure of his fingers spoke to me not through my intellect but through a more primitive emotional channel: the barrier of untold centuries which has grown up during the separate evolution of man and chimpanzee was, for those few seconds, broken down.

It was a reward far beyond my greatest hopes.

APPENDIXES

(with illustrations by David Bygott)

BIBLIOGRAPHY

INDEX

Appendix A

STAGES OF DEVELOPMENT

Some chimpanzees, like some humans, develop faster than others; moreover, the behavior of a chimpanzee's mother undoubtedly has a marked effect on his physical and social development; the same holds good for human mothers, too. A mother (chimp or human), for instance, may be permissive or restrictive toward her child's early attempts to walk; she may be tolerant or nervous about his initial contacts with others of his kind. The ages given here for the appearance of the different physical or social developments in chimpanzees are the *earliest* at which they were observed in any of our youngsters.

Month 2 refers to the second month of life: i.e., the infant is between 4 and 8 weeks of age. Similarly, year 3 refers to youngsters between 24 and 36 months of age.

	month first seen
Sucks thumb	2
Mother may tickle occasionally and briefly	2
Stares at object; reaches toward it	2
Struggles to pull from mother	2
Stands upright holding on to mother	2
Pushes and pulls itself forward on mother's body	3
Reaches toward object and grasps, showing coordination	3
First tooth	3
Mother plays frequently and for longer at a time	3
Infant shows play-face and laughing during tickling	3
Chews and swallows first piece of solid food	4

month first seen

Reaches to play with mother's hand during game	5
Starts to ride on mother's back*	5
Takes first step	5
Mother-infant contact broken	5
Climbs up sapling or branch	5
Kidnaped (a sibling may kidnap earlier, during 4th month)	5
Kisses another	5
Attempts to groom another, inefficiently	7
Attempts to make a nest	8
Attacked mildly by another	8
Mounts and thrusts "pink" female	9
Runs at and hits another infant aggressively	16
Reassures another in correct context	16
Grooms with adult technique	18

year

Charging display and rain dance in correct context	3 (early)
Violent attack on another youngster	3 (early)
Attempts tool-using in correct context	3 (early)
Weaned	by end of 5
Starts to lose milk teeth	6
May start to move around for short periods without mother	6
Attains puberty	about 8 or 9
First infant born	about 11 or 12
Male becomes fully socially mature	about 15

* One infant (Pom) rode in the dorsal position at 8 weeks; this was most unusual and was because she hurt her foot. See page 148.

Appendix B

FACIAL EXPRESSIONS
AND CALLS

1. Display-face

The DISPLAY-FACE is shown by aggressive chimpanzees, especially during their charging displays or when attacking others. It is not accompanied by calling.

The PLAY-FACE is shown by chimpanzees during play. When a game becomes vigorous the upper lip is often drawn back and up so that the front upper teeth are also exposed. The play-face is frequently accompanied by a series of grunting sounds or LAUGHING.

2. Play-face

3a and b, two of the facial expressions typically shown by chimpanzees as they utter a series of PANT-HOOTS. Pant-hoots are a series of *hoo* sounds connected by audible intakes of breath, gradually getting louder and usually ending with *waa* sounds also connected by panting intakes of breath. 3a shows the expression during a *hoo* and 3b, during a *waa*. Pant-hoots are given in a variety of contexts, especially when chimpanzees arrive at a food source, join another group, or cross from one valley to another. Pant-hoots serve as a contact call between spread-out individuals or groups of individuals; sometimes chimpanzees peacefully feeding in a tree will give this call, at which another group, some distance away, may respond. Quite often when groups of chimpanzees are sleeping within earshot of each other they may exchange pant-hoots during the night, particularly when there is a bright moon.

3a. *Hoo* part of pant-hoot

Grinning. A FULL OPEN GRIN (4a, upper and lower front teeth showing, jaws open) is usually shown by a chimpanzee who is frightened or very excited: during and after an attack, when a high-ranking male displays close to a subordinate, when a group of chimpanzees is confronted with a huge pile of bananas, and so on. If the chimpanzee is somewhat less frightened or excited, the upper lip may be slightly relaxed to cover the upper front teeth; this is the LOW OPEN GRIN. The full and the low open grins may alternate rapidly with one another and are nearly always accompanied by loud SCREAMING.

3b. *Waa* part of pant-hoot

A FULL CLOSED GRIN (4b, upper and lower front teeth showing, but with jaws *closed*) is the expression of a chimpanzee who is probably less frightened or less excited than one showing either of the open grins. A full closed grin may alternate with the low open grin or with a LOW CLOSED GRIN, in which only the lower front teeth show. Closed grins are usually accompanied by high-pitched SQUEAKING sounds that readily change to screams or WHIMPERS. Sometimes, however, a low-ranking chimpanzee may approach a su-

4a. Full open grin

perior in silence while showing a closed grin. If the human nervous or social smile has its equivalent expression in the chimpanzee it is, without doubt, the closed grin.

4b. Full closed grin

Pouting. As screams or squeaks change to WHIMPERING—a series of *oo* sounds repeated rapidly at different notes of the scale—the chimpanzee shows this HORIZONTAL POUT. After being attacked a youngster may gradually stop screaming and squeaking and start to whimper. Whimpering, however, does not only follow screaming and squeaking. A soft single-syllable HOO WHIMPER is the contact call between a mother and her infant. It is the sound made by a chimpanzee who desires food from a superior, who wants his companion to groom him, or who is frustrated in other ways. This soft *hoo* whimper is accompanied by a POUT when both lips are pursed together and pushed forward. If the frustration is not relieved, the call is repeated more frequently and more loudly until it becomes normal whimpering and the lips become increasingly parted. A pout looks almost identical with the expression shown in 3a.

5. Horizontal pout

Other expressions and calls

Chimpanzees GRUNT in a variety of contexts; these grunts may be high-pitched or low-pitched. Usually there is little change in facial expression during grunting, though the lips and jaws may be slightly parted. Grunts are given during feeding (FOOD GRUNTS), grooming, and as close-range contact calls between the individuals of a peaceful group.

A series of rapid grunts, connected by audible intakes of breath, are known as PANT-GRUNTS. A subordinate chimpanzee is likely to pant-grunt as he approaches a superior during a greeting or after being threatened or attacked. During pant-grunting the jaws are often partly open, the teeth normally concealed by the lips. If the superior behaves at all aggressively during the interaction, pant-grunting quickly becomes squeaking or screaming and the chimpanzee grins.

Loud BARKING often occurs when a group is socially excited; at the

same time some individuals pant-hoot others may bark. Very loud
FOOD BARKS often occur as chimpanzees arrive at a favored food source
and during the first few minutes of intensive feeding. The jaws open
slightly as each bark is emitted, and the lower front teeth may show
slightly.

When mildly threatening another chimpanzee (or animal of another `
species, including humans) a chimpanzee utters a SOFT BARK. This
sounds very like a single quiet cough; the jaws are very slightly parted,
with the lips covering the teeth.

When threatening more vigorously the chimpanzee often utters a
loud WAA BARK. The facial expression is very similar to that shown in
picture 3b.

The WRAAAA CALL of the chimpanzee is to me one of the most savage
sounds of the African jungle. It is a long drawn-out, clear sound,
pitched rather high, and is made when chimpanzees come across something unusual or slightly disturbing in the forest. It was with this call
that the chimpanzees acknowledged my approach in the early days once
they had overcome their initial terror of me. They may call thus when
they come across a herd of buffalo or a dead chimpanzee. The facial
expression is, again, very like that depicted in 3b. In similar contexts
some chimpanzees may utter long, loud screams.

Audible PANTING, rather like their laughing but without the grunting
quality, is sometimes heard when chimpanzees are grooming each other
intensively. Some males utter quite loud COPULATION PANTS during mating. No clear-cut facial expression accompanies panting.

Appendix C

WEAPON AND
TOOL USE

THE CHIMPANZEE uses the objects of his environment as tools to a greater extent than any other living animal with the exception of man himself. These drawings show:

1. Stick used as weapon.

2. Aimed throwing (see next page for illustration).

3. Investigation probe—chimpanzee sniffs end of stick after poking it

into a hole in dead wood. If insect larva is detected the wood will be broken open and the grub consumed. (A probe of this sort may also be used to investigate an unusual object such as a dead python.)

4. Stick used to feed on safari ants. These ants have a very painful bite and the chimpanzee tries to prevent them from crawling over his body while he plunges his stick into the ants' underground nest. A stick is also used to feed on ants living in hard football-sized nests constructed around the branches of trees.

5. Grass stems used to "fish" for termites (see top of page).

6. Tool*making*—leaves are stripped from a stem to make a tool suitable for termite-fishing. In addition, the edges of a wide blade of grass may be stripped off in order to make an appropriate tool.

7. Leaves, which the chimpanzee has made more absorbent by chewing, used as a sponge to sop up rainwater that cannot be reached with the lips. The initial modification of the handful of leaves provides another example of primitive tool*making* (see next page).

8. Leaf sponge used to wipe remnants of brain from inside the skull of a baboon (see next page).

9. Leaves used to dab at bleeding wound on bottom. Sometimes, when a chimpanzee has diarrhea, he uses leaves as toilet paper; he may also use them to wipe off mud, sticky foods, etc. (see next page).

In addition to the above examples of objects used by the Gombe Stream chimpanzees as tools, the chimpanzees were observed to use stout sticks as levers—to enlarge the opening of an underground bees' nest and, frequently, to attempt prying open banana boxes at the observation area. One chimpanzee used a twig as a toothpick and one picked its nose with a piece of straw.

Appendix D

DIET

LIKE MAN, the chimpanzee is an omnivore and feeds on vegetables, insects, and meat.

Vegetable Foods
More than 90 different species of tree and plant used by the Gombe Stream chimpanzees for food have already been identified. They have been seen eating over 50 types of FRUIT and over 30 types of LEAF and LEAF BUD. They also eat some BLOSSOMS, SEEDS, BARKS, and PITHS. Sometimes they lick RESIN from tree trunks or chew on wads of DEAD WOOD FIBER.

Insect Foods
Throughout the year the following kinds of insects may be eaten in large quantities: 3 species of ANT (*Oecophylla* spp., *Anomma* spp., *Crematogaster* spp.); 2 species of TERMITE (*Macrotermes* spp., *Pseudacanthotermes* spp.); 1 species of CATERPILLAR of a moth as yet unidentified.

These chimps also eat a variety of GRUBS—the larvae of different beetles, wasps, gallflies, etc. BEE LARVAE are eaten when chimpanzees raid bees' nests and feed on HONEY.

Birds' Eggs and Fledglings
Occasionally the chimpanzees take eggs or fledglings from the nests of a wide variety of birds.

Meat
The Gombe Stream chimpanzees are efficient hunters; a group of about

40 individuals may catch over 20 different prey animals during one year. Most common prey animals are the young of BUSHBUCKS (*Tragelaphus scriptus*), BUSHPIGS (*Potamochoerus porcus*), and BABOONS (*Papio anubis*), and young or adult RED COLOBUS MONKEYS (*Colobus badius*). Occasionally the chimpanzees may catch a REDTAIL MONKEY (*Cercopithecus ascanius*) or a BLUE MONKEY (*Cercopithecus mitis*).

Minerals

The chimpanzees sometimes eat small quantities of soil that contains some salt (sodium chloride).

Bushbuck

Red colobus monkey

Bushpig

Male chimpanzee slams a juvenile baboon against
the ground at the culmination of a hunt

Appendix E

CHIMPANZEE AND HUMAN BEHAVIOR

In what ways is the

study of chimpanzee

behavior relative to

the study of man?

THE CHIMPANZEE is our closest living relative. Recent research in biochemistry has shown that in some ways the chimpanzee is as close to man as he is to the gorilla. Neuroanatomists have pointed to the fact that the circuitry of the chimpanzee brain resembles the circuitry of the human brain more closely than does that of any other species. Observations at Gombe have highlighted striking similarities in the behavior of chimpanzee and man, notably in nonverbal communication patterns. Thus a thorough understanding of chimpanzee behavior will be of value in our efforts to understand our own.

The problem of human aggression is of vital importance. Before we can effectively control violence we must understand it. The studies of chimpanzee aggression in progress at Gombe may prove of immense significance.

The methods by which we raise our children should be a point of interest to all. Our studies at Gombe on different mothering techniques and on the stages of infant development have already proved of interest to child psychologists and psychiatrists. Our work highlights the importance of the mother-offspring affectionate bond in chimpanzees but we are not sure why some adult chimpanzees maintain closer bonds with their families than others. The answer may be significant to the understanding of some human family problems.

In humans, adolescence is a difficult time; it also is for chimpanzees. If we can learn more about the effect of physiological body changes in chimpanzees at puberty and how this affects their behavior, we may be able to understand and help our own teenagers.

Human mental illness causes untold suffering and is on the increase. Scientists working on, for example, the cure and prevention of clinical depressions, hope to induce similar symptoms in the chimpanzee and thus use him as an experimental model. However, such a scientist, before he can measure in full the success or failure of a given treatment, must have knowledge of the behavior of a normal chimpanzee. In addition he must be aware of the conditions that a captive chimpanzee must enjoy if it is *to be able* to show normal behavior. Our work at Gombe should provide this information.

Research at Gombe has encouraged collaboration between students from many different sciences—zoology, ecology, ethology, anthropology, psychology, and psychiatry. The participation of students and faculty members from the universities of Dar es Salaam, Cambridge, Stanford, Amsterdam, and other places will encourage further stimulating exchange of ideas. Such interdisciplinary collaboration will undoubtedly give rise to new lines of inquiry into many problems of human behavior.

Professor David Hamburg, of the Department of Psychiatry in the School of Medicine at Stanford University, is setting up a large outdoor chimpanzee enclosure at Stanford. Work on problems that cannot be solved in the field (such as the study of the hormonal changes occurring at puberty) will be carried out in close collaboration with research in progress at Gombe. The research on chimpanzee behavior will increasingly be related to programs of research into human behavior at Stanford.

A thorough knowledge of the behavior and diet of wild chimpanzees will be of great importance to the successful maintenance of captive colonies of chimpanzees. In particular, breeding colonies are of vital importance if we are to stop the constant drain on natural resources caused by the demands of science.

Conservation of the fauna of the world is another pressing problem. In order adequately to protect animals it is necessary to understand their requirements. Ecological and behavioral studies at Gombe are yielding a wealth of information that will be valuable to those responsible for the management of other parks and reserves where there are chimpanzees.

We aim to establish an observation area for tourists in the Gombe National Park. Thanks to the courtesy of the Tanzanian government, its President, Mwalimu Julius Nyerere, and the Tanzania National Parks, visitors from all over the world will have a unique opportunity to observe chimpanzees in all the splendor of their freedom.

BIBLIOGRAPHY

SUGGESTED READING

I HOPE that this book will stimulate interest not only in chimpanzees but also in other nonhuman primates, and in animal behavior in general. There are many detailed reports of chimpanzee behavior, both in captivity and in the wild, scattered throughout scientific journals, that are not for the most part readily available to the general reader. For this reason I suggest for supplementary reading only a few highly selected references that are accessible mainly in book form, are not overly technical, and summarize and give references to a good deal of the available information. Unfortunately, some major contributions are restricted to scientific journals and are not, therefore, appropriate for inclusion here; I refer in particular to articles by members of the Japanese Monkey Center in Inuyama, Drs. S. Azuma, M. Kawabe, T. Nishida, J. Itani, A. Suzuki, and A. Toyoshima and to articles by Dr. A. Kortlandt.

Chimpanzees in the Wild

Lawick-Goodall, Jane van. *My Friends the Wild Chimpanzees*, Washington: National Geographic Society, 1967.
Reynolds, Vernon. *Budongo: An African Forest and Its Chimpanzees.* Garden City, N.Y.: Natural History Press, 1965.

Chimpanzees in Captivity

Hayes, Catherine. *The Ape in Our House.* New York: Harper & Row, 1951.

Köhler, Wolfgang. *The Mentality of Apes*. New York: Harcourt, Brace, 1925.

Kohts, Nadie. *Infant Ape and Human Child* [in Russian], Scientific Memoirs of the Darwin Museum, No. 3 (1935), Moscow.

Yerkes, Robert M. *Chimpanzees: A Laboratory Colony*. New Haven: Yale University Press, 1943.

Nonhuman Primates Other Than Chimpanzees

Altmann, Stuart A., ed. *Social Communication among Primates*. Chicago: University of Chicago Press, 1967.

DeVore, Irven, ed. *Primate Behavior*. New York: Holt, Rinehart and Winston, 1965.

Harrisson, Barbara. *Orang-utan*. London: Collins, 1962.

Jay, Phyllis, ed. *Primates: Studies in Adaptation and Variability*. New York: Holt, Rinehart and Winston, 1968.

Kummer, Hans. *Primate Societies*. Chicago: Aldine Publishing Company, 1971.

Morris, Desmond, ed. *Primate Ethology*. Chicago: Aldine Publishing Company, 1967.

Schaller, George B. *The Year of the Gorilla*. Chicago: University of Chicago Press, 1964. Miss Dian Fossey is also working on the behavior of the mountain gorilla, in Burundi. She is now beginning her fifth year of observations and has published one article in the January 1970 issue of the *National Geographic Magazine*.

Some General Books on Animal Behavior

Eibl-Eibesfeldt, Irenaus. *Ethology: The Biology of Behavior*. New York: Holt, Rinehart and Winston, 1970.

Hinde, Robert A. *Animal Behaviour*. New York: McGraw-Hill, 1966.

Lorenz, Konrad. *King Solomon's Ring*. New York: Crowell, 1952.

Marler, Peter R., and William J. Hamilton III. *Mechanisms of Animal Behavior*. New York: Wiley, 1966.

REFERENCE SOURCES

The following represent important technical sources for facts referred to in this book.

For an account of Henry W. Nissen's observations, see "A Field Study of the Chimpanzee," in *Comparative Psychology Monographs*, Vol. 8 (1931), pp. 1–22.

Tool-using is discussed by Harry Beatty in "A Note on the Behavior of the Chimpanzee," under General Notes of the *Journal of Mammalogy*, Vol. 32 (1951), p. 118, and by Fred G. Merfield and H. Miller in *Gorillas Were My Neighbours* (London: Longmans, 1956). Wolfgang Köhler reported studies of tool-using and toolmaking by groups of captive chimpanzees in *The Mentality of Apes* (New York: Harcourt, Brace, 1925).

Details of the inability of one chimpanzee to use a hand ax for making a tool, which I mention in Chapter 19, are given by H. F. Khroustov in "Formation and Highest Frontier of the Implemental Activity of Anthropoids," a paper delivered at the Seventh International Congress of Anthropological and Ethological Sciences in Moscow, 1964.

The experiences with Washoe are told by R. Allen and Beatrice Gardner in "Teaching Sign Language to a Chimpanzee," *Science*, Vol. 165 (1969), pp. 664–72.

The Gombe Stream story is presented in very different form in my own monograph, *The Behaviour of Free-living Chimpanzees in the Gombe Stream Area*, which was published as Vol. 1, Part 3 (1968), pp. 161–311, of Animal Behaviour Monographs.

INDEX

Humphrey: pursuit of female, 182; relations with Mr. McGregor,
211–213, 215; candidate top-
ranking male, 248–250
Hunting techniques, 81–82, 190–191,
192–193; cooperation, 81–82,
191, 192; killing methods, 82,
192–193, 267; reactions of prey
species, 51, 198, 200

Illness, 87–88, 91, 204–213, 214–215,
218, 223, 244
Imitation, 104, 111, 115, 216, 228
Incest, lack of, 177
Infancy, 107–116, 146–158
aggression, in male, 156
aggression directed toward infants,
151, 157, 215–216
birth, reaction of group to newborn,
146–148
contact, importance of, 95–96, 219,
229
developmental stages in
communication patterns, 150, 216
feeding, 115, 218
locomotion, 110–112, 149–150,
151; experience in play, 154–
156
nest making, 150–151
play, 114, 154–156
sexual behavior, 156–157, 175
tool-using, 105, 115, 216–217, 228
(and see Appendix A, 255–
256)
imitation and practice of adult patterns, 105, 111, 115, 156–157,
216–217, 228
mother, relations with, see Mother-
offspring relations
observation of adults, 105, 111, 216–
217, 228
orphans, 214–220
play, 46, 153–154, 154–156, 231
protected: by males, 151–153; by
young females, 151, 175
sex differences, 156
sexual behavior, 156–157, 175, 177
siblings, relations with, see Sibling
relations
suckling, see Mother-offspring relations
tolerance, adult male, for infant, 92,
113, 151 et seq., 180
weaning, 95, 158 et seq., 221, 223

Ingratiation, 130, 216
Inspection of genital area, 96, 129;
chimp inspects baboon, 202
Intelligence, 103–104, 122, 142–143,
226–228
Interference with copulation, 92, 93,
157, 177
Interspecific relations, with baboons:
aggressive, 199, 200–201, 202;
hunted by chimps, 190 et seq.,
203–204; friendly, 161–162,
201–203; tolerance, 199, 201
Interspecific relations, with man: aggression to man, 49, 70–71, 72,
78, 84, 191–192, 195–196, 209;
communication with man, 234–
236, 251; experimental research
on chimp, 240–241; grooming
wild chimp, 85; hunting of
chimp by man, 192, 238–239;
play, chimp and man, 139–140,
250–251; predation on human
infants, 191–192, 242; tolerance
of human observers, 87, 145,
162, 196, 250; trust in man,
85, 139–140, 209, 213; zoos
and laboratories, 239–241

J.B., 73, 93, 99; friendship with Mike,
125–126, 164, 183; hits me,
195; steals baboon head, 198;
polio victim, 208
"Jealousy," 129
Juvenile, 159–168
abnormal behavior, 159–160, 223–
224
adopting sibling, 215, 218–219
independence: in nesting, 163; from
mother, 167
losing mother, 166–167
mother, relations with, see Mother-
offspring relations
play, 164
sexual behavior, in males, 168

Kidnaping, see Sibling relations, carrying infant sibling
Kissing, 46, 109, 118, 122, 168, 230,
233

Leakey (chimp): friendship with Worzle, 126, 127, 136, 171; preoccupation with females, 184–
185